Toward Two Societies

THE CHANGING DISTRIBUTIONS
OF INCOME AND WEALTH
IN THE U.S. SINCE 1960

Andrew J. Winnick

PRAEGER

New York
Westport, Connecticut
London

Library of Congress Cataloging-in-Publication Data

Winnick, Andrew J.
    Toward two societies : the changing distributions of income and
wealth in the U.S. since 1960 / Andrew J. Winnick.
        p. cm.
    Bibliography: p.
    ISBN 0-275-92899-3 (alk. paper)
    1. Income distribution—United States.   2. Wealth—United States.
3. United States—Economic conditions—1945-   I. Title.
HC110.I5W56   1989
339.2'0973—dc19   88-35980

Library of Congress Catalog Card Number: 88-35980
ISBN: 0-275-92899-3

First published in 1989

Praeger Publishers, One Madison Avenue, New York, NY 10010
A division of Greenwood Press, Inc.

Printed in the United States of America

The paper used in this book complies with the Permanent
Paper Standard issued by the National Information Standards
Organization (Z39.48–1984).

10 9 8 7 6 5 4 3 2 1

To the generation before me:
My parents, Marge and Leon Winnick,
who taught me to care about the world around me and
to change what needed changing, and
Jeannette and Ben Gray,
who dedicated their lives to the struggle to make
more equitable the distributions of income, wealth,
and power; and
to the generation which follows:
David, Shawn, and Hannah,
who will have to carry on the struggle to build a
more equitable world.

Contents

Tables   xiii

Preface   xvii

Chapter 1   Introduction   1
Background and Scope of this Study   1
Why Be Concerned with the Distribution of Income
  or of Wealth?   2
    Wealth vs. Income as a Focus   3
    The Significance of the Distribution of Income
      and Wealth   4
        Efficiency   4
        Equity   6
        The Ethical Basis of Both Efficiency and Equity
          Criteria   8
        Other Bases for Undertaking the Study of
          Distribution
              Social and Political Unrest   8
              Foreign Perceptions   10
              Simple Humanism   10
Conclusion   11
Notes   11
Table   13

PART I   THE DISTRIBUTION OF INCOME SINCE 1960   15

**Chapter 2   Developing a Standard Against Which to Measure
            the Distribution of Income**   17
Defining Income   17
The Shifting Tax Burden   19
Some Experimental Definitions of Income   20
Defining Family   21
Developing Standards of Comparison for Income Levels   22
    Defining the Official Poverty Level of Income   22
    The Bureau of Labor Statistics Income Standards   24
    Defining the Middle Class   26
Notes   27
Table   30

Chapter 3   The Historical Data on Family Income Since 1960   31
An Overview of the Data, Including by Race/Ethnic Group   31
Changes in the Number of Persons in Poverty: 1960-1987   34
A Closer Look at the Distribution in 1985   35
The Shrinking Middle Class   35
    Other Studies of the Shrinking Middle Class   37
        An International Comparison   39

Structural Change and the Movement to a Service
Economy   39
Changing Earnings Patterns Within Occupational
Categories   41
Possible Demographic Causes   43
The Growing Role of Part-Time Employment   43
The Growth in Contingent Workers   46
The Growth in Low Wage Jobs Across the Economy   47
The Possible Effects of the Business Cycle   48
Other Possible Causes of the Decline of the
Middle Class   48
Conclusion   49
Notes   49
Tables   54

Chapter 4   The Poor - Just Who Are They?   65
A Variety of Measurements as to the Extent of Poverty   65
The Poor Are Getting Poorer   66
The Deteriorating Relative Position   67
The Deteriorating Absolute Position   68
The Different Pattern of Change Before and
After 1973   69
The Situation for Minorities, Female-Headed Households
and Children   70
Racial/Ethnic Minorities   71
Racial/Ethnic Differentials in Unemployment   72
Children   73
Children and Welfare Programs   75
International Comparisons of Poverty Among
Children   76
Teenage Motherhood and Poverty   77
Female-Headed Households   78
The Employment History of the Poor   80
Low Income and the Minimum Wage   81
Employment Data on Those Below the Poverty Level   82
Secondary Workers in Poor Households   85
Employment Data on Those Below 125% of Poverty Level   86
Employment Data on Those Below the BLS Minimum
Adequacy Level   87
Some Historical Perspective   89
The Educational Experience of the Poor   89
Where the Poor Live   92
Conclusion   93
Notes   94
Tables   103

**Chapter 5   The Effects of Race, Sex, Education, Industry,
and Occupation on the Distribution of Income
Among Those Working Full-Time, Full-Year**   119
Racial and Sexual Discrimination Patterns Among
Full-Time, Full-Year Workers   119
Income Differentials by Race/Ethnic Group   119
Income Differentials by Sex   120

Some Conclusions Concerning the Pattern of Income
    Differentials 122
Looking at the Differentials in Earnings Instead
    of Income 122
An Alternative Analysis of Male-Female Income
    Differentials 123
The Impact of Education Upon Income 124
    The Data for 1986 124
    An Historical Perspective 126
    The Impact of Education Upon Income, Regardless of
        Employment Condition: A Comparison to Those Working
        Full-Time, Full-Year 127
The Pattern of Earnings Among Occupations 128
    Some Introductory Comments 128
    The Data for 1985 129
    Racial/Ethnic and Sexual Patterns in 1985 130
    The Trends in Occupational Earnings Data
        Since 1960 131
            Consistency Problems in the Data 131
            The Trends from 1960 to 1981 132
            The Trends since 1982 134
The Pattern of Earnings Among Industries 136
    The Historical Pattern from 1960 to 1987 137
    A Closer Look at the Data for 1987 138
Conclusion 139
Notes 141
Tables 143

PART II   THE CHANGING DISTRIBUTION OF WEALTH IN THE UNITED
           STATES 157

Chapter 6   The Sources of Data Concerning Wealth Holdings 159
Wealth as the Definition of Rich and Poor 159
Estate Tax Estimates of Wealth Holdings 160
The Efforts of the Federal Reserve System 160
The Bureau of the Census's New Survey and Data on Wealth 162
Weaknesses and Compatibility Problems in the Wealth Data 163
    The SCF vs. the SIPP Net Worth Figures 163
    The SCF vs. the Flow of Funds Net Worth Figures 165
    The SCF vs. Estate Tax Based Estimates of the
        Concentration of Wealth 166
    Other Issues in the Wealth Data 167
Notes 167

Chapter 7   The Changing Distribution of Wealth Since 1962 171
The Distribution of Net Worth in 1983 Compared to that
    in 1962 171
The Distribution of Net Worth Among Different Racial/
    Ethnic Groups and Different Types of Families 172
The Distribution of Net Worth Compared to the
    Distribution of Income 174

Comparative Wealth vs. Income Distributions Among
Different Racial/Ethnic Groups and Different Types
of Families   175
The Distribution of Net Worth by Family Income in
1983 and 1986   175
The Change in Wealth Holdings Within Families - 1983-1986 177
The Distribution of Family Net Worth Among Different
Assets   178
The High Degree of Concentration in the Ownership of
Wealth   180
The Concentration of Wealth in 1986   180
Changes in the Concentration of Wealth Since 1963   185
Conclusion   188
Notes   189
Tables   191

PART III   AN OVERVIEW OF WHAT IS AND WHAT COULD BE   201

Chapter 8   Summary and Recommendations   203
Summary: A Dozen Important Conclusions   203
Recommendations   211
Addressing the Basic Needs of Poor and Low
Income Families   212
Medical Care   212
Housing   213
Nutrition   214
Education   215
Child Care and Early Childhood Education   217
A Guaranteed Minimum Level of Income   217
Opening Up the Labor Market to All Who Want to Work   219
Creating Jobs: Reversing the Movement to
Part-Time and Temporary Jobs Instead of
Regular Full-Time Jobs   220
Creating Jobs: Redirecting the Flow of Private
Investment Funds   221
Creating Jobs: Social Investment Projects   223
A New Transportation Infrastucture   223
The Recycling Industry   225
Finding the Money for Social Investments   225
Training and Retraining the Labor Force   226
Reducing the Length of the Workweek and/or
the Workday   227
Improving the Wage Structure   229
Coming to Terms with the Distribution of Wealth   232
Taxes on Current Wealth Holdings   232
Taxes on Inherited Wealth   232
Wealth Taxes in Kind   232
Federal Chartering of Corporations and the
Redefinition of Boards of Directors   233
Conclusion   234
Notes   235

Bibliography   241

Index   255

Tables

1-1   Percentage of Eligible Voters Who Registered and/or
Voted in 1984 Presidential Election, by Income and
Education   13

2-1   Low, Moderate, and High Annual Budgets for a Four
Person Family, and Per Person Low Budget Levels
(in 1985 dollars)   30

3-1   Distribution of All Families Among Income Classes:
1960 to 1985 (in constant 1985 dollars)   54

3-2   Distribution of White Families Among Income
Classes: 1960 to 1985 (in constant 1985 dollars)   55

3-3   Distribution of Black Families Among Income
Classes: 1960 to 1985 (in constant 1985 dollars)   56

3-4   Distribution of Hispanic Families Among Income
Classes: 1960 to 1985 (in constant 1985 dollars)   57

3-5   Summary of the Distributions of All, White, Black and
Hispanic Families Among Income Classes in 1960, 1973,
and 1985 and Percentage Changes Between Those Years   58

3-6   Poverty Rate and Number of Persons in Poverty:
1960-1987   59

3-7   Distribution of All and Black Families by Designated
Income Categories: 1985   60

3-8   Nonagricultural Employment by Industry: 1960-1987   61

3-9   Employed Part-Time Workers as a Percent of All Employed
Workers by Age and Sex: 1968-1985   62

3-10   Average Weekly Hours of Production and Nonsupervisory
Workers in Private Nonagricultural Employment, by
Industry: 1960-1988   62

3-11   Percentage Changes in the Distribution of Families by
Income and by Race/Ethnic Group, Between 1973 and
1987 (in constant 1985 and 1987 dollars)   63

4-1   Percentage of Families Living Below Poverty Level by
      Size of Family and Comparative Data on Persons and
      Families Living Below Other Related Thresholds: 1985   103

4-2   Percentage Share of Aggregate Income Received by Each
      Fifth and Top Five % of Families: 1947-1986   104

4-3   Changes in the Gap Between Rich and Poor Families:
      1947-1987 (in constant 1985 dollars)   105

4-4   The Changes in Median Family Income: 1960-1987
      (in constant 1985 dollars)   106

4-5   Comparative Data on Persons and Children in Households,
      Families and Female-Headed Families Living Below the
      "Official" Poverty Level: 1960-1987   107

4-6   Comparative Data on Persons and Children in Households,
      Families and Female-Headed Families Living Below 125%
      of the 'Official' Poverty Level: 1970-1987   108

4-7   Children Living Below the Poverty Level as a Percentage
      of All Similarly Aged Children of that Racial/Ethnic
      Group: 1966-1987   109

4-8   Percentage of Families in Poverty by Type of Family and
      Race/Ethnic Origin: 1987   109

4-9   Work Experience of Working-Age Adults in Poverty, by
      Race: 1985   110

4-10 Work Experience of Head of Households in Poverty, by
      Race: 1985   111

4-11 Work Experience of Female Head of Households in
      Poverty, with No Husband Present, by Presence of
      Children and by Race: 1985   112

4-12 Work Experience of All Head of Households and of
      Female Head of Households Below 125% of Poverty,
      by Race: 1985   113

4-13 Number of Earners per Low Income Family and per Family
      Regardless of Income, by Race/Ethnic Group: 1985   114

4-14 The Educational Experience of the Poor and of the
      General Population: 1985   115

4-15 The Educational Experience of Poor Householders and of
      Poor Female Householders by Race/Ethnic Group: 1987   116

4-16 Where The Poor Live: 1987   117

5-1   Median Income by Race/Ethnic Group and Sex of
       Full-Year, Full-Time Workers and Ratios Between
       Incomes: 1939-1987 (in current dollars)   143

5-2   Median Earnings by Race/Ethnic Group and Sex and Ratios
       Between Earnings for Full-Year, Full-Time Workers:
       1975-1986 (in current dollars)   144

5-3   Median Income by Sex, Race, and Education for
       Full-Year, Full-Time Workers Age 25 and Older: 1986
       (in current dollars)   145

5-4   Ratios of Median Income by Sex, Race, and Education for
       Full-Year, Full-Time Workers Age 25 and Older: 1975,
       1980, 1985, and 1986   146

5-5   Median Income by Sex, Race, and Education for All
       Persons Age 25 and Older: 1986 (in current dollars)   147

5-6   Mean Earnings by Occupation, Sex, and Race/Ethnic
       Group, and Median Earnings by Occupation and Sex for
       Full-Year, Full-Time Workers: 1985   148

5-7   Ratios of Occupational Earnings by Sex and Race/Ethnic
       Group for Full-Year, Full-Time Workers: 1985   149

5-8   Percentage Changes in Constant 1985 Dollar Occupational
       Earnings, by Sex and Race/Ethnic Group: 1960-67,
       1967-73, 1973-75, 1975-81   150

5-9   Percentage Changes in Constant 1985 Dollar Occupational
       Earnings, by Sex and Race/Ethnic Group: 1982-85,
       1985-88-I   152

5-10   Average Gross Hourly Earnings of All Production and
       Nonsupervisory Workers in Private Nonagricultural
       Employment, by Industry, with Annual Equivalent
       Earnings: 1960, 1972, 1987 (all in constant 1985
       dollars)   154

5-11   Average Gross Weekly Earnings of All Production and
       Nonsupervisory Workers in Private Nonagricultural
       Employment, by Industry: 1960, 1972, 1987 (all in
       constant 1985 dollars)   155

7-1   Distribution of Families by Net Worth in 1962 and 1983,
       Using Federal Reserve Board's Survey of Consumer
       Finances (in constant 1985 dollars)   191

7-2   Distribution of Household Net Worth by Race/Ethnic
       Group, Income, and Type of Household, Using Bureau of
       the Census SIPP Data for 1984 (in 1985 dollars)   192

7-3   Median and Mean Net Worth by Income, Race/Ethnic Group,
      and Type of Household, Using Bureau of the Census SIPP
      Data for 1984 (in 1985 dollars)   193

7-4   Distribution of Net Worth by Family Income and by
      Race/Ethnic Group, Using Federal Reserve SCF for 1983
      and 1986 (in 1985 dollars)   194

7-5   Distribution of Net Worth Among Different Assets by
      Race/Ethnic Group, Using Bureau of the Census SIPP Data
      for 1984   195

7-6   Distribution of Net Worth Among Various Assets for
      Households with Heads Aged 25 or More Holding Varying
      Proportions of Total Net Worth, Using Federal Reserve
      1986 SCF Data   196

7-7   The Concentration of Wealth Holdings in 1983 and 1986
      Among Households with Heads Aged 25 or More by Types of
      Assets and by Percentage of Total Net Worth Held, Using
      Federal Reserve SCF Data   197

7-8   Concentration in the Dollar Holdings of Net Worth and
      in the Receipt of Income, and Mean Net Worth and
      Income, All by Percentile Holdings of Net Worth Among
      Households with Heads Aged 25 or More, Using Federal
      Reserve 1986 SCF Data (Assets in 1985 dollars)   198

7-9   Distribution Among American Families of Ownership of
      Publicly Traded Stocks from the Federal Reserve's 1983
      Survey of Consumer Finance   198

7-10 The Net Worth of the Wealthiest Americans in 1983
      (in 1985 dollars)   199

7-11 The Concentration of Wealth Holdings in 1963 and 1983
      Among Households with Heads Aged 18 or More by Types of
      Assets and by Percentage of Total Net Worth Held,
      Using Federal Reserve SCF Data   200

Preface

This book is the most recent stage of a project that has been an ongoing focus of my work since I began studying and teaching economics. For many of the reasons described in Chapter 1, I have long been convinced that the study of the distributions of income and wealth are, or should be, at the core of economics. That the level and rate of growth of the national product are important is clear. But a society that has a reasonable level of total output (on a per capita basis) and that maintains equitable distributions of both current income and wealth might well provide a far better standard of living for most of its people than a far richer nation with highly inequitable and very skewed distributions. Thus, I have made it a point to stress the importance of distributional questions in much of my teaching and research.

Moreover, while teaching and lecturing about economics for almost twenty years, I have never ceased to be amazed at the level of ignorance of most, even well-educated and otherwise fairly well-informed, Americans about the true dimensions of our nation's distributions of income and wealth. Although many know in a vague sense that we have a "poverty problem," they have little idea of the dimensions or extent of that problem. While many know that there are "some" very rich people, they have little sense of just how concentrated is the ownership of wealth. Even more striking are the misperceptions about the nature and extent of the middle class, variously defined. Most Americans seem to think that our nation has a vast middle class constituting on the order of eighty or ninety percent of American families, and that virtually all of these families live "the good life." They are amazed to find that this is not the case.

I have taught and lectured at fairly elite private colleges, at "historically Black" colleges where many of the students come from rather impoverished backgrounds, and at urban public colleges where many of the students might be viewed as working and lower-middle class. Surprisingly, these misperceptions about the nature of the distributions of income and wealth seem remarkably ubiquitous. So, I long ago began to accumulate statistics detailing the known facts about these distributions and laying that information out in handouts for my students and audiences. I typically began such lectures by having the students help me put together two budgets: one that they perceived as minimally necessary for a family of four to survive at a minimally acceptable level, and a second that they felt was the minimum necessary to live at a modestly comfortable level. It was interesting to see, time and again, how close these spontaneously defined budgets came to the Bureau of Labor Statistics Minimum Adequacy and Modest But Adequate budgets. It was even more interesting to see the shock that these audiences expressed when they found out how large a proportion of U.S. families lived below these levels.

Then, in 1985, I was asked to present a paper on this topic for the Families and Economic Distress Symposium organized by Linda Majka of the Department of Sociology and Patricia Voydanoff of the Center for the Study of Family Development, both of the University of Dayton, Ohio. That paper consisted of a brief overview of the changing pattern of the distributions of income and wealth from 1970 to 1983. Later, when these papers were published in a book of readings (Majka and Voydanoff 1988), I was invited by the organizers of the conference, now the editors of this book, to update and expand my paper "a bit." It was at this point that I decided to look at the full quarter century from 1960 to 1985, taking advantage of some new data, especially pertaining to the distribution of wealth (see Chapter 6). But I got carried away, and my expanded paper had to be cut by almost half to fit into the space restrictions of that book.

It was at that juncture that I approached Praeger Publishers about the possibility of further expanding the full paper into book form and updating the data to include the latest figures then available. Luckily for me, the idea appealed to James Dunton, Senior Editor for Economics and Business. Mr. Dunton was both very supportive and very understanding as the project took longer and got more complex than first planned. One of the problems I faced, like so many others in this field, is how to draw the line between the desires to make the work complete and current, especially the issue of when to stop adding new data. Mr. Dunton was patient with me as I tried to both fill in gaps and make the book as current as possible.

In the latter regard, I must thank two sets of researchers who were very helpful. Arthur Kennickell and his colleagues at the Division of Research and Statistics of the Board of Governors of the Federal Reserve System shared with me their most recent research findings on the distribution of wealth, including some, as of that time, unpublished papers. Enrique Lamas of the Poverty and Wealth Statistics Branch of the Population Division of the Bureau of Labor Statistics was very helpful in keeping me informed of their most recent work. A number of other researchers with the Bureau of Labor Statistics and with the Bureau of the Census generously shared unpublished, detailed data, helped with the interpretation of some of the published data, and sent me advance copies of materials as those become available. All of this made it possible for me to create that rare animal in economics, an empirical book that is still relatively current when it is published.

I also want to express my gratitude to the economics faculty and to the staff of the Institute for Research on Poverty at the University of Wisconsin-Madison. It was there that folks like Robert Lampman, Eugene Smolensky, W. Lee Hansen, and Burton Weisbrod began to provide me, as a graduate student in the turbulent 1960s, and the rest of the country, with detailed data that addressed so many of the issues upon which I focus in this book. My intellectual and inspirational debt to them is heartfelt. Moreover, the steady flow of empirical- and policy-focused research that has been generated by the Institute (much of it summarized in their journal *Focus*) has been a gold mine of important information that I, like so many other researchers in this field, have consistently employed.

I owe a very special expression of thanks to my colleagues in the Union for Radical Political Economics. It is that organization, now twenty years old, its members and journal (*The Review of Radical Political Economics*) that has provided the constant professional support and feedback that we all find so necessary. Over the years, as I have often served on the editorial board of that journal and attended and participated in many of the conferences, I have been able to test out ideas, and hear many new ideas, suggestions and criticisms. In particular, I have benefited from the work of Peter Meyer, Howard Sherman, Samuel Bowles, Thomas Weisskoff, Michael Reich, Richard Edwards, William Tabb, Barry Bluestone, Bennett Harrison, and David Gordon, among many others. Then, I owe a special acknowledgement to the students who, in so many classes, provided the motivation for this on-going project and also offered valuable feedback as it progressed. I also want to express my gratitude to Frank Welsch, my production editor at Praeger, for his cooperation and support during the final stages of getting the manuscript ready for publication.

As every author and every author's family knows all too well, no book ever got written without major sacrifices on the part of those who had the misfortune to have to live with the author while the book was in progress. Among academics, books almost always get written as an addition to all the regular demands of teaching and the university, and as an addition to the necessary demands of daily life. Without the understanding and support of their spouse and their children, either the books would not get written or all authors would shortly become unhappy, lonely bachelors. In my case, this book was written at the same time as my wife, Martina, wrote her Ph. D. dissertation, as our sons, David and Shawn, went through the process of applying for college, and as our daughter, Hannah, experienced her first years of life. The fact that we were all successful in our ventures is no small comment upon the strength and caring that we have been able to provide one another. I owe a special thanks to Martina for listening to me work out ideas, helping me to clarify my thoughts, and doing a great deal of proofreading in the midst of her own ordeal.

Finally, as always, I accept full responsibility for any errors of omission or commission that remain in this work. There are many unfinished tasks that one is constantly tempted to pursue -- lines of inquiry that should be explored, alternative policy proposals to be developed, supplementary statistical analysis that would make the work more elegant and more convincing, graphics that would make it more accessible and clearer to a wider audience. All of these pertain to this book. But, ultimately, if a book is ever to be published, one simply has to stop, let the work stand on its merits at a given point in its development, and be willing to listen to and seriously consider criticism. This is especially true when one is attempting to publish a book in the hope that its empirical work is still reasonably current. I can only hope that the material in this book stimulates new and on-going work, that it shines a bit of light and new understanding on some important topics, and that it leads to some renewed commitments to try to make the distributions of income and wealth in the United States more equitable.

Toward Two Societies

1

Introduction

BACKGROUND AND SCOPE OF THIS STUDY

The quarter of a century that has passed from 1960 to 1985 has been quite remarkable in many respects. It began with the liberal administration of John Kennedy and ended with the conservative one of Ronald Reagan. It began before most Americans had ever heard of Vietnam and ended long after that war was over, while we were in the midst of yet another conflict in the Middle East. More relevant to the specific concerns of this book, the period begins during the very earliest days of the civil rights movement, before the awareness brought by the famous TV special *Hunger in America*, before Johnson's Civil Rights Act and his War on Poverty, before the welfare rights movement, before the modern women's movement. It ends during a period of retrenchment, when many of the social programs of the 1960s have been cut back or eliminated, and when the civil rights movement is almost moribund (though a Black man ran for President in 1984, and then again in 1988). A time when, as we shall see, the level of poverty is once again almost as high as it was at the beginning of the period, and when the degree of polarization in the distribution of income is at the highest level since detailed records were first maintained.

The quarter century began just two years after the publication of John Kenneth Galbraith's *The Affluent Society* which argued that affluence, not poverty, should be the key to understanding our society. He stressed that, "The first task is to see the way our economic attitudes are rooted in the poverty, inequality, and economic peril of the past" and went on to argue that we needed to "escape from the obsolete and contrived preoccupations associated with the assumption of poverty" (Galbraith 1958: 3).[1] On the other hand, this period begins just two years before Michael Harrington was to publish his path breaking book, *The Other America: Poverty in the United States*, which looked at America from a very different perspective, arguing persuasively that poverty was a far more significant, pervasive, and difficult problem than we as a society had been willing to admit (Harrington 1962). In marked contrast the period ends with the publication of such very conservative books as George Gilder's *Wealth and Poverty* (1982) and Charles Murray's *Losing Ground: American Social Policy 1950-1980* (1984),[2] which attack the efforts in the intervening years to address the problems of the distributions of income and wealth as being either useless, or even worse, misdirected and misguided.[3]

As we look at the last few years of the quarter century that ended in 1985, and at the first few years of the next, we shall see that the period of the Reagan administration has seen an acceleration of major changes in the distribution of income, and also in the distribution of wealth, that have significantly affected the nature and structure of American society and affected the well-being of individuals and families. However, we shall also see that, in many respects, these changes were well under way long before Reagan took office.

The primary focus of this book is to identify the direction and pattern of changes that have occurred since 1960 in the distributions of income and wealth. Particular attention will be focused upon the rather abrupt change in the direction in which the distribution of income has moved, in a number of respects, since the early 1970s. Evidence from both the distributions of income and of wealth will be presented to support the contention that the middle class in America is shrinking as a proportion of the population and that an increasing degree of bipolarization is occurring, with the proportion of those who are poor and those who are quite affluent both increasing. We shall see that this polarization also has crucial racial/ethnic, gender, and family structure characteristics.

The primary concern is with the distributions of income and wealth among families in the United States and the effects on those families of changes in those distributions, though I also look at the patterns among unrelated individuals. This concern with the family is approached in a manner to highlight the differential effects upon families and persons of different racial and ethnic origins and upon the differential effects between men and women. There is a particular effort made to explore in some detail the varying impacts of education, occupation, and industry upon the income of persons of different racial/ethnic origins and sexes during this period and to also conduct a careful examination of the circumstances of those who are still in poverty today. Special attention is also directed at the effects of the distributions on children and upon households headed by women.

In Part I, the topic is the distribution of income, while in Part II attention will shift to the even wider disparities that occur in the distribution of wealth. Part III consists of my conclusions and some proposals as to what is needed to improve both the distributions of income and of wealth.

WHY BE CONCERNED WITH THE DISTRIBUTION OF INCOME OR OF WEALTH?

To the reader of this book, this may seem to be a useless question. After all, if you did not have some concern with these issues, you presumably would not have bothered to pick it up and begun to read. However, over the two or three centuries that political economy can be said to have existed as a reasonably well defined area of intellectual curiosity and analysis, the issue as to whether or not it is important to study either the pattern or the causes of the distribution of either wealth or income has been a topic of some debate.[4]

At an early point in this history, one could hear the three part argument -- (1) that there had always been rich and poor among us and always would be, (2) that this was largely a pattern of historical legacies with some allowance for new entrepreneurs, and (3) that, therefore, we should get on with the study of the more important micro questions of what gets produced and how and at what price, and of the more important macro questions concerning the size of the nation's economy, its overall rate of growth, and the changing level of prices.

Echoes of this perspective come down to us today. We hear the argument that poverty is largely a relative concept, that as the nation's overall income and wealth increase, so will the lot of the poor improve. Moreover, this perspective argues, ours is a nation with a massive middle class that is growing both absolutely and relatively, hence concern with the plight of the poor or the excesses of the rich are peripheral issues, more the proper concern of sociologists than of (political) economists.

On the other hand, there is another tradition of political economic thought, going back to Ricardo and John Bates Clark and to Marx and the early socialists, that argues that one of the primary concerns of analysis ought to be upon issues of distribution: What proportion of our population is rich or poor? How are these proportions changing? What is the gap between those at the top and at the bottom of the distribution and is that gap getting larger or smaller? What are the conditions of those at the bottom and are those conditions improving? Is the middle class growing or not and how does one define it? Those concerned with the issue of distribution are also at some pain to explain why it is what it is and what the forces are that shape it. This book is clearly within this latter tradition.

Wealth vs. Income as a Focus

In earlier periods, one discussed the distributional issues-- the questions of poor and rich--in terms of the holdings of wealth. The rich were those who owned and controlled great wealth, at first, largely in the form of productive land, later in more varied forms of property, both real (land and buildings) and financial (money itself, stocks or claims on the wealth of others). The poor were those who owned little or no wealth. It was simply assumed that those with large wealth holdings would also enjoy the benefits of large streams of current income, while those with little or no wealth would, at best, receive only such income as they earned in wages. These persons would be poor or not so poor depending on their contribution to production, which also allows for the questions of their motivational levels and the availability of jobs.

However, during the last century, the concern with distributional issues and the definitions of who are rich and who are poor, became to be defined more and more directly in terms of current streams of income. Those with large incomes, regardless of their underlying wealth holdings, were considered rich and those with very low incomes were considered poor, it being assumed that the latter could not have substantial wealth holdings.

After World War II, the U.S. government began to keep and publish data on the distribution of income. Following the growing concerns with the issue of poverty in the 1960s, it also began to keep and publish data concerning the poor, who were always so defined on the basis of their income. Only very rarely did the government gather data on the distribution of wealth. In fact, the regular governmental accumulation and publishing of extensive data on wealth holdings has only begun in the last few years. (Though a handful of economists did continue to study wealth holdings over the post-war period.)

In this book, I focus on the distributions of both income and wealth, although the far greater availability of data concerning income over the period in question, and the prevailing concern with that distribution, have led me to focus more heavily there.

The Significance of the Distribution of Income and Wealth

While it is clear that there has been debate among political economists as to whether or not distribution should be a major focus of analysis, we have not yet addressed the question as to why those who feel distribution needs to be studied hold that view. What is so important about the distributions of income and of wealth that warrants the commitment of intellectual resources, and of economic and political resources as well? In addressing this question, Lester Thurow argues that the primary issues can be grouped into two categories, those concerning the efficiency of an economy and those concerning the degree of equity that result from the functioning of the economy (Thurow 1975: ix). While I think these two categories are too narrow, they do serve as a good point from which to begin this discussion.

Efficiency
Let us turn first to the issue of the relationship between economic efficiency and the distribution of income. Economic efficiency can be defined in a number of ways. One of the most common is to resort to the Pareto concept that a society is producing in an efficient manner when it is not possible to increase the production of any one good or service without decreasing the production of some other good or service. Applied to the relationship between the well-being of the members of that society and its economic system, this can be restated as that system is economically efficient when any attempt to produce goods or services so as to increase the well-being of any one member of the society,

or any attempt to provide more income to one member of a society, can only be accomplished at the cost of decreasing the well-being of some other member, How do these concepts of efficiency relate to the distribution of income?

The theory of a properly functioning market system is that *given the existing distribution of income*, the market economy should produce a bundle of goods and services that meet the Pareto conditions indicated just above. If on equity or other grounds, one concludes that the distribution of income is not appropriate, the "efficiently" functioning market system will still adjust to it. Thurow put it well, when he stated:

> If income and wealth are not distributed in accordance with equity, individual preferences are not properly weighted and the market adjusts to an inequitable distribution of purchasing power. Technically, the market may be equally efficient in either case, but in the second case it is normatively inefficient just as a street-sweeper sweeping the wrong street is inefficient regardless of its technical street-sweeping ability (Thurow 1975: 21-22).

Thus, any attempt to ignore the issue of the normative acceptability of the distribution of income and wealth by hiding behind such a concept of efficiency is in effect to make the normative decision that the existing distribution is correct and should be the basis in terms of which the economy should attempt to adjust.

Other more micro concepts of efficiency can be identified. According to marginal productivity theory, the distribution of income among the economic actors should reflect, at least on average and short of market imperfections, their marginal contribution to the production of goods and services. If some actors are receiving either more or less than an amount equal to their marginal contribution, the system is functioning inefficiently. Even if one ignores the devastating attack upon the basic nature and validity of this theory mounted by Thurow (1975: 211-230), clearly ours is not a purely competitively market driven society. It never has been and never will be. Significant degrees of noncompetitive forces exist among producers, among workers, and even among consumers, especially when we view the government at its many levels and in its many forms as an important consumer. Moreover, ours is not even a purely market-driven society, even if one ignores the degree of competition within our markets. Government, at various levels, as a result of our political process, imposes a vast array of constraints upon the functioning of many markets. Thus, our society contains as a permanent and sometimes politically intended feature many so-called market imperfections. Hence, worrying about the efficiency of the distribution of income or wealth in terms of a flawed and not-very relevant marginal productivity theory does us little good. But that is not to say that efficiency concerns are not an important motivation for studying distribution.

If there is a pervasive ideology in our nation that states that people "should expect" to earn an amount proportionate to their contribution to society, and, at the same time, there is a widespread conviction among many of our citizens that they earn far less than what they are "worth" by this criteria, while others earn far more than they are worth, we have the basis for serious political discontent and instability, which in turn can lead to economic inefficiency.

Further, and perhaps more directly, if, as a result of the distributions of income and of wealth, many of our citizens are forced to live in conditions that lead to their not having the physical ability (due to illness or poor diet or to a lack of sleep due to overcrowded or inadequate or unavailable housing) to work, and in the case of a large proportion of our children an inability to study, our society is losing the production that these persons could contribute. Surely this must be viewed as an inefficiency. In addition, if one impact of these distributions is to generate a pattern of housing and access to education, reaching from preschool programs to graduate university and technical programs, which is such that a large proportion of our citizens do not receive the training needed to produce many goods and services in an increasingly high-tech environment, then we are again losing productivity and suffering inefficiency, even if they are physically able and willing to work.

Moreover, if, as another result of the distributions of income and wealth, our society as a whole is forced to expend vast sums of money on transfer payments to simply keep a large number of poor members alive and consuming at, at least minimal levels--monies that could otherwise be put to far more productive purposes--then this represents a further waste of resources. Finally, if the wealthiest members of our society have control of monies which are far in excess of what they need to expend for consumption, and if they are free, even encouraged, to employ a significant proportion of that money in a manner that does not make it available to productive investments, then our economic productivity and efficiency suffers even further.

Issues such as these can legitimately and reasonably be asserted to provide grounds on the basis of efficiency concerns to warrant the careful study of the distributions of income and of wealth.

Equity

Before proceeding to explore this motivational basis for the study of the distribution of income or of wealth, it is important to distinguish between a concern for equity and one for equality. For example, there are those who, on the basis of often strongly held philosophical views, argue that all members of a society are inherently equal and entitled to an equal share of that society's resources and goods and services simply on the basis of being a member (albeit in good standing) of that society.

Interestingly, those who employ Lorenz curves and Gini indexes are examining the distribution of income within a society on the criteria of equality. In a Lorenz curve analysis one plots the proportion of a nation's income received by various proportions of its population. Perfect equality exists when, for example, each 5 percent of the population receive 5 percent of the income. Inequality is indicated by a curve which reflects the fact that the poorest 5 percent of the population receives something less than 5 percent of the nation's income, while the richest 5 percent receive far more than 5 percent of the income.

The Gini index or coefficient is simply a ratio between, on the one hand, the area between the Lorenz curve and the 45 degree line of perfect equality, and, on the other hand, the total area between the line of perfect equality and the axes. Thus, if there is perfect equality, the numerator is zero (the Lorenz curve is identical to the line of perfect equality and there is no area between them) and hence the ratio is zero. Whereas, if there is perfect inequality (the richest individual has 100 percent of the income and everyone else has nothing, in which case the Lorenz curve lies alongside the axes), the Gini ratio is 1.

Those who are concerned with the issue of how equal or unequal is the distribution of income would therefore employ the Lorenz or Gini type of analysis. Numerous such studies have been done which conclude that the degree of inequality in the U.S. has been increasing over the past two decades.[5] Other studies using these techniques have been conducted in order to provide a basis upon which to compare different societies. These have concluded that the U.S. has come to have one of the more unequal distributions of income among the industrialized nations of "the first world." However, these measurements will not be a focus of this study.

The issue of the equity of a society's distributions of income and of wealth is far more subtle and illusive than the far simpler criteria of equality. Turning again to the work of Thurow, he identifies four "directions from which one can attempt to specify economic equity" (Thurow 1975: 23). With some paraphrasing and a bit of elaboration and modification, these can be expressed as:

1. The distribution is equitable if it results from fair and reasonable processes and procedures, if the rules of the economic game are fair and fairly administered.
2. The distribution is equitable if it reflects the political consensus of the individual preferences of citizens of that society, if it is the distribution that generates the most agreement.
3. The distribution is equitable if it has been made upon the basis of some agreed upon ideal of merit, for example, based upon marginal productivity, or upon the degree of social responsibility, or upon the extent of one's adherence to the "correct" religious practices.
4. The distribution is equitable if it is the one that maximizes the common good, the overall well-being of society, however that common good or well-being is defined within that society.

Those who are concerned with one or more of these concepts of equity will legitimately seek first to better define the particular criteria of a fair rule, or the nature of the political consensus, or the concept of merit, or of the common good and will then go on to study the extent to which the observed distribution of income or of wealth meets the standard so defined.

The Ethical Basis of Both Efficiency and Equity Criteria

Thurow goes on to make the important point that both efficiency and equity criteria are based upon value judgments, that efficiency criteria are no more value free than are equity criteria (Thurow 1975:24). I quite agree. Those economists and others who pretend to an "objective" analysis free of value or ethical judgments are simply trying to falsely cloak themselves in an aura of being "scientific" as a means to evade a discussion of the ethical basis, which in fact exists, for their analysis, conclusions, and policy prescriptions. It is far better to be open and honest about the value judgments one is making and to fairly allow others to join the debate on that essential ground, rather than to obfuscate and try to avoid such a debate by pretending to purely objective, value free analysis. Throughout this work, I will try to identify in a clear fashion the ethical value judgments I am making when evaluating the data that is presented concerning the distributions of income and of wealth and the impact of these distributions upon society.

Other Bases for Undertaking the Study of Distribution

Social and Political Unrest Aside from efficiency and equity, there are legitimate political, social, and cultural motivations for undertaking a study of the distribution of income or of wealth. One concern about how income and wealth are distributed stems from the conviction that when one or the other, or especially when both, reflect a pattern that violates the norms of equity that are ideologically supported in the society, a degree of social and political unrest may result that can come to threaten the very fabric of that society.

Moreover, here it is not just the distribution that exists at any given moment that is of paramount concern, but rather the nature of the changes that are occurring over time. If there is some general sense of the gap between rich and poor that is socially tolerable, and if that gap is steadily widening beyond what is seen as acceptable, then political and social forces may be called into play to force a closing of the gap either (1) by providing income (in money or in-kind) to the poorest, or (2) by attempts to confiscate some of the income, or even some of the wealth, of the richest, or (3) by attempts to change the way the market responds to the distribution of income, or (4) by attempts to change the way the market distributes income and allows for the accumulation of wealth. Ultimately, the social and political fabric of the society could be torn asunder.

In a famous passage, John Bates Clark made this point rather eloquently:

> For practical men, and hence for students, supreme importance attaches to one economic problem--that of the

distribution of wealth among different claimants. . . .
The welfare of the laboring classes depends on whether
they get much or little; but their attitude toward other
classes--and therefore, the stability of the social state-
-depends chiefly on the question, whether the amount they
get, be it large or small, is what they produce. If they
create a small amount of wealth, and get the whole of it,
they may not seek to revolutionize society; but if it were
to appear that they produce an ample amount and get only
a part of it, many of them would become revolutionists,
and all would have the right to do so (1899: i,4).

To put the matter in far more conventional terms, many students
of American society are quite concerned with the effect that the
distributions of income and wealth have upon the political process.
Unlike many other Western, democratic nations, access in the United
States to television and radio advertising as part of a political
campaign is largely dependent on the amount of money the candidate
has to spend. The very wealthy are simply in a better position to
run for office using their own funds. They also tend to be better
connected to other rich people who are able to provide needed funds,
either directly or through various devices, such as political action
committees. Is it an accident that more than two thirds of the U.S.
Senate are millionaires? However, beyond the issue of who runs for
office and who wins elections, there are also many ways in which
those with access to large sums of money can influence the path of
legislation, the establishment of executive directives, and the
manner in which laws are enforced.[6] To quote Thurow once more:
"With great inequalities in the distribution of economic power, it
is hard to maintain the equality of influence that is the backbone
of democracy" (1984).

Another avenue through which the distribution of income effects
the functioning of our political system becomes evident when one
examines the relationship between voting and income. According to
Bureau of the Census figures, supported by the analysis of various
political scientists, there is a direct and close relationship
between the amount of income a family enjoys and the likelihood that
voting age members of that family will actually vote. The amount
of income is also closely related to voter registration. Table
1-1 reveals the relationship between family income and both
registration and voting. The figures speak for themselves. As we
will see in later chapters, higher income is closely associated with
more education and education is also closely associated with
registration and voting. Table 1-1 displays these figures as well.
In the words of one study:

the American electorate is not a representative cross
section of the country's citizens. It is a distorted
sample that exaggerates the size of some groups and
minimizes that of others. The more money you have, the
more education you have, the more likely you are to vote.
. . . the electorate [is] stratified along class lines.
(McBride 1988).

Thus, the distributions of income and of wealth are of concern to all of those who worry about the issues of who registers and votes, who runs for office, and who is best able to influence those who hold political office. If one cares about the American political system and the exercise of democracy, one simply must be concerned with the distributions of income and of wealth.

Foreign Perceptions Above even our domestic concerns is the fact that the United States prides itself on its international image of democracy and fairness. However, we suffer as a nation, in terms of our own self-image and in terms of our image abroad, when it becomes clear, as is the case, that our distribution of income is more unequal than that in virtually every other major industrialized nation, and when the extent of the poverty and the conditions under which the poor are forced to live are made dramatically evident in the media, especially the foreign media.

Simple Humanism Finally, there is the very important, but very simple, issue of humanism. One can not study the distributions of income and of wealth and not come face to face with the terrible reality of the conditions facing a substantial portion of the American population, especially among our children. Simple decency requires us not to ignore this issue, but to study its extent and causes and to address the matter of how it can be corrected.

It is interesting in this light to read some of what John Kenneth Galbraith wrote two years before the period we are about to examine. He first cited the words of Marshall:

> "The study of the causes of poverty," Alfred Marshall observed at the turn of the century, "is the study of the causes of the degradation of a large part of mankind." He spoke of the contemporary England as well as of the world beyond. A vast number of people both in town and country, he noted, had insufficient food, clothing, and houseroom; they were: "Overworked and undertaught, weary and careworn, without quiet and without leisure." The chance of their succor, he concluded, gave to economic studies "their chief and their highest interest." (Galbraith 1958: 322)

But Galbraith then went on to state that: "No contemporary economist would be likely to make such an observation about the United States" (ibid.). Well, I am sorry, but during the 1960s and 1970s and again today, I and many other economists are making exactly that statement. When more than 33 million Americans live below the official poverty line, when more than 20 percent of all our children live in poverty, when about 35 percent of all American families live below a reasonably defined level of "minimum adequacy" in terms of income, and when we come to understand what this means in terms of poor housing, poor diet, inadequate medical care, and dysfunctional education, we should all have no choice but to speak out in such terms.

However to Galbraith's credit, while at that time he minimized the extent and the causes of poverty (as was quoted earlier), he did go on to acknowledge that:

> [Poverty] in part . . . is a physical matter; those afflicted have such limited and insufficient food, such poor clothing, such crowded, cold and dirty shelter that life is painful as well as comparatively brief. But just as it is far too tempting to say that, in matters of living standards, everything is relative, so it is wrong to rest everything on absolutes. People are poverty-stricken when their income, even if adequate for survival, falls markedly behind that of the community. Then they cannot have what the larger community regards as the minimum necessary for decency; and they cannot wholly escape, therefore, the judgment of the larger community that they are indecent. They are degraded for, in the literal sense, they live outside the grades or categories which the community regards as acceptable (Galbraith 1958: 323).[7]

CONCLUSION

For all of these reasons, analyzing the recent trends in our distributions of income and of wealth, and then using that information in the effort to make these distributions more equitable is truly a job worthy of the commitment of considerable time, effort, and resources. I can only hope that this study proves useful in that effort.

NOTES

1. To his credit, Galbraith does not deny that the problem of poverty exists. In fact, he stresses in one later chapter that poverty does survive and estimates that it effects about 7.5 percent of the population. However, he views poverty as either being a problem of special "cases" of individual situations or a situation of "insular poverty--that which manifests itself as an "island of poverty." He goes on to argue that: "Insular poverty has something to do with the desire of a comparatively large number of people to spend their lives at or near the place of their birth." Nevertheless, he sees it as a problem that should not be ignored or overlooked and one which "In the contemporary United States . . . is a disgrace."

2. An excellent, and I believe persuasive and rather complete, rebuttal and critique of Murray's book has been published as a Special Report by researchers at the Institute for Research on Poverty at the University of Wisconsin-Madison (McLanahan, et al. 1985). The debate continues with a follow-up article by Murray (1984).

3. To be fair, the period also ends with the publication of Harrington's *The New American Poverty* which opens with the words "The poor are still there" (Harrington 1984: 1). In this work, Harrington revisits the terrain of his earlier book, *The Other America*, (Harrington 1962/1981) and analyzes the differences in the nature of poverty in the 1980s, arguing that "Now there are new structures of misery." He also analyzes the very different and far more conservative social and political environment of the 1980s when " . . . America has lost its own generous vision of what might be" (ibid.: 4).

4. Martin Bronfenbrenner, in his classic book on income distribution theory, does a particularly good job of reviewing much of the historical literature, complete with many interesting quotes, in a chapter entitled "The Disputed Importance of Distribution" (Bronfenbrenner 1971: 1-24).

5. Among the studies reaching this conclusion are those by McKinley, Blackburn, and Bloom (1986), Grubb and Wilson (1987), and Tilly, Bluestone, and Harrison (1986).

6. This issue is not the major focus of this book, but the interested reader is referred to the vast literature in this area, including such books as *Who Runs Congress?* (Green et al. 1972), *The Washington Payoff* (Winter-Berger 1972), *The Politics of Power* (Katznelson and Kesselman 1979), and *The Irony of Democracy* (Dye and Zeigler 1978) to mention only a few well-known works.

7. By the way, it should be noted that Galbraith estimated that 7.5 percent of the American population fell into the poverty category in 1958. A few years later, official estimates were to increase that figure almost threefold (to 22.2 percent in 1960); and I will argue that even those "official poverty" estimates were and are far too low.

Table 1-1
Percentage of Eligible Voters Who Registered and/or Voted
in 1984 Presidential Election, by Income and Education

Annual Family Income	% Registered	% Voting
Under $5,000	50%	38%
$ 5,000 - 9,999	57	46
$10,000 - 14,999	63	54
$15,000 - 19,999	66	57
$20,000 - 24,999	69	61
$25,000 - 24,999	74	67
$35,000 and above	81	74
Education		
0 - 8 Years	53%	43%
1 - 3 Years High School	55	44
4 Years of High School	67	59
1 - 3 Years of College	76	68
4 or More Years College	80	79

Source: McBride 1988. (Based on U.S. Bureau of Census
November 1984 survey.)

PART I

THE DISTRIBUTION OF INCOME SINCE 1960

Developing a Standard Against Which to Measure the Distribution of Income

DEFINING INCOME

This portion of the study is primarily focused upon the changing distribution of family income. The first issue that faces us is how to define the concept of family income. Leaving aside for the moment the question of what is a family, we need to clarify our definition of income. Is it to indicate income before or after taxes? Should it include transfer payments, for example, welfare payments? Should we measure it in current dollars or in so-called real dollars, that is, dollars corrected for inflation? How do we handle in-kind transfer payments? All of these matters and others need to be addressed.

The primary source of data on income in the United States is that provided by the Bureau of the Census in two annual reports, both published as part of their Current Population Reports-Consumer Income, Series P-60 and both based upon the annual Current Population Survey normally conducted in March of each year to gather data about the calendar year just preceding.[1] Since this is the primary source that I am using for the income figures, it is essential to have a clear understanding of the definition of income used by the Bureau of the Census.

It is important to note first that the income figures reflect all regular money income received by the parties in question. This includes:

the sum of the amounts received from wages and salaries, self-employment income, Social Security, Supplemental Security Income, public assistance, interest, dividends, rent, royalties, estates or trusts, veterans' payments, unemployment and workers' compensations, private and government retirement and disability payments, alimony, child support, and any other source of money income which was regularly received (U.S. Dept. of Commerce 1986a: App. A, 33).

However, these figures do not reflect in-kind transfers, such as food stamps or medicaid. According to one study, if these in-kind transfers are evaluated in "market value" dollar terms and added to income, they result in a reduction of the official poverty rate by about one-third, for example, from 15.2 percent to 10.2 percent in 1983. Which is to say that about two-thirds of the poor are still poor even if this adjustment is done. Also, there is no evidence to suggest that these in-kind transfers move the persons affected very far beyond the poverty level of income, even if they are counted this way. Moreover, the trend as to the incidence of poverty over time remains virtually the same even if this adjustment is made, although the size of the adjustment varies somewhat when there are major contractions or expansions in the in-kind transfer (welfare) programs (Danziger, Haverman and Plotnick 1985).

The "market value" valuation technique has been severely criticized as overestimating the impact of in-kind transfers upon the poor.[2] In particular, if, for example, free medical care is valued at its market price, it tends to result in a vast overestimation of the actual income of the recipient, who would never have paid, or been able to pay, such a price for those services. If that presumed value is added to the family's income and their eligibility for other assistance programs is thus jeopardized, it is likely that the family's net position would be worse, not better, as a result.

Another study did examine the impact of such in-kind transfers under three different valuation techniques, that is, under three different methods of placing a dollar equivalent value upon them. One was the above-mentioned "market value" which is equal to the purchase price in the private market of the goods received. The second was the "recipient-cash equivalent" method which is the amount of cash that would make the recipient just as well off as the in-kind transfer. The third was the "poverty budget share" approach which limits the value of food, housing or medical in-kind transfers to the proportions spent on these items by persons at or near the poverty line in 1960-61, when such transfers were minimal. The effects of these different approaches upon the poverty rate was that in 1984, when the rate for all persons was 14.4 percent , it would have fallen to 9.7 percent with the "market value" method, to 12.2 percent under the "recipient cash value" approach, and to 12.1 percent under the "poverty budget share" approach; that is, the latter two methods resulted in a reduction in the rate of poverty only about half the size of the first (U.S. Dept. of Commerce 1986b).

Since such studies as these have been done using the data for only a few selected years and have used different approaches, it is simply not yet possible to do any comparisons over time that include in-kind transfers. Hence, for the remainder of this book, only cash income figures will be employed. Nevertheless, the importance of in-kind transfers should be kept in mind.

It also needs to be kept in mind that the income figures reported by the Bureau of the Census, and used in this study, are all on a pre-tax, pre-deduction basis. That is, all taxes (federal, state, and local), and all deductions for such items as Social

Security, Medicare premiums, private medical insurance, and union dues are still included in one's money income. That is why, in developing the Bureau of Labor Statistics standard budgets (discussed below), allowance has been made for the need to pay these amounts.[3]

THE SHIFTING TAX BURDEN

However, even though this study will focus on the distribution of pre-tax income, I would be irresponsible not to at least discuss in passing the nature of the shifting pattern of taxation upon the after-tax distribution of income. There have been a number of studies of this issue, perhaps the best known of which is that by Joseph Peckman, who has been examining this issue for years (Peckman 1987). Another major study, conducted by the Congressional Budget Office (CBO), examined the effects of taxation, especially federal taxes, through 1988 to specifically encompass the Tax Reform Act of 1986 and to place the effects of this law into a historical context (Congressional Budget Office 1987). The overall results of these and other studies conclusively demonstrate that the burden of taxation in the United States has become far more regressive over the recent decades, and that even the more progressive aspects of the 1986 Tax Reform Act are not sufficient to overcome that trend.

More specifically, using assumptions about the incidence of the various taxes that in the opinion of some researchers "tend to underestimate tax burdens on the poor" (Albelda 1988a: 11), Peckman found that the total burden of federal, state and local taxes upon the poorest 10 percent of the population had increased from 16.8 percent in 1966 to 21.9 percent in 1985, while the burden upon the richest 10 percent had decreased from 30.1 percent in 1966 to 25.3 percent in 1985. Under what Albelda considers "a more likely set of assumptions," Pechman found that by 1985 the overall tax system in America had become absolutely regressive, that is, the poor were paying a higher percentage of their income in taxes than the rich.[4]

In the CBO study, it was found that the poorest 40 percent of American families had real (inflation adjusted) average after-tax incomes in 1987 that were lower than in 1977, middle-income families had only about 1 percent more after-tax income in 1987 than in 1977, while the richest 1 percent had 74 percent more such income. In trying to place the effects of the 1986 Tax Reform Act in historical perspective, the CBO estimated that the poorest 10 percent of all households would still pay 20 percent more in federal taxes (including all income, excise, and payroll taxes) in 1988 (under the new act) than they did in 1977; while the richest 10 percent would pay almost 20 percent less. To look at this problem from a slightly different perspective, the overall federal tax burden on a family of four at the (pre-tax) poverty level[5] had increased, according to the CBO, from 1.8 percent in 1979 to 10.8 percent in 1986. The CBO estimated that the effect of the 1986 Tax Reform Act on such a family in 1988 would be to return the federal tax burden to the 1979 level.

However, before one gets too euphoric about that very real step forward, one should recall studies such as that by Reschovsky and Chernick that demonstrated that persons living below the poverty line in Massachusetts (one of the most progressive states) in 1986, paid about 9 percent of their income in local property taxes and about 8 percent in state and local sales and excise taxes, while only paying 0.5 percent in federal taxes (Reschovsky and Chernick 1988).[6] Thus, reforming the federal tax situation would only be a beginning, and the 1986 Act, as McIntyre (1988) makes evident, is only a very small beginning of even that effort.

From the perspective of this book, the point is that the reader should not assume that the impact of the American taxation system is such that the inequities in the distribution of pre-tax income that we will be analyzing were, or are likely to be, corrected when one looks at after-tax income. In fact, there is some basis to think that it might even be worse.

SOME EXPERIMENTAL DEFINITIONS OF INCOME

In late 1988, the Census Bureau released a major new study which had grown out of the many debates as to what definition of income to use when exploring the distribution of income in the United States. This study, entitled *Measuring the Effects of Benefits and Taxes on Income and Poverty: 1986* (US Department of Commerce, Bureau of the Census 1988d) actually provides data using 12 different definitions of income that build, one upon the other, beginning with the "official measure" that has been the standard and is used in this book (definition #1). This study, which the Bureau promises will be the first of an on-going series, looks at distributional questions and the incidence of poverty for each of these definitions.

What is done is to first eliminate all government transfers (definition #2), then add first capital gains (#3), and then employer paid health insurance (#4) to provide a new broad definition of private sector income. Then, to provide at least an initial look at after tax income, first federal income taxes (#5), then state income taxes (#6), and finally Social Security taxes (#7) are deducted. However, no attempt is made to allow for sales, excise, or property taxes. Then, to examine the effects of government transfer payments the value of nonmeans-tested cash transfers (#8), nonmeans-tested noncash transfers (#9), means-tested cash transfers (#10), and finally means-tested noncash transfers (#11) are progressively added. There are a variety of questions, similar to those presented earlier, that one could raise with the means used to evaluate the noncash transfers, but, in fairness, it would seem that the Bureau did employ a middle-of-the-road sort of approach here. Finally, there is an attempt to add in an imputed return on the value of the equity one has in one's own home (#12).

All of this data is presented for only one year, 1986; hence it is not possible to use these alternative, rather experimental, but interesting definitions for the longitudinal studies which are the primary focus of this book. Moreover, the data is presented for various types of households, rather than for families, which are the primary concern of the work presented in this book. Nevertheless, the results of this new research is quite interesting and as more such data become available in future years it will command closer study.[7]

DEFINING FAMILY

In analyzing the distribution of income, or of wealth for that matter, the issue arises as to what income earning, or wealth holding, units should be examined. The issue usually turns on the question of whether to use "family" data or "household" data. For a variety of reasons, this study focuses upon the family as the critical unit, although household data will be presented in some instances where that is the only available basis. Some analysis is also done concerning "unrelated individuals" in order to get at the issue of what might be called single member families. Before discussing the reasons for focusing on these categories, let us look at the various definitions.

The use of these terms is dictated by the Bureau of the Census and how they gather and report data. The Bureau employs the following definitions:

Family: A family is a group of two persons or more related by birth, marriage, or adoption and residing together; all such persons (including related subfamily members) are considered as members of one family.

Household: A household consists of all the persons who occupy a housing unit. A house, an apartment or other group of rooms, or a single room is regarded as a housing unit when it is occupied or intended for occupancy as separate living quarters. . . . A household includes the related family members and all the unrelated persons, if any, such as lodgers, foster children, wards, or employees who share the housing unit. A person living alone in a housing unit, or a group of unrelated persons sharing a housing unit as partners, is also counted as a household.

Unrelated Individuals: The term "unrelated individual" refers to persons 15 years old and over (other than inmates of institutions) who are not living with any relatives. An unrelated individual may (1) constitute a one person household, (2) be part of a household including one or more other families or unrelated individuals, or (3) reside in group quarters such as a rooming house (U.S. Dept of Commerce 1986a: 162-163).

Although I have been lecturing and writing about the distribution of income and wealth for years, the specific project which led to this book was the invitation to present a paper at a conference at the University of Dayton concerning the plight of the American family. Hence, my initial focus on the family as the unit of analysis. Beyond this, it seems to me that despite the new social patterns that became so evident in the 1960s, it is still the family which is the basic unit in the American social structure and it is the family which is the primary focus of interest when we raise questions about the distribution of income and wealth.

However, as a careful reading of the above definitions suggests, there are some important problems and limitations in using this Bureau of the Census category. To begin with, there is the problem of what might be called common-law relationships, two adults, one or both of whom may have children living with them, who are living together in one housing unit. According to the Bureau, this would constitute a household, but not a family. In fact, if both adults had children living with them, it would constitute two families. If either or both does not have children living with them, such adults would be considered unrelated individuals who together with the others present constitute a household. Since the institution of well-defined couples living together (often with children) and sharing resources, including income, is quite widespread, using the Bureau's definition of family probably misses some family units and double counts others. We can only hope that these two tendencies balance out.

On the other hand, if we use the concept of household, we run the even larger risk of counting as a single unit persons who are not sharing their income and wealth and should be counted separately in any meaningful discussion of the distribution of income or wealth.

We do need to look at the distribution among unrelated individuals since many of the elderly live apart from any other family members, as do many young people, and do constitute what we might call single member families. Again, if we use household data, we run the very real risk of lumping together into one unit, two or more single people who do not share their income or wealth.

The point is that there is no perfect solution to the problem of what unit to use. But it seems to me that the use of the family, augmented by some examination of the situation of unrelated individuals, presents the most fruitful approach.

DEVELOPING STANDARDS OF COMPARISON FOR INCOME LEVELS

In trying to appreciate the real meaning of the distribution of income, it is necessary to place the dollar numbers in some context that is understandable and meaningful in everyday terms. There are a variety of ways of doing this.

Defining the Official Poverty Level of Income

In 1985, the federal government's "official" definition of poverty for a "typical" family of four was $10,989. But most economists, especially those of a progressive nature, consider this to be a rather unrealistically low figure.

That "official" definition of poverty was based upon a rough estimate by the Social Security Administration of the cash income needed in early 1964 to provide an urban family of two adults and two children with a subsistence level diet. This, in turn, was based upon the Department of Agriculture's 1961 Economy Food Plan for a family with two adults and two school-age children. This plan allowed for $2.40 per person per day for food, in 1985 prices. In 1964, the Social Security Administration then accepted a 1955 Department of Agriculture study which estimated that providing such a diet for a family of three or more apparently accounted for about one-third of a family's budget. Hence, the subsistence food budget figure was merely multiplied by three to come up with a definition of poverty which was then rounded off to the figure of $3,000 per four member family. In computing the overall level of poverty, a sliding scale was developed to adjust the threshold level for family size.

Since then, despite reviews by federal interagency committees in 1969 and again in 1980, no attempt has been made by the Social Security Administration or the Bureau of the Census to modify that official definition of poverty in any substantial way. All that has happened is that, each year, the number is adjusted to take into account the larger amount of money that would be needed to overcome the effect of inflation.

Aside from the issue of in-kind transfers, already discussed, there are many other weaknesses and inadequacies about this definition. Thus, the official poverty index makes no allowance for regional differences in the cost of living. As Sar Levitan has pointed out: "It ignores the predominance of higher prices in central cities, where many of the poor are concentrated, and it also has not been modified to account for the added resources available to those living on farms" (Levitan 1985: 2).[8]

It also makes no allowance for the different tax burdens borne by families with the same income due to differences in the sources of that income. Even more obvious is the fact that the original 1955 Department of Agriculture Study employed a concept of food costs ". . . developed for 'temporary or emergency use', and do not reflect the costs of an adequate, permanent diet" (ibid.: 4). Even more important, as Levitan also points out: ". . . Americans now spend only one-fourth of their income on food, as opposed to the one-third spent by average consumers in the 1950s . . ." (ibid.). Hence, the poverty level should now be set at four times a minimum food budget, not three times.

Finally, there is the whole issue of whether the appropriate definition of poverty should be absolute or relative. The official government definition is absolute. By adjusting only for price, it holds constant the real amount of purchasing power that defines poverty. It makes no allowance for the changes in productivity in the society which make possible substantial changes in what is considered a minimal standard of living. Thus, our society's values change; for example, we now consider it a norm for there to be indoor plumbing and for there to be separate sleeping rooms for parents and children. The definition of minimally required dental and medical care has changed. However, none of this is reflected in an absolute measure such as the official definition of poverty.

A relative measure would tie the definition of poverty to some figure like the median family income; for example, setting it at 50 percent of median income. But being an absolute figure, the official poverty level has slipped far below the relative position it held when it was first defined. In 1960, the poverty level for a family of four reflected an income about 53 percent of the median family income, but by 1985 that had fallen to below 40 percent. Thus, many families that given their relative income in 1985 would have been considered poor by the standard in 1960, are now not counted as part of the poverty problem. This tends to give us a false sense of progress on this issue. Thinking about the issue of using an absolute versus a relative measure to define poverty, it is useful to again recall the comments of John Kenneth Galbraith quoted toward the end of the previous chapter:

> just as it is far too tempting to say that, in matters of living standards, everything is relative, so it is wrong to rest everything on absolutes. People are poverty-stricken when their income, even if adequate for survival, falls markedly behind that of the community. Then they cannot have what the larger community regards as the minimum necessary for decency; and they cannot wholly escape, therefore, the judgment of the larger community that they are indecent. They are degraded for, in the literal sense, they live outside the grades or categories which the community regards as acceptable (Galbraith 1958: 323).

The Bureau of Labor Statistics Income Standards

The Bureau of Labor Statistics (BLS), on three different occasions since World War II, had undertaken detailed studies to try to define what they originally called the Low, the Modest But Adequate, and the High budget levels for American families. The middle standard was later renamed the Moderate Budget level. Unfortunately, the last such detailed study was done back in 1967.[9] Thus, from 1967 to 1985, this too must be considered an absolute standard, though it was intended to be a relative one.

From 1967 until the Reagan administration, these numbers, were adjusted annually, or in some cases quarterly, for inflation and then published in the BLS's *Monthly Labor Review*. The Reagan Administration, according to staff members at the BLS with whom I have spoken, stopped this process and no longer publishes these standards.[10] However, I have updated them through 1985 and report that information in Table 2-1, which is found at the end of this chapter.[11]

In considering these BLS standards, it is important to consider the criteria that were used. The Moderate, or Modest But Adequate, standard was carefully designed so that:

It provides for the maintenance of health and social well being, nurturance of children, and participation in community activities . . . the standard reflects the collective judgement of families as to what is necessary and desirable to meet the conventional and social as well as the physical needs (of the family).

Then the lower and higher standards were defined by refining this moderate standard. The bare adequacy of the lower standard was noted explicitly by the BLS when it stated that:

The lower standard budget will represent a minimum of adequacy. Substantial downward adjustments will be made in the content and/or manner of living of the moderate standard, where this is possible without compromising the family's physical health or self-respect as members of the community...the lower standard budgets are expected to be more appropriate than the moderate budgets for establishing goals for public assistance and incomemaintenance programs

However, sometime later, the BLS admitted that it outdid itself in cutting back the food budget and had to admit that it was not really adequate by its own standards, stating: "It has been estimated that only about one fourth of those who spend amounts equivalent to the cost of the lower budget food plan actually have nutritionally adequate diets." [12]

Therefore, most responsible economists, when working with these standards, adjust the Low Budget's food allowance to that of the Moderate (or Modest But Adequate) Budget. In Table 2-1, this has been done, but the originally defined lower food budget is also shown in parentheses.

It should be noted that, throughout this book, all dollar figures have been converted to constant 1985 dollars of purchasing power. This was done to allow for meaningful comparisons of figures between various years, that is, for comparisons between dollar figures that represent levels of purchasing power unaffected by changes in the price level. This is necessary due to the almost constant presence of some level of inflation in the American economy and is especially critical given the quite severe inflation that occurred during the 1970s.

To summarize this part of the discussion, in 1985, the official definition of poverty was $10,989, while the adjusted Low BLS budget, which one might think of as a reasonable definition of a "low income" or "minimum adequacy" level, was $20,207. At this time, the Moderate (or Modest But Adequate) budget was $30,177, while the High budget stood at $44,884. Thus, roughly speaking, we can use the figures of $10,000, $20,000, $30,000, and $45,000 as meaningful benchmarks against which to compare the actual distribution of income, so long as we are dealing with 1985 constant dollar figures.

However, while the adjusted BLS figures do overcome some of the limitations which were noted as applying to the Social Security Administration/Census Bureau official poverty threshold, it must still be viewed as an absolute, not a relative, standard since no new market baskets of goods and services upon which to base the budgets have been developed since 1967. This is significant since the median family income in 1985 ($29,152), though below that achieved from 1972 through 1979, was still, in terms of constant 1985 dollars, 43 percent higher than in 1960, the beginning of the period examined in this study, and 14 percent higher than that in 1967, when the BLS last reevaluated the makeup of the budgets. Hence, it is likely that some significant changes in the buying patterns and standard of living have occurred which are not reflected in these figures. Nevertheless, the use of these adjusted BLS standards provide a very useful elaboration and comparison to the even more limited official poverty threshold standard.

Defining the Middle Class

One of my concerns in conducting this study is to examine what has been happening to what is referred to as the American middle class. The question that concerns us at this juncture is how to define the middle class. Given the BLS adjusted budgets, it would certainly be reasonable to argue that no family that has an income below that considered minimally adequate, that is, about $20,000, should be included within the category. On the other side, families earning above about $50,000, that is, families earning at least $5,000 more than the BLS High budget, might reasonably be considered to be living at a standard above that of the middle class. Thus, it is not surprising that the category of families earning between $20,000 and $50,000 is one that has often recently been used, at least initially, to define the middle class; and it is the one I will use in this study. [13]

Admittedly, such a definition of "class" is very limited and is quite economistic in a rather narrow sense, since even life-cycle concerns about consumption patterns are ignored and the definition considers income, but not wealth or asset holdings (except to a limited extent in Part II). Moreover, this definition of middle class does not deal with the vast array of sociological, political, ideological and other considerations that are required for a full definition of class boundaries. However, this study is not intended to get into these other areas.[14] Rather, using this admittedly limited definition, I will demonstrate that the widely held perception that, at least in terms of income, most Americans are middle class, is not true. Moreover, I will demonstrate that the proportion of American families with constant dollar earnings in this range has been shrinking as a percentage of the population as a whole. I will examine a number of other studies that try to explain why this has been happening, will offer some of my own conclusions, and will discuss some of the important implications of this situation.

NOTES

1. The first of the two annual documents has in recent years carried a title such as *Money Income of Households, Families, and Persons in the United States: 1985* (U.S. Department of Commerce 1987a). This volume with data for 1985 was published in August 1987 based upon the survey taken in March 1986 concerning the situation in 1985. The other annual document has recently carried a title such as *Money Income and Poverty Status of Families and Persons in the United States: 1985 (Advance Data From the March 1986 Current Population survey)* (U.S. Department of Commerce 1986a). This volume was published in August 1986 and contains only a small portion of the data available in the later more complete release, but it does contain more detailed tables focusing on the specific characteristics of the poverty population in the given year.

2. See, for example, "Defining Away the Poor - Reducing the Poverty Rate Without Reducing Poverty" (1987).

3. It should be noted that recently adopted changes in the income tax laws, especially when combined with the rapid increase in Social Security taxes, will require that these budgets have their allowance for taxes adjusted in future years.

4. Another recent study which looked at the burden of taxes paid to all level of governments found that taxes hit the poorest harder than all but the very richest, and even that result required making assumptions that imply that all corporate taxes, in effect, are passed on to and paid by stockholders. This study by the Tax Foundation found that those earning under $10,000 in 1986 paid 49.5 percent of their income in taxes, as compared to 31 to 35 percent for those earning beween $10,000 and $90,000. Even with the very conservative assumption about corporate taxes, those earning above $90,000 paid only slightly more (51.6 percent) than the poorest. When the effect of the 1986 tax reforms, with their lower marginal rates, are then considered, it was thought most likely that as the title of one article about this study put it "US Taxes Hit Poorest Hardest" (Francis 1989).

5. A careful and critical examination of how the official poverty level was/is determined and of possible alternative standards is contained in the next chapter.

6. See also the study by David Kahan (1987) on the need to reduce the burden of state and local taxes upon the poor.

7. Nevertheless, a few observations are in order about the patterns which begin to emerge from this new data. The distribution of private sector income (definition #4) is far more unequal that of the "official measure." The effect upon this private sector distribution of federal and state income taxes and Social Security taxes (as revealed using definition #7) is *very* mildly progressive. The effect upon that distribution of government transfer payments (definition #11), on the other hand, is quite progressive, with,

surprisingly, nonmeans-tested transfers having more of an effect that those that are means-tested. The added impact of imputing a return on home equity is insignificant. These results are summarized in a short article by Amott (1989), which is one of the first to use this new data. Finally, it should be noted that the Bureau's study also presents data on the income distribution patterns by race/ethnic group, sex, and household composition for each of the 12 definitions of income.

8. However, there is some serious debate about whether the cost of living for the rural poor really is any lower than for the urban poor when, for example, transportation costs are taken into account. This point was made in an interview with the author of a study on the extent of rural poverty in American, Kathryn Porter of the Center on Budget and Policy Priorities (Hey 1989)

9. Moreover, the last "direct pricing" of the separate items included within the market baskets of goods defined in the standards was done in 1969. Between then and and the autumn of 1981, the last time the BLS published these standards, all of the categories were simply adjusted using the broadly based Consumer Price Index.

10. In the news release, dated April 16, 1982, when the BLS published these figures for the last time (for autumn 1981), it was stated that "The Bureau of Labor Statistics eliminated the program as part of the recent budget reduction." That release also stated the BLS's awareness of and desire to update and revise the expenditure and price data in order to bring the standards up to date, but then went on to indicate, with an obvious tone of regret, that ". . . funding was not available."

11. In December 1980, the BLS published a report of a study it had commissioned from the Wisconsin Institute for Research on Poverty as to how these standard budgets should be revised and/or updated (Watts 1980). The body of the report recommends the creation of four, instead of the then current three, budget levels identified as the Social Minimum Standard, the Lower Living Standard, the Prevailing Family Standard, and the Social Abundance Standard. These are apparently, from the language of the report, designed to be roughly equivalent to the official definition of poverty and the three BLS standards discussed in this chapter.

However, instead of being based on new original research into the bundles of goods, and their prices, appropriate to such standards, the majority of the committee recommends the expedience of adopting the convention of simply assigning the median expenditure of a two-parent family with two children to the Prevailing Family Standard. They would then make percentage adjustments of that figure to arrive at the other standards for such a family and another set of percentage adjustments to create standards at each level for families with different numbers of members and aged or nonaged (65 and older or not) parents. The Social Minimum would be set at one-half, the Lower at two-thirds, and the Social Abundance at 50 percent above the Prevailing Standard.

Unfortunately, except for a vague reference to the apparently rather arbitrary view of the majority of committee members, some seven individuals, no evidence or strong rationale is provided, or even hinted at, to justify the percentages chosen. (The adjustments for family size and age would use percentages developed in research by Orshansky and Fendler, cited in the report, which was based only upon the relative cost of U.S. Department of Agriculture "Thrifty Food Plans.")

A stongly worded minority report, which was published as part of the overall report, attacked this methodology arguing pursuasively, in my view at least, for the need to conduct the research necessary to develop meaningful current standard budgets rather than simply adopting rather arbitrary percentages of median expenditures for a "typical" family. I agree with this minority view and for that reason chose not to use the recommended figures contained in the body of this report. Also, since this report is not widely known and has never been implemented, in part due to the budgetary priorities of the Reagan administration, it seemed to be far better to stick with adjusted numbers from the established and widely used BLS standards in effect until 1981.

However, for the interested reader, the figures for these proposed new standards are presently below, alongside those developed in the text, for comparison. All of these are expressed in 1985 dollars to make that comparison meaningful.

			New as % of
New Standard		Existing Standard	Existing
Social Minimum:	$11,951	Poverty: $10,989	108.8%
Lower Living:	15,936	Min. Adeq: 20,207	78.9%
Prevailing:	23,903	Moderate: 30,177	79.2%
Social Abun.:	35,854.	High: 44,884	79.9%

A quick look at the percentages in the last column would strongly suggest that the committee's choice of percentage adjustments to define their new standards were pretty clearly aimed at developing new standards that would, on the one hand, only very slightly improve on the current official definition of poverty and, on the other hand, adjust the existing BLS standards downward by about 20 percent. But, as the minority report indicates, no substantive research supported the choice of the percentage ajustments adopted. Moreover, as this dissenting view argued: "The postulate that adequacy at prevailing levels of living is always at median consumption, and that other standards remain in fixed percentage relationships to the median, is inherently insupportable" (Watts 1980: 10). I quite agree.

12. The above three quotes are all taken from (Meyer 1977).

13. See for example the study entitled "The Shrinking Middle Class" which is discussed later in the book (Bradbury 1986).

14. For those who want to delve more into the matter of a class analysis of the United States, I recommend two works as good starting points: Erik Olin Wright's *Class, Crisis & The State* (1979) and *The American Class Structure* by Dennis Gilbert and Joseph Kahl (1987). Moreover, both of these contain excellent and extensive bibliographies that will allow the interested reader to go as deeply as wanted into this subject.

Table 2-1
Low, Moderate, and High Annual Budgets for a Four Person Family,
and Per Person Low Budget Levels (in 1985 dollars)

Budget Category	Low or Minimum Adequacy Budget	Moderate or Modest But Adequate Budget	High or Quite Comfortable Budget	Average per Person, Using Low Budget
Food	$7,268 ($5,636)	$7,268	$9,162	$4.98/day ($3.86/day)
Housing	3,401	6,661	10,105	$59.50/month
Transportation	1,513	2,670	3,589	$7.02/week
Clothing & Personal Care	1,643	2,300	3,335	$34.22/month
Medical Care	1,693	1,700	1,773	$35.27/month
Other Consump.	779	1,447	2,385	$16.22/month
Other Items	760	1,248	2,100	$15.83/month
Social Security & Income Taxes	3,150	6,793	12,435	$65.63/month
Total Budget	20,207 (18,576)	30,177	44,884	420.98/month

Source: Developed from earlier B.L.S. work—see text for details.

3

The Historical Data on
Family Income Since 1960

AN OVERVIEW OF THE DATA, INCLUDING BY RACE/ETHNIC GROUP

The significance of the alternative income standards developed in the preceding chapter becomes clear when we look at the overall distribution of income in the U.S. in 1985[1] and compare it to that in selected years back to 1960. This is done in Table 3-1 through 3-4, with the results summarized in Table 3-5. Table 3-1 reports the data for all families, while Tables 3-2, 3-3, and 3-4 report that for White, Black, and Hispanic families, respectively.[2] The data for 1973 and 1983 are reported, in addition to that for each fifth year in the period, because those years have special significance.

Nineteen Seventy-three was the year when the incidence of poverty, using the Social Security Administrations "official" definition, reached its lowest point since these records have been kept--11.1 percent of all persons and 9.7 percent of all persons living in families; whereas, 1983, in the aftermath of the Reagan recession, saw the highest incidence of poverty since the mid-1960s with 15.2 percent of all persons and 13.9 percent of all persons in families living below the "official" poverty level. Moreover, as will become clear, 1973, or more generally the early 1970s, represents a major turning point in the distribution of income in many different respects.

Before proceeding, it should be pointed out that the consistently higher incidence of poverty among "all persons" as compared to "all persons living in families" reflects the fact that poverty occurs more often among "unrelated individuals," to use the Census Bureau term, than among persons who live in families, that is, with other persons related to them by blood or marriage. The higher incidence of poverty among these single persons, who are not counted as constituting single member families, pulls the poverty rate for "all persons," which does include them, above that for "all persons living in families" which does not. Thus, it should be kept in mind when looking at the data for families that the extent of poverty is consistently understated.

In Tables 3-1 through 3-4 (all of which refer to the family category), along the left margin, the data have been broken down by income levels and descriptive labels have been attached to the various levels to help the reader place these numbers in some meaningful context. Cumulative figures for 1985 are also presented which simply reflect the results of adding the numbers as one goes down the page.

Keeping in mind that the percentages in every year reported are presented in terms of income levels in constant 1985 dollars of purchasing power to allow for meaningful comparisons, one sees that whether one looks at all families or at White and Black families separately (data were not reported for Hispanics until 1972), there was a consistent pattern from 1960 to 1973--to wit: the percentage of families in each of the three lowest income categories fell, while that in the upper three categories rose. However, from 1973 to 1983, the percentage of families, whether one considers all, White, Black, or Hispanic, living at the three lowest levels of income turned around and rose, reaching levels higher than that in 1970 and, in the case of Black families at the lowest income level, higher even than that in 1965. In the two years, from 1983 to 1985, there was some significant improvement with the percentage of families in these lowest categories again falling, but that improvement so much ballyhooed by the Reagan administration looks good only in comparison to the even worse percentages in the earlier Reagan years. Looked at from a longer term perspective, the 1985 figures are worse (higher) for White families in all three lower categories, for Black families in the lowest category and for Hispanic families in the lowest two categories than was the case back in 1970, fifteen long years ago. Moreover, in some important regards the figures got even worse in 1986 and 1987.[3]

This picture is confirmed by the official poverty figures which show that for most categories the percentage levels of poverty in 1985 (and in 1986 and 1987) were higher than those in 1980, and in many cases higher than in 1975 or even 1970. More detailed numbers concerning the incidence of poverty are presented in Table 4-5 which will be discussed in the next chapter, although an initial look is presented in Table 3-6.

Returning to Tables 3-1 through 3-4, we find that, in 1985, 4.8 percent of all American families, 13.5 percent of Black, and 8.3 percent of Hispanic families, lived with income of less than $5,000 a year; that is, at an income level that represented only 45 percent of even the official poverty level (for a family of four) and less than 25 percent of our BLS adjusted low income level. Moreover, for every group for which we have data, this was the highest proportion of that population living in such condition of abject poverty in any year since 1965, except during and immediately after the Reagan recession, that is, in 1982-83. Thus, while the 1985 numbers represent an improvement over the figures of 5.2 percent for Whites, 14.4 percent for Blacks, and 9.0 percent for Hispanics reached in 1982/83, they are hardly numbers to be proud of when one considers the longer historical period of the last 20 years.

To move from an absolute measure to a more relative one and with all figures again expressed in constant 1985 dollars of purchasing power, it should be kept in mind that whereas even $5,000 represented 24.5 percent of median family income in 1960 and 21.1 percent in 1965, by 1985 it represented only 18 percent. Hence, in 1985, we not only had a larger proportion of our population living below this inhumane $5,000 level than at any point since 1965, (again excepting 1982/83), but, relatively speaking, this level was itself considerably further below the norm.[4]

Moving to the next bracket, we find that 13.3 percent of all families, and fully 30.6 percent of Black and 25.3 percent of Hispanic families, had to make do with $10,000 or less in 1985 (compared to the official poverty level of $10,989). These are the highest percentages since 1968, again with the exception of the 1982/83 period. Looking at this level in relative terms, it is instructive to note that in 1960, $10,000 (in 1985 dollars) represented almost exactly 50 percent of the median family income, whereas in 1985 this represented only 36 percent. Or to view it in slightly different terms, in 1960 the poverty threshold represented an amount of purchasing power about equal to half of the median family income in the U.S.; whereas, by 1985 this threshold was set a little above about a third of median income. Relatively speaking, the poor were much poorer, even if the threshold was held constant in terms of absolute purchasing power.[5]

When we go on to the $20,000 level, we find that more than one third of all American families (34 percent) lived, in 1985, on less than $20,000 at a time when the Low BLS Budget, with the lower inadequate food allowance, was $18,575 and the more reasonable adjusted Lower Budget was $20,207. While this was the condition for 31.2 percent of White families, some 52.3 percent of Hispanic, and 57.9 percent of Black families suffered a similar fate. Thus, more than one-third of all families and more than half of all Black and Hispanic families lived below the adjusted BLS Minimum Adequacy level. Moreover, while the figures for 1970 were a vast improvement over the 1960 figures for all of these groups, all of these percentages were considerably worse (that is, higher) in 1985 than they had been in 1970 (or 1968-69, for that matter).

Looking at the $35,000 level, and keeping in mind that the BLS Moderate (or Modest But Adequate) Budget was $30,177, one finds that almost two-thirds (62.9 percent) of all American families and some 79.6 percent of Hispanic and 81.2 percent of Black families lived, in 1985, at no more than $5,000 above the Moderate level. For the categories of all, White, and Hispanic families, the percentages living below $35,000 (in 1985 dollars) were worse (that is, higher) in 1985 than in 1973, and for Black families the figure was only 0.9 percentage points better. In fact, 54.1 percent of all families (51.6 percent of White families and 74.8 percent of Black families) had incomes in 1985 below $30,000.

Recalling from the earlier discussion that this Moderate level was defined as being the minimum necessary to provide "for the maintenance of health and social well being, nurturance of children . . . ," (Meyer 1977: 3) it is hard to maintain the image of an affluent America when more than half of all families and three fourths of Black and Hispanic families live below this level.

Moreover, preliminary data for 1987 paint the same grim picture. Thus, using the latest data as this book was going through final editing, for 1987: the BLS Low and Moderate budgets, adjusted to 1987 (all figures in this paragrapth are in 1987 dollars) are $21,351 and $31,885, respectively, while the High budget is $47,424. In 1987, according to the preliminary numbers, 30.3 percent of all American families had incomes below $20,000, that is, at least $1,351 or more below the Low budget, and 57 percent had incomes below $35,000, that is, had at most $3,172 above the Moderate level. For Black families, the figures were 54 percent and 77.4 percent, and for Hispanics they were 59.4 percent and 75.3 percent, respectively. Looking at a $30,000 cut off figure in 1987, we find that 54.8 percent of White families and 72.4 percent of Black families lived below this benchmark, which was itself $1,885 below the BLS Moderate budget for that year. Thus, the statements made above concerning the picture in 1985 remain true in 1987.

In fact, one very recent study (Danziger, Gottschalk, and Smolensky 1989) concluded that, ". . . the current recovery has been atypcial--inequality increased and is now [1987] higher than at any time since 1973 (ibid.: 314). Using adjusted (for family size) family income for persons (including single persons) living in families headed by nonelderly males in order to avoid the special situations affecting either the elderly or families headed by single women, they found that the percentage of income going to each of the poorest five deciles (50 percent of the population studied) fell from 1973 to 1987, that going to the 6th and 7th deciles held virtually constant, and that going to the highest two deciles increased. Then, using a fixed threshold (9 times the poverty level or about $95,000 in 1987 dollars) to define "the rich", they found that, "Between 1973 adn 1987, the percent rich more than doubled from 3.1 to 6.9 percent" (ibid.: 312) due in large part, especially since 1982, to the earnings of the wives.

CHANGES IN THE NUMBER OF PERSONS IN POVERTY: 1960-1987

However, talking in percentage terms at all is a bit deceptive, for it clouds the true picture as to the total number of persons who are affected. Moreover, switching for a moment to the issue of the number of individuals living in poverty, as opposed to the poverty rates for families, captures the situation of the so-called "unrelated individuals" to which we referred earlier. For after all, not only was there a higher percentage of poor people in the U.S. in 1985 and even in 1987 than in 1980 or 1970, but the population had been increasing over this whole period. Table 3-6 makes this point clear.[6]

Thus, except for the Reagan years (1981-87), only if one goes back 20 years do we find a higher percentage of our nation's people living in poverty. Even then (1967--14.2 percent), there were 4.7 million fewer people in poverty than in 1987 and 7.7 million fewer than in 1983, the worst of the Reagan years. Indeed, one must go back to 1964 to find a time when more Americans (36.1 million) suffered the terrible burden of poverty than has occurred during Reagan's administration. It was the conditions prevailing in those years of 1960 to 1965, that finally led this country to declare a "War on Poverty." Then, under conditions as bad or worse, President Reagan cut back and severely weakened many of those hard won and much needed programs. In these circumstances, President Reagan's efforts to paint a rosy picture of the economic situation facing the American people under his administration seem saddly hollow.

A CLOSER LOOK AT THE DISTRIBUTION IN 1985

Moving to Table 3-7, an attempt has been made to try to develop more precise estimates of the number of families in the various conceptual categories developed earlier, by interpolating, for 1985, between the detailed income categories which the Bureau of the Census uses in reporting its data, which, given the published data, was not feasible for Hispanic families. Hence, the data are reported for "all families" and for "Black families."

One finds that in 1985 more than a third of America's families (34.5 percent) and more than half of its Black families (58.3 percent) lived at incomes below the Minimum Adequacy level, while more than half of all families (54.4 percent) and fully three-fourths of Black families (75.1 percent) lived below the Moderate level. Indeed, only 23.3 percent of all families and only 9.9 percent of Black families lived at or above the Quite Comfortable level. Hardly a picture of an affluent America with a vast middle class living in material comfort.

THE SHRINKING MIDDLE CLASS

This brings us to an important aspect of this study. One of the major distributional issues popularly discussed in recent years has been the plight of the middle class. For many decades, it has been a mainstay of American ideology that the middle class is the backbone of the nation. Judging from the responses I have received over the years from my students at various universities and from audiences at public lectures throughout the United States and Europe, the popular image of the U.S. is that we are a nation that is characterized as having a vast middle class, with a small wealthy class above it, and a small, albeit very significant, poorer class below it. The figures that have already been presented demonstrate that the number of officially poor and the number of those suffering below the low income level; that is, at an income below the BLS Minimum Adequacy level, can hardly be considered small. But for now, let us turn from an examination of those at the lower end of the distribution to look more directly at those in the middle class.

How big is this group and what has been happening to it relative to the population as a whole?

When one exempts the families in the highest reported income bracket (those who received more than $50,000) and those earning less than $20,000, we find, in 1985, using this $20,000 to $50,000 as a broad and generous first approximation, that the so-called vast American middle class contains less than one-half (47.7 percent) of all American families. Even among White families, only 49.3 percent are in this middle-class category; while only 35.1 percent of Black families and 39.8 percent of Hispanic families enjoy that status. Thus, a bit less than 50 percent of White families and only a few more than one-third of Black and Hispanic families can be considered middle class in terms of income. A far different picture than that often presented by the media.

Aside from the issue of the current size of the middle class, there is perhaps the even more interesting and important matter of whether this portion of our population has been shrinking in recent years. If it has, and there is compelling evidence to support this contention, then serious issues are raised about the bipolarization that is implied. Indeed to the extent this is occurring, we must question whether our society has begun to move away from the popular image of it as being predominately made up of a vast middle class, with a small lower or underclass and a small upper class, and is, instead, moving toward a form of American apartheid characterized by a large, relatively permanent, and relatively powerless underclass, a large, rather permanent and powerful upper class, and a shrinking middle group of increasingly less importance.[7] Tragically, this does seem to be occurring and on some fronts the debate has turned from whether this is happening to why has this been occurring. But before taking this question up, let us look at some of the evidence concerning the changing relative size of the middle class.

Referring back to Table 3-5 and even using our very broad definition of middle class, that is, the $20,000 to $35,000 and $35,000 to $50,000 brackets, it is quite instructive to compare the changes here to those that have occurred at the lower and at the highest categories. Table 3-5 makes this picture quite clear. Here, for clarity of presentation, the income categories have been collapsed to four. What one finds is that during the 13 year period from 1960 to 1973, the proportion of the families in the lowest two categories (the poverty and low income groups) decreased dramatically (by more than 40 percent for all or White families and by 38 percent and 12 percent in the two categories for Black families)[8] while the proportion in the middle and upper levels increased, most dramatically at the highest level. This represented a significant improvement in the distribution of income with a smaller proportion of the population in the lower brackets and a larger proportion in the middle and upper categories.

However, from 1973 to 1985, among White families, the percentages at the lowest two levels--the poverty and low income levels--turned around and increased, while the highest level also continued to increase, though at a much slower rate. That is, it was not that the proportions of poor and low income Whites merely slowed their rates of decrease. The proportions actually increased during this 12 year period and did so significantly. The proportion in the highest bracket continued to rise. On the other hand, the percentage receiving a middle income decreased by almost 10 percent. For Black and Hispanic families, the picture of emerging bipolarization since 1973 was even more vivid with the percentages in the lowest (poverty) and highest levels increasing while the percentages in both the low income and middle income groups decreased. Thus, the proportion of both rich and poor has been increasing since about 1973 in the U.S., while the proportion of middle-class families has been decreasing, as has the proportion of low income families in the Black and Hispanic communities.[9]

Other Studies of the Shrinking Middle Class

Other studies have found the same result. After a detailed examination, Bradbury (1986), in an article entitled "The Shrinking Middle Class," found that whether she defined the middle class as those families within the $20,000 to $50,000 range, or alternatively as those in the $15,000 to $40,000 range, between 1973 and 1984 there was a 5.1 percent or a 4 percent drop, respectively, in the proportion of families within that income category, while the proportion of families at the higher and lower levels increased. Moreover, she found that most of those who left the middle-class category, however defined, fell into the lower income brackets, rather than moving up to the higher brackets. Bradbury goes on to examine various theories as to why this occurred. Similarly, McMahon and Tschetter (1986), in an article entitled "The Declining Middle Class: A Further Analysis" first refer to earlier work showing that the middle class is indeed shrinking and then go on to evaluate conflicting theories as to why this is occurring.

Finally, a rather detailed study by two economists with the BLS, Horrigan and Haugen (1988), entitled "The Declining Middle-Class Thesis: A Sensitivity Analysis" examined a myriad of data for the broader period of 1969 to 1986. They evaluated the use of alternative income levels for defining the three classes, ultimately testing seven different lower limits (for the middle class) ranging from $17,676 to $26,514 and eleven different upper limits ranging from $39,999 to $63,999 (all in constant 1986 dollars). They tested different methods for measuring the changes in class size over time including that which I used earlier, dollar intervals adjusted to represent constant purchasing power; as well as intervals representing fixed percentages above and below the median income. When testing the latter approach, they again employed seven possible lower limits, this time ranging from 60 percent to 90 percent of the median, and eleven possible upper limits ranging from 136 percent to 244 percent of the median.

They also made both year-to-year comparisons of class size and conducted regression analyses to establish long-run trends. Finally, in establishing constant dollar limits, they tested three different price indexes: the most commonly used Consumer Price Index for All Urban Consumers (CPI-U), which I employ throughout this book, the Fixed Weight Personal Consumption Expenditure index (FW-PCE) developed by the Bureau of Economic Analysis, and an experimental index developed by the BLS to overcome some statistical consistency problems in the use of the CPI-U over long periods. The latter is known as the CPI-U Experimental Measure I--Rebased, which they denote as CPI-U-X1. After some discussion of alternatives, they chose to use the family, as opposed to households as their base unit, as is done in this book; and they chose to focus on total, before-tax, family money income, as opposed to some measure such as total earnings or wage and salary earnings or some after-tax measurement--again, the same decision as I made, and for much the same reasons as were explained earlier.

Interestingly enough, the one element around which they did not conduct any sensitivity analysis was the issue of the starting point for the comparisons. Given the evidence that I presented earlier and that which is developed later, it would seem that it was during the early 1970s, in particular about 1973-75, that the critical turning point in the U.S. economy was reached. As we will see, it is around this time, in looking at a wide variety of data, that one finds important trends reversing direction. Hence, taking as the beginning point in their analysis only the year 1969 may be a bit limiting.

Their conclusions are that, indeed, "These results support the declining middle-class thesis" (ibid.: 6). Specifically, they found that this holds true for lower limits ranging from $17,676 to $24,000 and upper limits ranging from $39,999 to $59,999. Only if they use a lower limit of $24,000 or above in combination with an upper limit of $61,999 or above does the secular decline not appear in evidence. But, in no case do they find any secular increase in the size of the middle class. With regard to the use of different price indexes to set the constant dollar limits for the definition of the middle class, they found that: "Results using all three price indexes show a decline in the relative size of the middle-class between 1969 and 1986" (ibid.: 7). Finally, when they tested the use of fixed percentages of median income, as opposed to the constant dollar boundary limits, to define the middle class, they found that: "Here, the middle-class declined for an even broader range of income intervals than for the interval deflator approach" (ibid.: 7). The result of this study, especially in combination with the earlier work done by others, simply leaves no doubt about the fact that the U.S. has been experiencing a decline in the relative size of our middle class.

The other issue that Horrigan and Haugen address is "where did the middle go." With regard to the lower class, they found that when they used the CPI-U-X1 index with the fixed dollar boundaries that it has been secularly fairly stable in relative size, but that:

> The secularly stable trend in the size of the lower-class has been accompanied by a secular *decline* in the share of the aggregate income held. . . . Thus, the picture which emerges is one of a lower class that, although stable in size, is receiving a *declining share of the pie over time* (ibid.: 6).

When they employed the more commonly used CPI-U ". . . the lower class exhibited a secular increase . . ." (ibid.: 7) which would compound the effect of the decreasing share of income upon the families involved. In all of these situations the upper class secularly increased.

When they tested the fixed percentage of median income boundaries, they found that:

> For each interval, as the middle declines in relative size, both the lower and upper classes experience secular *increases* in relative size. . . . [while] . . . the share of aggregate income held by [the lower class] has either remained the share or declined . . . (ibid.).

Which leads them to conclude that no matter what methods are employed, the evidence ". . . points to a fundamental *decline* in the lower-class per-family share of total aggregate income."

Thus, the evidence is overwhelming that for more than a decade, and perhaps close to two decades, the US has been experiencing a decline in the relative size of its middle class, an expansion of its upper class, and a deteriorating situation for the families within a lower or underclass that most evidence would argue has also been expanding. One issue that needs to be addressed is why this has been happening. In what follows in this chapter, I will attempt to outline some of the underlying causes of this phenomenon.

An International Comparison

As discussed in more detail in Chapter 4, we are now beginning to get a stream of data emerging from the Luxembourg Income Study that allows us to make meaningful international comparisons concerning the distribution of income in some 10 industrialized nations. One recent study (Coder, Rainwater, and Smeeding 1989), divided each country's population into four groups--poor, near poor, middle class and well-to-do. Using comparable definitions of income and group boundaries, this study found that during the period of 1979-83 the United States had the smallest proportion of the population in the middle class, 53.7 percent, compared to over 70 percent in Germany, Sweden, and Norway and to an average of 64.4 percent for the other 9 nations taken as a whole. The US also had the largest proportion of its population in poverty and, by a variety of measures, the most unequally distributed income.

Structural Changes and The Movement to a Service Economy

Much of the analysis as to why the middle class has been shrinking has built upon the seminal work by Bluestone and Harrison in their book *The Deindustrialization of America* (1982).[10] This perspective argues that there has been a decline in the relative proportion, and in some regions, in the absolute number of reasonably well paid, good fringe-benefit granting, typically unionized jobs in the so-called smokestack and goods-producing industries, while simultaneously there has been a significant increase in the low paying, poor fringe-benefit granting,[11] typically non-unionized service industry on one hand and in the often high paying, but also nonunionized, high-tech area.[12] Bluestone and Harrison argue that from 1969 to 1982, 63 percent of the millions of new jobs created were in those industries which paid, on average, the lowest wages. They also indicate that from 1973 to 1980, while the number of production workers in the manufacturing industries declined by 5 percent, there was a slight increase in the overall employment in these same industries due to increases in the number of supervisory and managerial level positions (Bluestone and Harrison 1984).

The steel industry is often cited as an example of the decline of an industry that once provided many relatively well-paying, blue collar jobs. However, recently there has been some increase in employment in that industry and this has been used by some to argue against the Bluestone-Harrison sort of analysis. But the facts are these: In 1988, steel industry employment did increase by 6.2 percent, to almost 170,000. However, during the pre-1982 recession period during the 1970s, steel industry employment averaged 435,000, and even this was a far cry from the 650,000 employed at the all-time peak year of 1953 (Hicks 1989). Thus, the most recent increases must be seen as a relatively minor upturn along a path that, from a long-term perspective, is clearly downward sloping.

The data in Table 3-8 provide a rather complete picture of both the relative and absolute growth patterns of employment in the production of goods, in the private provision of services, and in the government (most, though not all, of which is service type employment). As the Table reveals, employment in the manufacturing industries, which represents the bulk of employment in the production of goods, has been rather stagnant since about 1965, certainly since 1970, fluctuating with the business cycle between about 18 and 20 million. Total employment in the goods producing sector has also fluctuated since 1970, but at no point between 1980 and 1987 did it reattain the peak of 26.5 million workers achieved in 1979. Overall, from 1960 to 1987, employment in this sector increased by 4.4 million (an increase of only 21.6 percent in 27 years), in the context of total employment almost doubling, from 54.2 to 102.3 million. Thus, the relative size of employment in this sector steadily decreased from 37.7 percent of total employment in 1960 to only 24.2 percent in 1987.

On the other hand, employment throughout the service sector has steadily and rapidly increased, especially in the retail sales and general services areas (which includes personal and business related services) at a rate even faster than that of the total, going from 25.3 million in 1960 to 60.5 million in 1987--an increase of 139 percent. The impact of this was that of the 31.4 million net new jobs created since 1970, 25.9 million, or 82.5 percent, came in the service sector .

Government employment, most of which is service, not goods, producing also increased considerably--by 102 percent over the 27 year period, including a 35 percent increase (4.4 million net new jobs) since 1970. However, during the early years of the Reagan

Administration, federal government employment fell slightly from 1980 to 1982, but then, despite the continuing rhetoric, began to slowly increase, surpassing the 1980 figure in 1985 and continuing on to a new peak in 1987. State and local governmental units, taken together, followed a similar pattern though they did not hit their low point until 1983. However, taken as a whole, in relative terms, government has seen its share of total employment fall since 1975 (which one might note was five years before Reagan took office), from a peak of 19.1 percent to 16.6 percent in 1987, the same relative level it had been in 1965.

Yet another indication of the trend toward a service providing economy is indicated by the fact that from 1960 to 1986, the proportion of real (constant dollar) GNP resulting from goods production (agriculture, mining, manufacturing, and construction) declined from 39.9 percent to 32.2 percent--including a decrease from 35.8 percent to 29.6 percent for nonagricultural goods production. On the other hand, the share derived from the private service producing sector expanded from 46.2 percent in 1960 to 56.3 percent in 1986--or from 60.7 percent to 67.2 percent when one includes government within a larger vision of the service sector (Economic Report of the President 1988: 296-297).

Finally, the Bureau of Labor Statistics recently completed a projection of the United States economy to the year 2000. Based upon a range of assumptions, they report projections based upon high, moderate, and low growth rates. Using their moderate projections, Kutscher reported upon the BLS's projections as to the composition of the labor force, employment, and industrial growth patterns anticipated during this period. He indicates that the "Goods-producing industries are projected to experience almost no change in employment over the 1986-2000 period. Service-producing industries, therefore, will account for nearly all of the projected growth . . . [of] 21 million new jobs . . . " (Kutscher 1987). Agricultural wage and salary jobs are expected to grow, but this will be offset by a decline in agricultural self-employment, resulting in a net loss of 300,000 jobs in this sector. Within the goods-producing sector, construction is expected to increase by 890,000 jobs, while mining decreases by 59,000 and manufacturing decreases by 834,000, for a net loss 3,000 jobs. Every one of the major industrial groups in the service-producing sector are seen as likely to experience substantial growth, with the retail trade industry growing by 4,857,000 jobs (27.2 percent), wholesale trade by 1,531,000 (26.6 percent), finance, insurance, and real estate by 1,620,000 (25.7 percent), and the (other) services category by an astounding 10,014,000 jobs (44.4 percent). Government is anticipated to grow by 1,618,000 jobs (9.7 percent). Hence the patterns we have experienced in recent years are likely to continue and even accelerate.

Changing Earnings Patterns Within Occupational Categories

Moving from consideration of the pattern among industries to that among occupations, Rosenthal, studying the changing pattern of median weekly earnings by occupation from 1973 to 1982, did find a small shift away from the middle earning jobs, but also found that the proportion of lower paying jobs also declined, which seemingly contradicts the Bluestone-Harrison argument (Rosenthal 1986). On the other hand, Lawrence found an increasing degree of bipolarization from 1969 to 1983, but attributed this primarily to the changing age structure of the labor force (Lawrence 1985).

McMahon and Tschetter, in the article already cited, replicated the work of both Rosenthal and Lawrence and extended it to cover the same 1973 to 1985 period often discussed in this book. They found that both studies were correct in their conclusions and found that the missing factor necessary to reconcile these two earlier works was "that within occupational earnings groups, the earnings distributions had shifted downward, that is, each group included more lower paying positions" (McMahon and Tschetter 1986: 22). Thus, the earnings patterns among occupational groups have contributed to the polarization of our society. It may also account for part of the fall in average hourly earnings discussed in Chapter 5. In that chapter, we will discuss the issue of earnings by industry and by occupation, both currently and historically, in much more detail.

If we again turn to the BLS's projections for the period of 1986-2000, we find that the White labor force is expected to grow by 15 percent, while the Black labor force grows by 29 percent and the Hispanic by 74 percent. In fact, ". . . if non-Hispanic white women are included (with Black, Hispanic, Asians, and other races), the[ir] combined share of future growth reaches more than 90 percent." Thus, the future labor force ". . . is projected to become increasingly minority and female" (Kutscher 1987). If we combine this information with the projections as to the occupational categories that are expected to experience the most growth and if the women and minority workers primarily go, as they have in the past, into the lower paying occupational groups of salesworkers (which is expected to grow by 29.6 percent) and service workers (32.7 percent anticipated growth), while the White males disproportionately go into the high paying executive and managerial positions (28.7 percent growth) and professional occupations (27.0 percent growth), the sexual and racial/ethnic aspects of the polarization of our society are also likely to continue and even worsen.

However, given the relative and absolute growth in the numbers of women and minority workers compared to that of White males, there will be more opportunities for the women and minorities to move into the better paying positions. Whether those opportunities, in fact, are realized is another matter.

It might also be noted that another fast growing occupational group, in fact the one projected to grow the fastest in percentage terms (38.2 percent), is that of technicians, which may hold out some hope for some middle class jobs.[13] However, the total number of these anticipated new jobs, only 1,428,000, pales in comparison with the number of expected new service worker jobs (5,407,000) and salesworker positions (3,728,000), and even with the new administrative support (including clerical) jobs (2,258,000).

Hence, there is little in the projections concerning the occupational location of the jobs likely to be created between now and the year 2000, to warrant much hope that the shrinkage in the middle class will be reversed.

Possible Demographic Causes

Bradbury examined the many demographic factors that some have hypothesized may be responsible for the shrinking middle class and concluded that all of those factors, even in combination, could explain only 8 percent (0.4 percent out of 5.1 percent) of the decline in the percentage of families receiving a middle class income and only 10 percent (0.7 percent out of 7.3 percent) of the decrease in median family income. The factors she considered were: (1) changes in family size, (2) regional shifts in population and regional differences in income, (3) the changing structure of families (that is, the increase in female-headed vs. married couple families), (4) the changing age of the head of the household (the so-called "maturing baby-boom" issue), and (5) the changing labor force participation rates of spouses.

Interestingly, Bradbury found that the first three factors did contribute to both the decrease in the middle class and the decrease in median income, but that the latter two factors worked in the opposite direction, resulting in the small net effect cited above. She concludes "that demographic changes are not responsible for the bulk of the 1973-84 decline in the size of the middle class or in median family income . . . [and that] it seems that the dwindling of the middle class is real and probably not transitory" (Bradbury 1986: 52).

Recent work by Bluestone and Harrison, reported upon in more detail just below, found that neither the growth in the female workforce nor the entrance of the baby-boom generation were significant in explaining what they refer to as the U turn in the proportion of low wage work that occurred during the 1963-1986 period they studied (Bluestone and Harrison 1988a).

Given Bradbury's negative findings, and given the results of McMahon and Tschetter and of Bluestone and Harrison, it would seem that shifts within industries and occupations, as well as between them, are indeed essential casual factors for the increasing degree of inequality within the American society. However, by the same token, it would appear that demographic factors, on balance, are not a major causal factor.

The Growing Role of Part-Time Employment

Another structural factor that can be cited as a contributing cause for the increased polarization in the income distribution within the US is the increasing importance of part-time work--work that is very often low paying and carries few, if any, benefits. Part-time work is defined as regular employment for less than 35 hours per week. However, that rather simple sounding definition in fact covers a rather complex set of circumstances. An important study of the nature and extent of part-time work in the U.S., a study which cast new light on this complex area, was done by Thomas Nardone (1986) for the Bureau of Labor Statistics (BLS).

As Nardone points out, those workers who are employed part-time "for economic reasons" (a BLS term that includes such circumstances as slack work, partial layoffs, material shortages, can not find full-time job, etc.) are all included in the full-time labor force. However, he demonstrates that these part-time workers, in fact, are composed of two groups of workers in rather different circumstances. The first is those who "usually work full-time," but have been forced to work part-time due to circumstances like slack work, material shortages or repairs to the plant or equipment; while the second group is composed of those workers who have been *forced* to accept *regular* part-time work ("usually work part-time") because they can not find a full-time job, even though they continue to want one. Nardone argues rather persuasively that this latter group of workers should more correctly be included as part of the part-time, not the full-time, labor force. He has apparently convinced the BLS which is now beginning to publish data with this revised definition. The effects of this change in taxonomy are rather startling.

For example, Nardone cites the fact that between 1979 and 1985, while employment in the retail trade and service industries increased by about 7 million, according to the traditional definition (those voluntarily working part-time) only 560,000 (8 percent) of these were part-time workers--a result many found surprising given the extensive use of part-timers in these industries. However, when he adds in as part-time workers those who, though wanting full-time work, "usually work part-time for economic reasons", the number of part-timers increased to 2.4 million or 34.3 percent of the increase in employment (Nardone 1986: 15).

Using this revised definition, Nardone demonstrates that from 1968 to 1985 the proportion of employed persons who worked part-time increased from 14.0 percent to 17.4 percent (See Table 3-9). He concludes that:

> Further, the part-time employed measure shows that during the 1970s and early 1980s, part-time employment grew more rapidly than full-time employment. The rapid growth of part-time employment has led to some restructuring of the work force (Nardone 1986: 15).

In addition, he presents figures to show, for example, that in 1985, among those who worked part-time for economic reasons, but usually worked full-time, on average 55.1 percent worked less than 30 hours and 12.2 percent less than 15 hours per week. Whereas, among those who worked part-time for economic reasons and who usually had to work part-time, 75.5 percent worked less than 30 hours and 20.7 percent less than 15 hours per week--a startling difference, especially when one realizes that the latter group is more than twice as large as the former. Moreover, these latter figures are very similar to the pattern of work among voluntary part-time workers and is further evidence of the appropriateness of counting these "usual," but not voluntary, part-time workers as part of the part-time, not full-time, labor force.

Beyond the work by Nardone, it is important to note, as shown in Table 3-10, that there has been a gradual reduction in the number of hours worked, at least for all production and nonsupervisory workers in private nonagricultural employment,[14] pretty much across the entire American economy during the period from 1960 through the first quarter of 1988 (the very latest available data as this is written). For this group as a whole, the average hours worked weekly dropped rather steadily from 38.7 to 34.4, so that by 1985 and thereafter, the "average" such worker was technically working only part-time, not full-time. However, as the industry breakdown in Table 3-10 reveals, it is the retail trade and service industries that bear the primary responsibility for pulling the overall average down, though the rest of the non-goods producing industries contributed to this decline by having shorter average work weeks. In the retail trade and service industries, the average work week fell below 35 hours way back in 1968, and in the retail trade industry the figure fell below 30 hours in 1982.

Thus, the impact of the drift away from a goods producing economy not only has produced more lower paid jobs on a hourly pay basis, but has also resulted in a serious decline in the number of hours worked. The combined effect is an important element in the structural changes within the American economy which have led to the shrinking of the middle class. Larry Mishel, research director of the Economic Policy Institute, in an article by Laurent Belsie, is quoted as arguing that:

> the shift from a manufacturing to a service-based economy has left too many former full-time workers out in the cold. . . . since 1979 [through 1987], part-time jobs accounted for more than a fifth of all net new jobs created in the United States[15] . . . Just over half of these new part-time jobs were filled by people who wanted full-time work (Belsie 1988).

This conclusion is reinforced by recent work by Bluestone and Harrison in which they conclude that "more than 90 percent of the net additions to the low-wage labor force between 1979 and 1984 were part-time or part-year workers" (Bluestone and Harrison 1988a: 124).

There is one ironic note that needs to be added to this discussion. Over the last hundred years, the industrialized nations have gradually, but steadily, moved to shorten both the standard workday and the number of hours and days that defines the standard workweek. Noting the continuing historically high levels of unemployment that have persisted since the early 1970s and the increases in productivity that have been experienced since these standards became the eight-hour workday and the five day-a-week, 40 hour work week, many in the labor movement have issued notice that the time is ripe to move again to shorten one or both of these.

In fact, a major strike in the Federal Republic of Germany in the early 1980s was based upon the call for "30 for 40"; that is, 30 hours of work as the accepted new standard, without a reduction in pay. More progressive elements within the American movement have also begun to issue this call. This is seen as a preferable way to spread the available work, reduce unemployment, and improve the distribution of income via the redistribution of current productivity-based and historic profits. The German strike was only very partially successful, with a reduction in the workweek from 40 to 37 hours in a series of steps.

Ironically, in the U.S., as we saw in Table 3-10, we have succeeded in shorting the average workweek to below 35 hours for the majority of at least nonsupervisory and production workers. But, we have done so almost totally in the service sector and by the disproportionate growth in that sector; and we have done so without any attempt whatsoever to maintain the weekly base pay. Hence, the result has been some spreading of the work and a lot of new jobs in the service industries; but, at the same time, we have undercut the earnings base of many families and made it virtually impossible for those families to survive on the earnings of only one worker.

Then, we compounded the problem by providing no child care for the children of the parents, both of whom must work for the family to survive, or for the single mother's children, who even when she does work can not adequately support her family. Perhaps a bit of rational planning, a legally enforced shortened workweek that acknowledges and validates what is already occurring, combined with some reasonable social programs, could have avoided, or at least softened, the dire effects of this historical development.

We will speak more about the effects of the distribution of income upon the all too many less fortunate within our society in the next chapter and more about the pattern of earnings among occupations and industries and the effect on those earnings of the shortened work week in Chapter 5.

The Growth in Contingent Workers

Recently, studies have begun to recognize the growing numbers of workers in the American economy who are only very loosely tied to their current employers. Richard Belous of the Conference Board has labeled these as "contingent" workers, whom he differentiates from what he calls "core" workers. He characterizes the core workers as having at least an implicit contract with the firm, tending to work a regular schedule, with a fairly stable salary and a reasonable level of benefits. Contingent workers, however, have only a short-term relation with their employer(s), often (but not always) earn less than regular employees, and almost always receive a poorer benefit package, if any.

Belous includes in the contingent category part-time workers, temporary workers, consultants, leased workers, and life-of-the-contract workers. Halverson, in a report citing the work of Belous, indicates that from 1980 to 1986, while the U.S. work force grew by about 10 percent, the contingent work force grew by 20 percent -

from 28.5 million people to 34.3 million. He concludes that 52 percent of the growth in jobs during this period was among contingent workers, with the fastest growth, 75 percent, occurring among temporary workers. (Halverson 1988) Thus, problems associated with the emergence of growing numbers of contingent workers must be seen as a broader issue than that of part-time workers alone. Moreover, this phenomenon provides yet one more explanation for the changing distribution of income.

The Growth in Low Wage Jobs Across the Economy

Recent work by Bluestone and Harrison (1988a) is primarily an attempt to trace the pattern of change in the proportion of low wage versus middle and high wage employment during the period from 1963 to 1986. In order to avoid the issue of part-time and/or part-year workers, they focused their analysis on those working full-time, full-year--or YRFT (year round full-time) workers. Following upon earlier work by the Joint Economic Committee of Congress, they define low wage as wages below one-half of the 1973 real median wage and high wage as wages above 200 percent of that benchmark. They conclude that:

> Put simply, the low-wage share has taken a great U turn, with over half of the improvement in the low-wage share between 1963 and 1970 (when it declined from 21.4 percent to 12.5 percent) reversed by 1986 (by which time it had increased to 17.2 percent). . . . The trends in the size of the middle- and high-wage strata are equally striking, the middle stratum share falling from nearly 81 percent in 1970 to only 74 percent in 1986. In contrast, the high stratum share of YRFT employment peaked in 1973 at 9.1 percent, fell to as low as 6.5 percent during the recession year 1981, and then recovered to 8.8 percent by 1986. Taken together, the three trajectories indicate an acute increase in wage polarization since the late 1970s (Bluestone and Harrison 1988a: 127-128).

A study by the Economic Policy Institute reached similar conclusions, reporting that between 1979 and 1986, ". . . more than 3 million workers moved down the ladder, from jobs with mid-level to jobs with low-level earnings" (1988).

Moreover, consistent with the findings reported above from a variety of studies, Bluestone and Harrison find that:

> the U turn in the low-wage employment trend and the drift toward polarization are found among most demographic groups, across most regions, and within both manufacturing and service industries. The pattern of a shrinking middle found for the YRFT workforce as a whole is mirrored among men and women, and generally among whites and nonwhites.

What differences do exist are in degree rather than direction (Bluestone and Harrison 1988a: 126).

The Possible Effects of the Business Cycle

Finally, while various macroeconomic factors, such as recession and inflation, may have contributed to the decline of the middle class, the fact that the trend has continued for a decade and a half and under varying macroeconomic conditions suggests that a broad, underlying structural change, rather than a cyclical one, is occurring within the American economy. This conclusion is supported by the recent work of Bluestone and Harrison who used six different variables to try to "decycle" the trend they found in the proportion of low wage jobs among even the full-time, full-year workforce. They concluded that, "No matter which variable is used . . . the U turn remains strongly in evidence." (Bluestone and Harrison 1988a: 125).

Other Possible Causes of the Decline of the Middle Class

In discussing the possible causes of the U turn in the proportion of low wages that occurred during the 1963-86 period (discussed earlier), Bluestone and Harrison identify a number of candidates, including slow productivity growth and the shift of employment out of manufacturing. They go on to point out that *within* both the service and goods producing sectors there are factors which have led in recent years to "a slippage in wages at the bottom and polarization throughout." The factors they identify in this regard are:

-- the decline in unionization
-- the erosion in the real value of the minimum wage
-- wage concession bargaining
-- two-tier wage structures
-- "outsourcing," replacing "in-house" production
-- a secular shift from productive to overtly speculative
   investment (Bluestone and Harrison 1988a: 127-128).

A number of these factors relate to the nature and role of trade unions and to the changing content of collective bargaining. Others relate to some changed patterns in production management and investment practices. Aside from their direct effects, all of these factors may play a role in the slow growth in productivity that has occurred in the U.S.

In any event, while I agree that, on the face of it, these factors seem likely to be quite relevant and worthy of study,[16] an in-depth examination of them simply goes beyond the scope of this work. However, taken as a whole, consideration of such factors further supports the concept that there are a variety of institutional and structural problems, beyond those discussed earlier, which can help us to understand the pattern of change that has occurred in the distribution of income in the U.S. since 1960 and especially since the early 1970s.

CONCLUSION

The historical data concerning the distribution of income in the United States for the quarter century from 1960 to 1985, plus the preliminary data for the period since then, as well as the many studies of all that data, paint a rather clear picture. During the first half of this period, from 1960 to about 1973, the distribution became considerably more equitable, with the proportion of families falling below both the poverty and low income levels declining, while both the middle and upper classes (as measured in terms of income) expanded. In addition, the percentage differentials between the incomes of Whites and Blacks narrowed, though that between males and females widened. However, during the second half of the period, the middle class shrank, while the proportions of those in the lower or underclass and those in the upper class expanded. During much of this latter period, those in poverty increased both in absolute numbers and relatively. For the Black and Hispanic communities, the polarization was even more pronounced as those in both the middle class and low income group declined while the poverty and upper-class groups expanded. Only the situation as between males and females improved. Moreover, the phenomenon of the shrinking middle class was shown as likely to be a reflection of long term structural and institutional changes that will continue to affect the American social fabric for many years to come. It would indeed seem that during the period since the early 1970s, America has been moving rather dramatically toward becoming two societies, separate and quite unequal.

However, it is not enough to merely note the relative degree of inequality in income between these two societies within America; one must also inquire as to the actual characteristics and conditions of those who suffer on the lower end of the distribution and also inquire further as to the causes of this distribution and the effects of race, gender, education, occupation and industry upon it. This will be done in the next two chapters.

NOTES

1. At the time the detailed work for this book was being done and the manuscript prepared, the latest available data was for 1985. Then, as the last chapters were being written and the manuscript went into the editing stage, preliminary data from the March 1987 Current Population Survey, which reports on the distribution of income in 1986, became available. Still later, as the final editing was underway, full data for 1986 and preliminary data for 1987 became available, the latter as a courtesy of staff at the Bureau of the Census who were good enough to send me an advance copy. Rather than delay publication of the book and redo the entire

analysis to include this new data and to place the constant dollar figures onto a 1987 basis, the detailed analysis for 1985 is retained and all figures, including those for later years, were expressed in terms of 1985 constant dollars. However, wherever feasible, data for 1986 through early 1988 is either included or references are made to it in endnotes. Hopefully, this will suffice to satisfy the twin goals of timely publication and the use of data as up to date as is possible.

2. Unless otherwise noted, all figures in Tables 3-1 through 3-5, and later income tables, are either directly taken, or are developed, from either U.S Dept. of Commerce 1987a, U.S. Dept. of Commerce 1986a, or from earlier numbers in these same series.

3. The data for 1986 and 1987 paint a much more disturbing picture. However, because of the way the data are reported and the consequent difficulty in employing income brackets identical to those in the text, in talking about this most recent data we must convert 1987 brackets of $5,000, $10,000, etc., to their 1985 dollar equivalents so that comparisons with the figures in the main text can be made. Thus, the dividing points for the brackets, in 1985 dollars, for discussing the most recent data are: $4,744, $9,488, $18,975, $33,207 and $47,438, that is, 5.4 percent below the figures in the text due to the inflation from 1985 to 1987. Looking at the data for 1986 and 1987, one finds that while there continued to be some improvement in the proportion of White families in the lowest income categories, the proportion of Black and Hispanic families actually turned around and rose again.

Thus, this latest data reveal that the proportion of Black families below $4,744 (in 1985 dollars) increased from 12.4 percent in 1985 to 13.4 percent in 1986 and to 13.5 percent in 1987. There was a slight improvement for those between $4,744 and $9,487 (from 16.8 percent in 1985 to 16.5 percent in 1987), but the proportion of Black families living with between $9,488 and $18,974 steadily grew from 19.2 percent in 1985 to 24.1 percent in 1986 and to 24.3 percent in 1987.

For Hispanics, the proportion of families at the lowest level (below $4,744 in 1985 dollars) increased from 7.4 percent in 1985 to 8.2 percent in 1986 and to 8.6 percent in 1987. However, there did continue to be some small shrinkage in the proportions within the next two brackets.

Thus, even with the modest improvement in the proportion of White families in the three lowest brackets (0.8 percentage points or less from 1985 to 1987), the proportions of White and Hispanic families in the lowest two brackets (as defined in this note) were still higher in 1987 than they had been 14 years earlier in 1973, as was the proportion of Black families in the lowest bracket. It is thus clear that the overall picture painted in the text of the relative conditions in 1985 was still quite accurate at the end of 1987, and for Blacks and Hispanics the picture in 1985 is even a bit too positive compared to that two years later in 1987.

4. Median family income actually peaked in 1973 at $29,172 (in 1985 dollars) and in 1985 stood at only $27,735, or more than 5 percent below the 1973 peak. By 1986, median family income had increased to $28,909 (in 1985 dollars), which was still 1 percent

below the peak. By 1987, after 14 long years, it reached $29,272 (again in 1985 dollars), finally surpassing, by a meager $100, the 1973 level. Thus, while the 1985 to 1987 figures were above the $26,116 median income experienced in 1982, such a performance is only something to rave about if one overlooks the fact that the 1982 figure represented the lowest such number in 12 years and a fall of almost 12 percent from the 1973 peak. More discussion of the changing pattern of median family income is presented based upon Table 4-4 in the next chapter.

5. The official poverty level for a family of four in 1986, in 1986 dollars, was $11,203, and, by 1987, the poverty level was defined as $11,611 (in 1987 dollars). Both of these figures represent only about 38 percent of that year's median family income--only a slight improvement (2 percentage points) from the 1985 percentage.

6. The differences in the number of persons living below the poverty level in 1986 (32.4 million) and in 1987 (32.5 million) were not statistically significant from that in 1985 (33.1 million), according to the Bureau of Census's own calculations. Nor were the poverty rates of 13.6 percent and 13.5 percent statistically significantly different (at the 95 percent confidence level) from the 14 percent figure in 1985.

7. The term "underclass" is one that some readers may find objectionable and a bit pejorative; however, it is a term that is beginning to be used more and more to describe the unfortunate situation that has been developing in America. For example, Mayor Coleman Young of Detroit has said: "We've seen regression . . . We have begun to develop an underclass." Mayor Henry Cisneros of San Antonio, one of the most prominent Hispanic politicians, stated that: ". . . the nation can not survive if does not deal with the problem of a growing underfed, undereducated underclass." Quotes are from Saikowski 1988.

8. As was pointed out in Table 3-3, until 1967, the data for Black families are only available within the category "Black and Other Races." In 1967, Blacks constituted 91.4% of the Blacks and Other Races group (sometimes referred to as "Nonwhites" by the Census Bureau). To examine the possible bias this inconsistency imposes on our analysis, it should be noted that in 1967, Blacks had a larger proportion of their population in every income bracket below $20,000 (in 1985 dollars) and a smaller proportion in every bracket above that figure than did the group referred to as "Black and Other Races." Thus, in using the larger group for 1960 and 1965 and the more narrowly defined group thereafter, one actually makes the distribution seem better in the earlier years than it was. That is, the degree of improvement shown from 1960 or 1965 to 1970 or 1973 is actually understated for Blacks, as is the contrast with what occurred after 1973.

9. If one uses the preliminary figures for 1987, makes the same comparisons between 1973 and 1987, but in constant 1987 dollars, and uses the same categories (which actually have a purchasing power about 5.4 percent below that in 1985), one gets a picture that is exactly the same in terms of the direction of changes for each racial/ethnic group in each bracket as that

discussed in the text. To see this, one can compare the last column for each group in Table 3-5 to the columns in Table 3-11. Clearly the nominal brackets in the two tables are identical, while the price level has changed; hence, exact comparison is not possible. Nevertheless, to help make some comparison feasible, the income brackets in Table 3-11 are expressed both in the terms of 1985 and 1987 dollars. Thus, for all families the newest data show that from 1973 to 1987, using the brackets shown in Table 3-11, the proportion of those in the highest and in the two lowest categories increased while the proportion in the middle-class bracket decreased. Thus, the thrust of the remarks made in the text is not changed.

However, aside from the direction of change is the issue of the size of the changes. The newest data indicate that the increase in the lowest (well below poverty) category is larger among Blacks (21.0 percent for 1973-87 compared to 13.8 percent for 1973-85), but considerably smaller among Whites (17.0 percent compared to 23.1 percent) and slightly smaller among Hispanics (50.3 percent compared to 52.4 percent). Overall, the increase is smaller--17.0 percent for 1973-87 compared to 22.0 percent for 1973-85. This reflects the sad fact that the proportion of Black families in this lowest bracket turned around to increase from 1985 through 1987, after decreasing from 1983 to 1985. For Hispanic families in this bracket, the decrease continued to 1986, but also increased from 1986 to 1987. This turnaround for minority families, but not for White families, in the midst of the much bragged about (at least by Bush and Reagan) expansion, is quite disturbing. We will have to see just what this portends for the future. But for now it would seem that the increasing racial/ethnic polarization is worsening yet again.

On the other hand, the overall (all families) decrease in the middle-class group is slightly larger (10.3 percent compared to 9.7 percent). This is the result of a larger apparent decrease in the middle class among all three racial/ethnic groups when one looks at the data through 1987 using these brackets of slightly lower purchasing power. The largest apparent difference is the much more rapid growth in the upper class (overall, 18.7 percent compared to 10.9 percent), which is evident for all groups.

It should be noted that since each of the brackets when expressed in 1987 dollars represents about 5.4 percent less purchasing power than when the same dollar figures were expressed in 1985 dollars, some families whose income held its purchasing power (that is, increased at just the rate of inflation) would creep over into a higher bracket. This statistical artifact accounts for part, but certainly not all, of the changes noted.

The essential point is that even if the analysis discussed in the main body of the text were conducted using 1987 instead of 1985 as the terminal year for comparative purposes, the analysis would not be altered in any significant way.

10. Other articles along the same lines include Kuttner 1983, Thurow 1984, Steinberg 1985, Harrington and Levinson 1985. Others (Eberts and Swinton 1988; Cohen and Zysman 1987) argue that goods production, particularly manufacuturing, continues to be vitally important to the U.S. I quite agree, but that point does not weaken

the argument that the reduced employment in goods production and the changing occupational structure within that sector have been an important factor in the shrinking of the middle class and in the changing distribution of income.

11. One study reported that, in 1982, only 22% of personal service workers, 38% of retail trade workers, and 49% of business service workers had group health coverage, compared to 82% of manufacturing workers (*Dollars and Sense* 1986a)

12. Later, we will discuss the effect of wages by industry on the distribution of income and at that time it will be clear that the average wages in the service industries, including wholesale and retail trade, finance, insurance and real estate, and the personal and protective services, are considerable lower than in the manufacturing, mining, or construction industries (See Tables 5-10 and 5-11 for details). However, as is discussed in the body of this chapter, there are also important wage differentials within the latter industries, often between those actually engaged in the production of goods and those performing clerical and related services. On the other hand, some of those providing sophisticated legal, accounting, or computer services are quite well paid.

13. Almost twenty years ago, I analyzed the growth patterns in the technician occupations and explored the feasibility of focusing job training programs on these occupations, rather than on the mostly dead-end jobs that was then the rule. I found that given the background typical of people in these occupations, such job training efforts indeed were quite feasible; however, little has been done in the years since that study (Winnick 1970).

14. It is quite possible that among supervisory workers and among salaried nonproduction workers the average weekly hours may have increased or decreased. The BLS simply does not record hours of employment for such workers. Moreover, for those who are paid on the basis of a salary, typically an annual salary, the number of hours worked does not effect their income in a direct manner, while it may be a matter of interest in other regards.

15. From 1973 to 1985, to look at the period upon which we have often focused in this study, 24.2 percent, or nearly one quarter, of the increase in employment was accounted for by part-time jobs, using Nardone's revised definition.

16. Bluestone and Harrison indicate in their article (1988a) that they plan to discuss these topics in some detail in a forthcoming book (1988b) which is not yet available as this is being written.

Table 3-1
Distribution of All Families Among Income Classes:
1960 to 1985 (in constant 1985 dollars)

	All Families								Cum in '85
	1960	1965	1970	1973	1975	1980	1983	1985	
Less Than $5,000 "The Truly Destitute"	8.0%	5.5%	3.8%	3.1%	3.3%	3.9%	5.2%	4.8%	4.8%
$5,000 to $9,999 Below the '"Official" Poverty Line*	11.8%	10.1%	8.2%	7.8%	8.9%	8.9%	9.2%	8.5%	13.3%
$10,000 to $19,999 Above "Poverty", But Below "Minimum Adequacy"*	33.4%	28.1%	20.7%	19.7%	21.5%	21.5%	21.8%	20.7%	34.0%
$20,000 to $34,999 "Minimum Adequacy" to 14% Above "Modest-But Adequate"	30.3%	33.8%	35.1%	31.8%	32.3%	31.1%	29.9%	28.9%	62.9%
$35,000 to $49,999 Up to 9% above the BLS "High Budget" Line	11.3%	14.7%	19.3%	21.0%	20.0%	19.5%	18.3%	18.8%	81.7%
$50,000 and above From the Lower-Upper Class to the Super Rich	5.2%	7.8%	13.0%	16.5%	13.9%	15.1%	15.6%	18.3%	100.0%

Note: Social Security official "Poverty" level for a family of four in 1985 was $10,989.
The adjusted Bureau of Labor Statistics "Minimum Adequacy" or "Low Budget" was $20,207,
while the adjusted "Moderate" or "Modest-but Adequate" budget was $30,177 and the "High"
budget was $44,884.

Source: U.S. Department of Commerce 1987a and earlier numbers in this eries.

Table 3-2
Distribution of White Families Among Income Classes:
1960 to 1985 (in constant 1985 dollars)

	White Families								Cum in'85
	1960	1965	1970	1973	1975	1980	1983	1985	
Less Than $5,000 "The Truly Destitute"	6.6%	4.6%	3.2%	2.4%	2.7%	3.0%	3.9%	3.7%	3.7%
$5,000 to $9,999 Below the "Official" Poverty Line	10.6%	8.9%	7.1%	6.7%	7.7%	7.6%	7.7%	7.5%	11.2%
$10,000 to $19,999 Above "Poverty", But Below "Minimum Adequacy"	33.3%	27.3%	19.7%	18.4%	20.7%	20.9%	21.4%	20.0%	31.2%
$20,000 to $34,999 "Minimum Adequacy" to 14% Above "Modest-But Adequate"	31.7%	34.3%	35.9%	32.5%	33.0%	31.9%	30.9%	29.6%	60.8%
$35,000 to $49,999 Up to 9% above the BLS "High Budget" Line	12.0%	16.0%	20.2%	22.2%	21.0%	20.5%	19.3%	19.7%	80.5%
$50,000 and above From the Lower-Upper Class to the Super Rich	5.8%	8.9%	13.9%	17.6%	14.9%	16.1%	16.8%	19.6%	100.0%

Source: U.S. Department of Commerce 1987a and earlier numbers in this series.

Table 3-3
Distribution of Black Families Among Income Classes:
1960 to 1985 (in constant 1985 dollars)

	Black Families *								Cum in'85
	1960	1965	1970	1973	1975	1980	1983	1985	
Less Than $5,000 "The Truly Destitute"	21.5%	13.2%	9.9%	8.7%	8.5%	11.4%	14.3%	13.5%	13.5%
$5,000 to $9,999 Below the "Official" Poverty Line	21.9%	21.3%	17.4%	18.2%	20.3%	19.3%	20.1%	17.1%	30.6%
$10,000 to $19,999 Above "Poverty", But Below "Minimum Adequacy"	34.7%	36.8%	30.2%	30.4%	27.9%	27.5%	25.9%	27.3%	57.9%
$20,000 to $34,999 "Minimum Adequacy" to 14% Above "Modest-But Adequate"	16.8%	20.1%	27.4%	26.0%	27.2%	25.1%	23.9%	23.3%	81.2%
$35,000 to $49,999 Up to 9% above the BLS "High Budget" Line	4.6%	6.5%	10.7%	10.7%	11.2%	11.3%	10.2%	11.8%	93.0%
$50,000 and above From the Lower-Upper Class to the Super Rich	0.9%	2.1%	4.5%	6.0%	4.9%	5.5%	5.7%	7.0%	100.0%

Note: * For 1960 and 1 965, the figures are actually for the category "Black and Other Races."
Separate data for "Blacks" was not reported until 1967, at which time Blacks represented
91.4% of the "Blacks and Other Races" group (sometimes referred to by the Census Bureau
as simply "Nonwhites").

Source: U.S. Department of Commerce 1987a and earlier numbers in this series.

56

Table 3-4
Distribution of Hispanic Families Among Income Classes:
1960 to 1985 (in constant 1985 dollars)

| | Hispanic Families | | | | | Cum in '85 |
	1973	1975	1980	1983	1985	
Less Than $5,000 "The Truly Destitute"	4.0%	6.5%	7.1%	8.9%	8.3%	8.3%
$5,000 to $9,999 Below the "Official" Poverty Line	12.8%	15.7%	15.6%	16.9%	17.0%	25.3%
$10,000 to $19,999 Above "Poverty", But Below "Minimum Adequacy"	30.6%	31.0%	29.8%	28.8%	27.0%	52.3%
$20,000 to $34,999 "Minimum Adequacy" to 14% Above "Modest-But Adequate"	31.2%	31.0%	28.2%	26.9%	27.3%	79.6%
$35,000 to $49,999 Up to 9% above the BLS "High Budget" Line	14.3%	10.8%	12.7%	11.3%	12.5%	92.1%
$50,000 and above From the Lower-Upper Class to the Super Rich	7.3%	4.9%	6.4%	7.2%	8.1%	100.0%

Note: * 1972 is the first year in which data is available for Hispanic ("Spanish Origin")
families. "Spanish Origin" families and persons "may be of any race."

Source: U.S. Department of Commerce 1987a and earlier numbers in this series.

Table 3-5
Summary of the Distribution of All, White, Black, and Hispanic
Families Among Income Classes in 1960, 1973 and 1985 and
Percentage Changes Between Those Years

Income in 1985 Dollars	ALL FAMILIES						WHITE FAMILIES				
				Percentage Change						Percentage Change	
	1960	1973	1985	'60-'73	'73-'85		1960	1973	1985	'60-'73	'73-'85
$0 to $9,999	19.8%	10.9%	13.3%	-44.9%	22.0%		17.2%	9.1%	11.2%	-47.1%	23.1%
$10,000 to 19,999	33.4%	19.7%	20.7%	-41.0%	5.1%		33.3%	18.4%	20.0%	-44.7%	8.7%
$20,000 to 49,999	41.6%	52.8%	47.7%	26.9%	-9.7%		43.7%	54.7%	49.3%	25.2%	-9.9%
$50,000 and over	5.2%	16.5%	18.3%	217.3%	10.9%		5.8%	17.6%	19.6%	203.4%	11.4%

Income in 1985 Dollars	BLACK FAMILIES						HISPANIC FAMILIES		
				Percentage Change					Percentage Change
	1960	1973	1985	'60-'73	'73-'85		1973	1985	'73-'85
$0 to $9,999	43.4%	26.9%	30.6%	-38.0%	13.8%		16.6%	25.3%	52.4%
$10,000 to 19,999	34.7%	30.4%	27.3%	-12.4%	-10.2%		30.9%	27.0%	-12.6%
$20,000 to 49,999	21.4%	36.7%	35.1%	71.5%	-4.4%		46.1%	39.8%	-13.7%
$50,000 and over	0.9%	6.0%	7.0%	566.7%	16.7%		6.3%	8.1%	28.6%

Source: U.S. Department of Commerce 1987a and earlier numbers in this series as summarized in Tables 3-2 to 3-4.

Table 3-6
Poverty Rate and Number of Persons in Poverty
1960-1987

Year	Official Poverty Rate (%)	Number of Persons Living below Poverty Level
1987	13.5	32.5 million
1986	13.6	32.4
1985	14.0	33.1
1984	14.4	33.7
1983	15.3	35.5
1982	15.0	34.4
1981	14.0	31.8
1980	13.0	29.3
1975	12.3	25.9
1970	12.6	25.4
1967	14.2	27.8
1965	17.3	33.2
1960	22.2	39.9

Source: U.S. Department of Commerce 1987a,d and 1988c.

Table 3-7
Distribution of All and Black Families by Designated Income Categories
1985

	All Families			Black Families		
	At Each Level		Cummulative Percentage	At Each Level		Cummulative Percentage
	Number of Families*	% of Families		Number of Families*	% of Families	
A. Below the Poverty or Physical Subsistence Level of $10,989	9,791	15.4%	15.4%	2,337	33.7%	33.7%
B. From "A" to the BLS Low or Minimum Adequacy Level of $20,207	12,153	19.1%	34.5%	1,697	24.5%	58.3%
C. From "B" to the BLS Moderate or Socially Necessary Level of $30,177	12,668	19.9%	54.4%	1,160	16.8%	75.1%
D. From "C" to the BLS High or Quite Comfortable Level of $44,884	14,132	22.3%	76.7%	1,036	15.0%	90.1%
E. From "D" to the Upper or Affluent Level of $60,000	7,766	12.2%	88.9%	464	6.7%	96.8%
F. Above Mere Affluence **	7,048	11.1%	100.0%	226	3.3%	100.0%

Notes: * Number of families in 1,000's.
       ** The top 5% bracket for All Families starts at $77,706.

Source: Calculated on basis of figures from U.S. Department of Commerce 1987a.

Table 3-8
Nonagricultural Employment by Industry: 1960-1987
(in millions)

		The Goods-Producing Sector			
Year	Mining	Manufacturing	Construction	Total Employ. in Sector	Sector as a % of Total Employment
1960	0.7	16.8	2.9	20.4	37.6
1965	0.6	18.1	3.2	21.9	36.0
1970	0.6	19.4	3.6	23.6	33.3
1975	0.8	18.3	3.5	22.6	29.4
1980	1.0	20.2	4.3	25.5	28.2
1985	0.9	19.3	4.7	24.9	25.5
1987	0.7	19.1	5.0	24.8	24.2

			The Service Sector				
Year	Transport. & Pub.Util.	Wholesale Trade	Retail Trade	Finance & Real Estate	Other Services	Total Employ. in Sector	Sector as % of Total Employment
1960	4.0	3.1	8.2	2.6	7.4	25.3	46.7
1965	4.0	3.5	9.3	3.0	9.0	28.8	47.4
1970	4.5	4.0	11.0	3.6	11.5	34.6	48.8
1975	4.5	4.4	12.6	4.2	13.9	39.6	51.5
1980	5.1	5.3	15.0	5.2	17.9	48.5	53.7
1985	5.2	5.7	17.4	6.0	22.0	56.3	57.7
1987	5.4	5.9	18.5	6.5	24.2	60.5	59.1

	The Government Sector		
Year	Government	Sector as a % of Total Employment	Total NonAgricultural Employment
1960	8.4	15.5	54.2
1965	10.1	16.6	60.8
1970	12.6	17.8	70.9
1975	14.7	19.1	76.9
1980	16.2	17.9	90.4
1985	16.4	16.8	97.5
1987	17.0	16.6	102.3

Source: U.S. Department of Labor 1988.

Table 3-9
Employed Part-Time Workers as a Percent
of All Employed Workers by Age and Sex
1968-1985

Year	All Workers	Men 20 years and older	Women 20 years and older	Both sexes 16-19 yrs
1968	14.0%	4.8%	22.5%	48.8%
1970	15.2	5.4	23.4	51.8
1975	16.6	6.2	24.4	53.6
1980	16.9	6.4	23.6	55.0
1985	17.4	7.3	23.9	61.0

Source: Nardone 1986.

Table 3-10
Average Weekly Hours of
Production and Nonsupervisory Workers
in Private Nonagricultural Employment
by Industry: 1960-1988

Year	Mining	Constr.	Manuf.	Transp. & Pub. Util.	Whsl. Trade	Retail Trade	Finance & Real Estate	Other Serv.	All Indus.
1960	40.4	36.7	39.7	n/a	40.5	38.0	37.2	n/a	38.6
1965	42.3	37.4	41.2	41.3	40.8	36.6	37.2	35.4	38.8
1970	42.1	37.3	39.8	40.5	39.9	33.8	36.7	34.4	37.1
1975	41.9	36.4	39.5	39.7	38.7	32.4	36.5	33.5	36.1
1980	43.3	37.0	39.7	39.6	38.5	30.2	36.2	32.6	35.3
1985	43.4	37.7	40.5	39.5	38.4	29.4	36.4	32.5	34.9
1987	42.3	37.7	41.0	39.1	38.2	29.3	36.2	32.5	34.8
1988*	41.1	37.6	40.9	38.6	37.8	28.6	35.7	32.3	34.4

Note: * Data are for the first quarter of 1988, and are preliminary and not seasonally adjusted.

Source: U.S. Department of Labor 1988 and earlier years in this series.

Table 3-11
Percentage Changes in the Distribution of Families by Income
and by Race/Ethnic Group, Between 1973 and 1987
(in constant 1985 and 1987 dollars)

Income in 1987 Dollars	Income in 1985 Dollars	% Change in Proportion of Families			
		All	White	Black	Hispanic
$0 to $9,999	$0 to 9,487	17.0	14.8	21.0	50.3
$10,000 to 19,999	$9,488 to 18,974	0.5	3.5	-17.1	-8.3
$20,000 to 49,999	$18,975 to 47,437	-10.3	-10.2	-6.7	-17.2
$50,000 and over	$47,438 and over	18.7	18.4	39.7	43.4

Source: U.S. Department of Commerce 1988c.

4

The Poor—Just Who Are They?

As has been already suggested by the earlier discussion of the Social Security Administration's "official" definition of poverty versus the measurement based on the Bureau of Labor Statistics Lower or Minimum Adequacy Budget level, there are a number of competing definitions of what one might consider "being poor in America." Table 4-1 gives us an opportunity to explore some of these alternative definitions using data for 1985.[1]

Until this point, most of our analysis has been based upon some concept of a typical family, which, though less and less true, is still thought of as consisting of two adults and two children. However, the Social Security Administration, when it calculates the number of poor families, does so based upon a sliding scale depending on family size (and upon the number of related children under the age of 18 in the family).[2] The "official" poverty thresholds for various sized families, the distribution of families by size and the distribution of poverty, by this definition, among families of different sizes and race/ethnic origin, are all presented in the top portion of Table 4-1.

What emerges from these figures is that while, in the general population, there is a greater proportion of families of two or three persons than there is of families greater than four, the incidence of poverty is higher among the larger families. In fact, depending upon the racial/ethnic origins of the family, the rate (or incidence) of poverty for families of size seven and more is two to four times as high as among families of only two persons. If one compares the average incidence of poverty taking into account family size, that is 11.4 percent in 1985, and compares it to the figure when one simply uses the four-person threshold and applies it to families without regard to family size (15.4 percent, as shown in the second portion of Table 4-1), the bias involved is clear. The larger proportion of small families outweighs the higher incidence of poverty among large families and the figure that does not take into account family size is four percentage points higher. This is the case across race/ethnic groups, where the differential varies from three to five percentage points.

However, there are many other subtleties that also effect "the poverty rate".   Moving down Table 4-1, we see that while 11.4 percent of families, adjusted for size, are poor, 12.6 percent of the people living in families are poor, reflecting again the incidence among large families.   Moreover, we find that the incidence of poverty among those living alone is far higher, 21.5 percent, which yields the result that the incidence of all persons living in poverty is higher than that for persons living in families, to wit, 14 percent.

Moreover, for a number of years, the Bureau of the Census has tacitly conceded the inadequacy of the poverty threshold by publishing data on those who fall below 125 percent of the "official" poverty threshold, taking into account family size. For 1985, this represented, for a family of four, a threshold of $13,736, which was still only two-thirds (66.8 percent) of the adjusted BLS Minimum Adequacy standard. The poverty rate using this 125 percent threshold level was 18.7 percent. Finally, this figure can be compared to 34.4 percent of families (undifferentiated by size) below the Minimum Adequacy level and the 53.9 percent below the Modest but Adequate level. Even if these latter two numbers are upward biased by about 4 percent or so because of the family size issue, these figures are still very useful in obtaining a first approximation as to the number of American families who are forced to live in conditions of poverty or low income.

At the bottom of this table are presented some numbers as to the mean size of families and mean number of children in families with children, for each racial/ethnic group. While the size of poor families tends to be significantly larger than that of the population as a whole, the mean difference is consistently less than half a child.

There are obviously a number of other criteria that might be used to set different poverty level thresholds, such as regional differences in the cost of living, whether the family is living in a rural or urban setting, and if urban, whether the family lives in the suburbs or in the central city. However, these distinctions, some of which were made in earlier years, are no longer employed.

THE POOR ARE GETTING POORER

With an awareness of the complexity of defining "the" poverty level, let us now return to the key focus of this work--how has the distribution of income been changing, especially since 1960. Aside from the problems associated with the bipolarization implied in the shrinking proportion of the middle class, there are the problems inherent in the falling standard of living, in both relative and absolute terms, of the poorer portions of our society.

The Deteriorating Relative Position

One way to view this effect of growing polarization, or growing inequality, is to look at the data in Table 4-2, which gives us an overview of the full period from 1947 to 1986. As is summarized in the comments along the right hand side of that table (augmented by notes below the table), we see that in 1986 the poorest (in terms of income) 20 percent, 40 percent and even 60 percent of our families shared among themselves the smallest proportions of our nation's income ever recorded by each respective group (except in the case of the very lowest 20 percent for which in three years-- 1949, 1950, and 1954--a figure of 4.5 percent was recorded, compared to the 4.6 percent in 1985 and 1986). Even those in the fourth 20 percent, those between the 60th and 80th percentile points, were at the lowest level since 1974; although still tied for the highest level from 1947 to 1974. So even this group, which had 1986 incomes between \$34,362 and \$49,432 (in 1985 dollars of value), that is, the upper portion of the middle class, while still at high historical levels, has seen their relative position weaken in recent years.

To take a bit broader view, at the bottom of this table, one sees that the poorest 40 percent of America's families received in 1986 only 15.4 percent of family income, while the richest 40 percent received 67.7 percent, or more than four times as much. Despite the slippage in the proportion of income received by those in the fourth quintile, the figures for both of these groups are, respectively, the lowest and the highest on record.

Looking more closely at those at the highest levels, we see that the proportion of income received by the richest 20 percent, including that received by the richest 5 percent, represented the largest proportions of total income ever recorded by those groups. Thus, the poor, the lower class, and the lower-middle class are sharing among themselves smaller proportions of our nation's income than ever before. Even the upper-middle class has begun to slip in terms of the income available to it. Only those at the highest relative levels have larger proportions of the nation's income of which to dispose. There can be little doubt that the relative position of the poor has worsened considerably, as has that of the lower- and, in recent years, even upper-middle class.[3]

Recalling that cash transfer payments are included in the income figures cited, it is important to understand that this deteriorated relative income position of the poor has occurred despite the increased transfer payments that followed the War on Poverty.[4] In this regard, Bradbury commented that:

Readers may be surprised that income was more unequally distributed in 1984 than in 1973, since the amounts of social security, welfare, and other transfers have grown considerably . . . . This distribution has become more unequal in spite of increases in "pro-poor" transfers because the distribution of pre-transfer income has become even more unequal (Bradbury 1986: 54).

There is one important exception concerning the effectiveness of cash transfer payments upon the distribution of income. As we will see in Table 4-5, the one group that has seen its poverty rate drop dramatically since 1960 are those over the age of 65. This is due in large measure to increased Social Security benefits and to the indexing of those benefits to the cost of living. Danziger of the University of Wisconsin's Center for Research on Poverty estimates that more than two-thirds of the decline in the rate of poverty among the elderly since 1959 is due to increased Social Security benefits.[5]

The Deteriorating Absolute Position

It is important to note that the deteriorating position of the poor is not just a relative phenomenon. From 1973 through 1982, while the absolute purchasing power available to American families decreased generally, the situation for the poorest portion of our society was considerably worse than the average overall. Moreover, while there was some improvement during the 1982-87 period, the absolute purchasing power available to the poorest 20 percent of American families was still less in 1987 than it had been in 1973, more than a decade earlier. It should be noted that the poorest 20 percent of American families in 1987 were those who had a total income under $13,710 (in 1985 dollars), which was just under the 125 percent of poverty threshold of $13,770 for a family of four.

Thus, as one can see in Table 4-3 (in which all figures are in 1985 constant dollars), from 1973 to 1982, the median income of the poorest 40 percent of the American population (the 20th percentile income) *fell* by $2,244, from $14,726 to $12,482, an amazing 15.2 percent decrease in real, inflation adjusted, 1985 dollars. While there was an 9.8 percent improvement in the next five years (a slower rate of improvement than that enjoyed by those families already at the upper end of the income distribution), it still left the median for the poorest 40 percent some 6.9 percent below the 1973 level. To place this in context, the upper income limit for a family to be included in the poorest 40 percent was $23,814 in 1987 (in 1985 dollars again), or just $3,607 above the BLS Minimum Adequacy level.

During the 1973-82 period, the median income of the upper 40 percent of the population (the 80th percentile income) also fell, but by $2,052 from a base more than three times higher, that is, from $46,623 to $44,571--only a 4.4 percent drop. Thus, the gap between those at the 20th percentile and those at the 80th percentile (that is, between the median income of the poorest 40 percent and the richest 40 percent) widened during that decade from $31,897 to an even worse $32,089. During the next five years, the upper 40 percent saw their median income go up by 12.6 percent, leaving them 7.7 percent better off in 1987 than in 1973 and the gap yet even wider at $36,489. Again, to put this situation in context, the median income of the upper 40 percent in 1987 was some $5,315 above the BLS High or Quite Comfortable level.

If we turn to the richest 10 percent of American families, we see an even more startling picture. During the period for 1973-82, their median income did fall, but only by 1.9 percent, to $71,328. Then, from 1982 to 1987, their median income increased at the fastest rate (14.8 percent), to cross the $80,000 threshold. The gap between the median income of the poorest 40 percent and that of the richest 10 percent, thus widened to over $68,000 by 1987.

What may surprise the average reader is the fact that there has been a clear and persistent pattern--stretching back to the beginning of the recording of modern data right after World War II (1947)--of a steadily and vastly widening gap in the purchasing power available to the poorer families of America as compared to that of the richer and of the richest families in America. To further look at this growing gap, in absolute terms, between the rich and the poor, consider the data in the center of Table 4-3. Here, we see that the gap in actual (1985) constant dollars of purchasing power between the 20th percentile and the 95th percentile of income, the medians of the lower 40 percent and upper 10 percent, respectively, has steadily widened since 1947, as has the gap between the 20th and 80th percentiles, the medians of the lower and upper 40 percent, respectively. In both cases, the absolute difference in purchasing power in 1987 was more than twice that of 1947 and 75 percent and 67 percent greater than in 1960, respectively.

To look at it in a slightly different way, the purchasing power of the income of a family at the 20th percentile level as a percentage of the income of a family at the 95th percentile level, had fallen, by 1987, to 16.7 percent, its lowest level in the 40 years of these records. Similarly, the purchasing power of a family at the 20th percentile as a percentage of one at the 80th percentile had fallen from just under one-third, 32.2 percent in 1947 to just over one-quarter, 27.3 percent in 1986. Thus, by 1987, a family at the 80th percentile had more than 3.7 times as much income, and a family at the 95th percentile had almost 6 times as much income, as the family at the 20th percentile.

The Different Pattern of Change Before and After 1973

However, this broad view clouds another very interesting phenomenon: namely, that the changes in the real income figures at the three levels show a different pattern before and after 1973. Looking at the lower portion of Table 4-3, one sees that from 1947 to 1960 there were significant increases in all three levels of (constant dollar, real) income, but with the highest growing at the *slowest* rate. From 1960 to 1973, all three continued to grow, but now at slightly higher rates the higher the income level.

However, from 1973 to 1982, there was a major divergence. As we discussed earlier, all three income categories fell, with a very pronounced pattern of the rate of decrease becoming faster the lower the income level. Since 1982, we seem to have returned to the relative pattern of growth of 1960-73 with those with the highest incomes also enjoying the fastest growth rates, but with even wider differentials in those growth rates than was true in the earlier period. The net results, as discussed earlier, were that those at the 20th percentile found themselves 6.9 percent *worse* off in 1987 than in 1973, while those at the 80th and 95th percentiles found themselves 7.7 percent and 12.7 percent *better off*, respectively.

One summary measure of the dramatically different pattern of changes in income since 1973, especially during the 1973-82 period, is shown in Table 4-4. Here, one finds that median family income increased substantially from 1960 to 1973. However, from 1973 to 1982, despite some minor ups and downs during the late 1970s, it decreased for all families, taken as a whole (one of the issues that Bradbury addressed), as well as for White, Black and Hispanic families considered separately. Since 1982, there has again been some substantial improvement. Nevertheless, as of 1987, while the median family income for White families had very slightly (0.4 percent) surpassed the level that had been achieved in 1973, that for Black and Hispanic families remained 2.4 percent and 8.7 percent *below* the 1973 level. A sad record of achievement after 14 long years.

If one recalls the oft-quoted remark of Franklin Delano Roosevelt in the early 1930s that he looked out over a nation where one-third of its people went to bed every night either ill-fed, ill-clothed, or ill-housed, the horrible truth is that, in the mid 1980s, by the reasonable standards defined by the Bureau of Labor Statistics (recall the description of these standards as discussed in Chapter 2), that is still the case in America. Moreover, among the minorities of our nation, the situation is far worse even than that. In addition, there are the hard facts that the gap between rich and poor has been steadily widening, that the relative size of the middle class has been shrinking, that the median family income fell for almost a decade and remained in 1987 barely above (for Whites) the level first achieved in 1973, and that the proportion of the nation's income available to the lower 60 percent of our families has been decreasing. Faced with these economic pressures, is it any wonder that we hear so much about the distress of the American family.

THE SITUATION FOR MINORITIES, FEMALE-HEADED HOUSEHOLDS AND CHILDREN

Now let us look in more detail at how the incidence of poverty has been changing over the period in question and how the burden of poverty has affected various groups such as different racial/ethnic groups, female-headed households, and children. Before analyzing the data in Table 4-5, it is important to note that the definition of poverty used there is the official Social Security Administration/Bureau of the Census standard--with all its advantages and disadvantages which have been explored above, and which, it should be recalled, is more than 50 percent lower in 1985 dollars than the far more appropriate BLS Low income standard. A bit later, in Table 4-6, is presented data based upon 125 percent of the poverty level, which stood at only 66.8 percent of the Low income standard. Hence, what follows may be viewed as a far more positive and conservative description than that which indeed faces the American people.

Table 4-5 presents data for every five years from 1960 to 1980, plus 1987 which is the latest available,[6] with an added column for the peak year since 1980 for that particular category. The data presented along the right-hand side of the table all relate to families, while that along the left-hand side relate to all persons in that group, whether or not they lived in families. Table 4-6 provides some similar data, but with regard to the 125 percent of poverty threshold.

Racial/Ethnic Minorities

Looking at Table 4-5, the first thing one should note is that except when dealing with female-headed households or families, the rate of poverty within the Black community is about two to three times higher than that among Whites, and the poverty rate for Hispanics is generally at about the same level as that for Blacks, sometimes a bit higher, sometimes a bit lower, depending on the particular category under investigation. On the other hand, it is important to note that of the 32.5 million persons living in poverty in the U.S. in 1987, 21.4 million, or 65.8 percent, were White; that is, two out of every three poor people were White.

The simple fact is that while the rate of poverty is far higher within the minority communities, the far larger number of Whites living in America, combined with the significant degree of poverty in that community (10.5 percent in 1987), means that about two-thirds of the poor in the U.S. are and have been White. The media image of the poor as being predominately people of color is not and never has been true. In this context, the tendency of authors such as Charles Murray to write in such a manner as to imply that being poor and being Black are virtually synonymous is, at best, inappropriate and misleading (Murray 1984).

Moreover, it should also be pointed out that a similar picture emerges when one looks at the welfare figures. In 1985, 2.1 million White families received welfare benefits compared to 1.4 million Black families. Moreover, while about 31 percent of Blacks lived below the poverty line in 1985, only 21 percent received public assistance. More than 2 million Black people living below the poverty line were not "on welfare."[7]

Returning to Table 4-5, we see that for all persons whether living is Census defined families or not, the incidence of poverty in 1987 is more than three times higher for Blacks than for Whites and only a bit lower for Hispanics than for Blacks. Among unrelated individuals, the differential is a little more than 2 to 1, reflecting the high level of poverty (20.8 percent) even among White unrelated individuals.

Before one leaps to any conclusions as to the cause of poverty among unrelated individuals, it is important to note that the poverty rate among our senior citizens, regardless of race/ethnic origin (12.2 percent in 1987), is significantly lower than that for unrelated individuals (21.6 percent). That is, the high rate of poverty among unrelated individuals is not primarily due to single older persons, quite the contrary. In fact, one striking fact is that for all racial/ethnic groups, the incidence of poverty among the elderly has consistently fallen and this has contributed to a similar fall in the rate for unrelated individuals. This improvement in the circumstances facing the elderly is largely a result of expanded Social Security benefits, as discussed earlier.

If we look at the changes in the incidence of poverty among the racial/ethnic groups over time, focusing first on Whites, one finds that in general (that is, for "all persons") and for those in families, the poverty rate was higher in 1987 than it was 16 years earlier in 1970.[8] In fact, in 1987, the poverty rate for all White persons living in families stood 32 percent above its low point of 6.9 percent reached in 1973.

Among Hispanic persons in general and for those living in families, the poverty rates in 1987, 28.2 percent and 27.7 percent, respectively,, were higher than at any time prior to 1982 and only 1.7 to 1.5 percentage points below their 1982 peaks. Moreover, the rates for 1987 were higher than for 1986. In fact, in 1987, Hispanics constituted 16.8 percent of the officially poor, a historic high. For Blacks, poverty rates for all persons and for those in families increased substantially in 1987 from 1986 (by 2 percent and 2.1 percent respectively) and, except for the peaks reached during the 1980s, one has to go back to 1966 to find levels substantially higher. That is, the rates for all of these groups have shown little or no improvement over the last 15 or even 20 years. It is, of course, true that the rates in 1987 are a bit lower than their peaks during the Reagan recession, but from a longer term perspective, they remain very high.

Looking at the data in Table 4-6 pertaining to those living below the threshold defined as 125 percent of poverty, what the Government often refers to as the "near poor," we see a generally similar picture to that just discussed. The "near poverty" rate runs two to three times as high in the Black community as in the White and only slightly lower in the Hispanic community than in the Black. Looking at the top portion of Table 4-6 we see that for Whites, the figures for 1987, while below their Reagan peaks, are above the 1970 levels. A similar picture emerges for Hispanics for whom the 1987 rates are above those in 1980, the first year these data were reported for that group. However, by this standard, the figures for Black persons and families do show some modest improvement from those in 1970, though little or none since 1980, in part due again to the increase suffered in 1987.

Racial/Ethnic Differentials in Unemployment
It might be mentioned at this juncture that it is quite true that the unemployment rate among Blacks during the mid-1980s has run at about two and a half times that for Whites--on average during 1986, for example, at 6.0 percent for Whites and 14.5 percent for Blacks and in 1987 at 5.3 percent and 13.0 percent, respectively. It is also quite true that this differential had increased from about 2:1 during the mid-1970s.[9] It is also important to understand that the overall average annual unemployment rate of 6.2 percent in 1987 that is touted for being such an improvement compared to the terrible modern peak rate of 9.7 percent in 1982, only looks good

when one chooses to ignore the fact that that rate never exceeded 5.9 percent, and averaged only 4.8 percent, during the 13 year period from 1962 through 1974.

Related to these unemployment figures is another interesting facet of the recent recession period, which might rather broadly be viewed as 1979-83. To wit, 62 percent of the White workers who were laid off were then rehired by the same firm during that period, while this was true for only 42 percent of the Black workers. Moreover, of those not rehired, 17 percent of the Blacks as compared to 14 percent of the Whites were unable to find another job (Helmore and Laing 1986c: 20).[10]

Nevertheless, as severe as the unemployment problem has been in recent years, and despite the vast disparities in unemployment between Whites and Blacks, unemployment is only one part of the poverty problem. Chapter 5 examines the pattern of wages among those employed full-time, full-year, and examines the reasons people did not work *other* than traditionally defined unemployment.

Children

The poverty situation for children in America is truly horrible. Again referring to Table 4-5, we see that, in 1987, one out of every five children in the U.S. (20.0 percent) who were living in families, lived in poverty. We see that far more than one-third (39.3 percent) of all Hispanic and almost half (45.1 percent) of all Black children under 18 in families were being forced to live in those conditions. Overall, 36.4 percent of the poor were children under the age of 15, and more than 47 percent of the poor were age 21 or less. Children under the age of 6 actually experienced the highest incidence of poverty of any age group - 22.1 percent.[11] Moreover, the situation in 1987, while a bit better than during the 1981-87 peak, is considerably worse than it was for any year back to the late 1960s. Thus, the overall poverty rate in 1987 of 20 percent for children under the age of 18 living in families must be compared to the fact that from 1966 through 1979, that figure never exceeded 17.4 percent and averaged 15.5 percent. In fact, for White kids, one has to go back to the early 1960s to find conditions as bad.

Turning to Table 4-7, one sees clearly the growing plight of very young children, those under the age of 6, and those ages 6 to 15. In 1987, more than one-fifth (22.7 percent) of all such young children and very close to half (49.0 percent) of Black and 41.8 percent of Hispanic young children lived in poverty. For such young children as a whole and for Whites and Hispanics separately, except for a year or two during the 1980s, these are the worst figures since these records have been kept. For Blacks, the 1987 figure for the youngest children (49 percent) was above even the recent peaks, having increased by 3.4 percentage points just since 1986, and was only slightly below the all-time peak. It was well above the figures recorded during the 1970s. For the Black children ages 6 to 15, the figure of 45.2 percent is the highest in almost 20 years. When one turns to the 125 percent threshold (Table 4-6), one finds that for children under 18 living in families, the incidence of poverty is 1 in 4 (25.1 percent) for all such children and more than 1 in 2 (52.8 percent) for Black children. Overall, the situation was summed up rather well by Edward Zigler, director of the Bush Center in Child Development and Social Policy at Yale University, when he stated that, "Children are in the absolute worst status they have been in during my 30 years of monitoring child and family life in this country . . . Every day more and more children are slipping into poverty, which immediately puts them at very high risk . . ." (Gardner 1986).

Some important symptoms of the high risks to which our children are subjected, especially our Black and Hispanic children are indicated by the following facts. Sixteen percent of White 17-year-olds and 47 percent of Black 17-year-olds are functionally illiterate. Black children drop out of college at almost twice the rate of White children.[12] In 1976, the proportion of Black high school graduates going on to college was 33.5 percent, which, amazingly, was slightly above the 33.0 percent rate among Whites. But, by 1985, the figure for Blacks had *dropped* to 26.1 percent, while that for Whites had *increased* to 34.4 percent. Moreover, this occurred in the face of the fact that the proportion of Blacks graduating from high school, that is, not dropping out, increased during this period from 67.5 percent to 75.6 percent. Black enrollment in graduate programs has also slipped in recent years from 5.5 percent in 1980 to 4.8 percent in 1984. It should also be noted that the fall in Black college enrollments would have been even worse had there not been an increase in the proportion of Black women going on to college. In the words of Xavier University President Norman Francis: "When it comes to college enrollment and retention, Black males are becoming an endangered species" (Marshall 1987: 46).

These findings were confirmed in a later report by the American Council on Education, Office of Minority Concerns (1989). This study found,

> A dramatic decline in the number of Black men in college . . . Overall, the study found that Black enrollment in higher education peaked in 1980 at 1.1 million, of a total of 11.8 million undergraduate and graduate students. By 1986, total enrollment in higher education had increased to 12.5 million students. but the total number of Black students had fallen by 30,000 . . . The slippage was in Black male students. In 1976, they numbered 470,000; but by 1986 that figure had fallen 7.2 percent, to 436,000. In the same period, the number of Black women in college increased to 645,000 from 563,000 (Daniels 1989: 1).

The article by Daniels (1989) reporting on this study also discusses some of the problems for the Black community, and for the nation, raised by this phenomenon and some possible actions to confront it.[13]

In addition, looking back at our primary and secondary educational system, "Black students are placed in classes for the mildly mentally handicapped more than three times as often as white students. But they are placed in classes for the gifted and talented only half as often as white students (Helmore and Laing 1986d: 29-30).

Children and Welfare Programs

Given the poverty under which increasing numbers of our children must live and the likely consequences of such conditions, it is particularly disturbing to find that the welfare programs designed to help such children have been reduced significantly in their reach and effectiveness under the Reagan administration. According to a study by the House Select Committee on Children, Youth and Families (1986), between 1979 and 1984, while there was a 30 percent increase in the number of poor children (from 9.9 to 12.9 million), there was a 20 percent decrease in the rate of participation in the Head Start and the Aid to Families with Dependent Children (AFDC) programs.

The study did find that there was a 22 percent increase in the rate of participation in the Supplemental Food Program for Women, Infants and Children (known as WIC), but that even so, this program reached only one-third of the eligible children in 1984. Moreover, the study found that 332 counties in 19 states did not have any WIC or other food program at all. Amazingly, the Committee reported that the number of children receiving AFDC benefits in the "high poverty counties" actually dropped 10 percent from 1979 to 1984 and that in 30 states the number of children receiving AFDC benefits dropped, despite increases in the number of poor children. The committee concluded that "funding had not kept pace with increased demand" and that "The record growth in poverty among children has not been accompanied by increased availability of key safety net programs" Commenting on the study, the committee chairman, George Miller, stated that, "The so-called 'safety net' has turned into a sieve" (*Columbus Dispatch* 1986).

Moreover, there has come to be a *de facto* situation of institutional racism in the funding levels of the programs that effect children. Within the overall structure of the Social Security system, there are two programs that were defined specifically for the care of children in single parent situations. One is the Aid to Families with Dependent Children (AFDC) program, which became part of the Social Security structure with the original act in 1935. Despite its use of the undifferentiated word "families," it was designed "... to provide for the needs of poor fatherless children, most of whose fathers had died" (Garfinkel 1988: 11). It has been administered in such a manner as to exclude families in which an "able-bodied" male is living in the home. In fact, some have argued that the way it has been administered has virtually forced husbands without jobs to leave their families so as to entitle their children to support. Garfinkel concludes that ". . . some research has shown that . . . It (AFDC) may break up marriages; it clearly seems to retard remarriage and to encourage young girls with babies to live in separate households from their extended families . . ." (ibid.).

The second program is Survivors Insurance (SI), which became part of the Social Security system in 1939. It was designed to provide income to single parent families in situations where one parent had died. This program only covers those whose employment history in so-called "covered" jobs qualifies them for Social Security. It was the AFDC program that was seen as filling in any gaps left by deceased parents whose employment history did not entitle their children to SI.[14]

Looking at these two programs, Senator Moynihan has stated:

in providing such assistance, we have created an extraordinary institutional bias against minority children. . . . The characteristics of these two populations (of children in the two programs) are quite different. The majority of the children receiving SI benefits are white. The majority of the children receiving AFDC are black or Hispanic. Since 1970 we have increased the real benefits received by children under SI by 53 percent. We have cut the benefits of AFDC children by 13 percent. The U.S. government, the American people, now provide a child receiving SI benefits almost three times what we provide a child on AFDC. . . . We do care about some children. Majority children. It is minority children--not only but mostly--who are left behind. . . . [Overall] Poor children on average receive less support today than they did 20 years ago. Is it any great wonder, on the edge of privation or worse, that they do not become model scholars? (Moynihan 1988: 5).[15]

If it can be said of any nation that a crucial basis upon which to judge it is the way it treats its children, then America is damned by its perpetuation of a distribution of income that forces such a large proportion of its children to grow up under circumstances of absolute poverty and then does so little to alleviate those conditions.

International Comparisons of Poverty Among Children

It is sad to note that a host of recent work, much of it based upon data developed as part of the Luxembourg Income Study (LIS),[16] reveals that the incidence of poverty among American children is perhaps the highest in the industrialized world. For example, in one recent study (Coder, Rainwater, and Smeeding 1989), it was reported that of ten industrialized Western nations,[17] the United States had the highest incidence of poverty among its children. In fact, the study indicated that the U.S. rate of poverty among its children (21.4 percent) was more than 7 times higher than in West Germany (2.8 percent), 2.5 times higher than the average for the other nine nations (8.7 percent), and a full 6 percentage points higher than the next worst case, Australia (15.4 percent). This and other studies indicate that a major cause of the difference lies in the failure of U.S. social programs to provide an adequate level of benefits for most of our poor children (Palmer, Smeeding, and Torrey

1988 and House Select Committee on Children, Youth and Families 1986).

However, the root cause is that when looking at the distribution of disposable income across these 10 nations, the United States has the highest incidence of poverty (16.6 percent), an incidence almost twice that of the average for the other nine nations (8.6 percent). Also, using any one of the three most popular criteria of the overall degree of inequality, the Gini, Theil, and Atkinson measures, the US has the most unequal distribution of income, including the smallest middle class (Coder, Rainwater, and Smeeding 1989).[18]

Teenage Motherhood and Poverty

One critical risk to which our children are subjected is that associated with teenage pregnancy and teenage parenthood. Since the teenage fathers often escape responsibility, this is typically discussed as the problem of teenage motherhood and has become associated with the larger problems of female-headed households which we will discuss below. For now we need to deal with the misperceptions about the issue of teenage motherhood that often view it as largely a racial or a moral problem, rather than one associated with poverty.

However, one can legitimately argue that teenage motherhood (which is not to say teenage pregnancy) is closely tied to the incidence of poverty and that this is true regardless of race. For example, the number of births per 100 poor White teenage girls is 21.2 and for poor Black girls, it is 22.6--very similar figures. On the other hand, in 1985, Black teenage births amounted to 25 percent of all Black births and the Black poverty rate was about 31 percent, while White teenage births accounted for 12 percent of White births and the White poverty rate was 11 percent. As for the myths concerning sexuality in the Black community, the U.S. Department of Health and Human Services found that between 1970-85, the birthrate among Black teenage girls dropped by 10.1 percent, while it increased by 74.3 percent among White teenage girls. Moreover, a study at Johns Hopkins University showed that,

> low-income black teenage girls generally have their first sexual experience about six months earlier than their white counterparts. However, low-income black teenage girls have fewer partners and engage in sexual intercourse less often than low-income white teenage girls.[19]

Speculation as to the possible reasons for the clear correlation between the incidence of poverty and teenage motherhood runs the gamut from an inability to obtain adequate contraceptive devices or medicines to the inability to obtain abortions to the issue of the so-called "culture of poverty" which, supposedly, is more accepting of teenage motherhood. One can even turn this argument around and contend that teenage motherhood is a significant cause of children living in poverty. This is not a debate into which I wish to enter here except to note that a recent study by the Children's Defense Fund concluded that,

> a sharp decline in recent years of the earnings of young American men of all races, except for college graduates . . . has been a sharp deterrent to the formation of stable families. The earnings decline has greatly exacerbated the teen pregnancy problem and the declining marriage rates among young black men and women (Hey 1987).

It would seem clear that it is highly unlikely that we can adequately deal with the problem of teenage motherhood without at the same time addressing the problems associated with the high incidence of poverty among our children and among young adults as well.

Female-Headed Households

In recent years, there has been a good deal of concern expressed about the situation facing households headed by women. The concern is fully warranted. Looking yet again at Table 4-5, one sees that there was rather significant improvement made in reducing the incidence of poverty in female-headed families and households during the period from 1960 to 1980. In fact, 1979 represents the lowest incidence of poverty for both female-headed households (32.0 percent) and families (34.9 percent); although neither figure is something about which anyone should want to brag. Then, these figures worsened dramatically in only a few years, quickly reaching peaks in 1982 that were higher than in 1973 for such households and higher than in 1966 for such families. What is particularly disturbing is that after some modest improvement following the 1982 peaks, the figures for 1987 are worse than those for 1985. Thus, the situation remains at a crisis level, especially for non-Whites.

In 1987, one-third (33.6 percent) of the persons living in female-headed households and 38.3 percent of persons living in female-headed families, had to try to survive at or below the official poverty level of income, while for both Black and Hispanic female-headed households the figure remained well over 50 percent. Even among White female-headed households and families, the figures stood at well over one-fourth (26.4 percent, and 29.5 percent, respectively) who lived in poverty. Moreover, it is quite troubling to note that while the poverty rates for White and Hispanic female-headed families and households have fluctuated over a narrow range during the 1985-87 period, the figures for Blacks have steadily worsened.

Looking at the families themselves, Table 4-8 reveals the incidence of poverty among the three different types of families for each racial/ethnic group in 1987. It is clear that, with one exception, the poverty rate was considerably higher for families headed by either a single male or a single female than was the case with married couple families across all racial/ethnic groups. The exception was for Hispanic male-headed families which actually showed in 1986 and 1987, though not in 1985, a lower incidence of poverty than did Hispanic married couple families. With this exception, the effect of having only one primary breadwinner was obvious. However, the poverty rate among female-headed families was two to three times higher than for single male-headed families. Among Black and Hispanic female-headed families the poverty rate exceeded 50 percent, while it stood at 26.7 percent for White female-headed families. It should be noted that the incidence of poverty among White female-headed families decreased in 1987 from 1986, while it increased for both Blacks and Hispanics, demonstrating again the racial/ethnic trends in the latest data. However, among male-headed families, the incidence of poverty decreased slightly in 1987 among Blacks, but increased among Whites and Hispanics. It is too early to tell if these represent the beginnings of any significant trends.

To look at the issue from a slightly different perspective, more than half of all poor (by the official definition) households in the U.S. in 1985, and 48 percent of all poor families, were headed by a woman with no husband present and just under half of all the poor people lived in female-headed households. By 1986, this latter figure had increased to 52.3 percent. Thus, by 1986, we had reached the point where more than half of all the poor people lived in female-headed households with no husband present. By 1987, 51.5 percent of all poor families were female-headed.[20]

Focusing once again on the plight of our nation's children, it must be kept in mind that in 1986 almost one-fourth (23.5 percent) of all our children lived in single parent family homes, and in 89 percent of these cases, encompassing some 14.8 million children, they lived with their mothers. Overall, 18.3 percent of White children, 53.1 percent of Black children, and 30.4 percent of Hispanic children lived within households headed by a woman without a husband. Historically, the proportion of children living with a single parent in 1986 was two and one-half times that in 1960. Most of these mothers were divorced or separated from the fathers of their children. But, in a growing number of cases, the mothers have never been married. For example, between 1970 and 1985, the proportion of Black children living with a never-married parent increased from 5 percent to 24 percent, while the proportion of White children in that situation increased, but only to 2.1 percent (Helmore and Laing 1986b: 26).

When one looks at the economic conditions facing the related children in female-headed families (see Table 4-5), not unexpectedly, given what has already been shown, the situation can only be described as a disaster. More than half (54.7 percent) of all such children live in poverty and more than two-thirds of Black and Hispanic children (68.3 percent and 70.1 percent, respectively) in female-headed families live in poverty. Needless to say, all of these figures worsen when the threshold is increased to the 125 percent of poverty level (Table 4-6). Here, we find that more than half of White children and about three-fourths of Black and Hispanic children in female-headed families live at or below this level.[21]

However, while it is true that the number of female-headed households has increased in recent years, it is perhaps surprising to note that there is little evidence, especially in the case of Black and Hispanic households, to support the contention that that is a cause of poverty. Many of the people who newly create these households would have been poor even if they had stayed in their previous situations, that is, with parents or husbands. Mary Jo Bane of Harvard University, concluded in a recent paper that,

> Though there has been a dramatic, and shocking, increase in female-headed households among blacks, and an equally dramatic "feminization" of black poverty, one cannot conclude that much of the poverty could have been avoided had families only stayed together (Bane 1984).

Thus, she found that more than two-thirds of the Black women who created new households were already poor before they made the transition. Among White women the pattern was somewhat different. Most of them were not poor either before or after the transition into a newly created female-headed household. However, of those White women who were poor during their first year in the new household, three-quarters of them were coming from nonpoverty situations.

On the other hand, given the problems encountered by any single parent/single earner family in securing a high enough income to avoid poverty, and given the sexual and racial discrimination in wage and earning patterns even among full-time, full-year workers in similar industries and occupations, which will be analyzed in Chapter 5, it is easy to understand why female-headed families, especially where the woman is Black or Hispanic, have a very high vulnerability to being poor.

THE EMPLOYMENT HISTORY OF THE POOR

The classical image of the poor is very much associated in many people's minds with unemployment. It is certainly true that being unemployed, especially in America,[22] may soon force a family into poverty, the truth is that a significant proportion of the poor work. Indeed, some poor persons, especially poor heads of families[23] even work full-time full-year and still live below the poverty level. The concept of the working poor, as they have come to be known, is now often discussed in the daily press and most people no longer even stop to think about this strange contradiction in terms. Too often, elsewhere in the same newspaper will be an article claiming that the way to solve the poverty problem is to put the poor to work.

There is a real contradiction, perhaps even a real degree of hypocrisy here; for while it is true that for those of the poor who are able to work, but can not find a job, this would help, it is hardly a solution in itself--else we would not be faced with the millions of working poor, people who work and are still officially poor. Moreover, if one recalls our earlier discussion about the absolute inadequacy of the official poverty standard and the need to think instead in terms of the adjusted Bureau of Labor Statistics

Minimum Adequacy or Low Income standard, we will see that more than two-thirds of families below this level have at least one person workings and more than 20 percent have two or more workers.

Low Income and the Minimum Wage

How can this be? Consider the fact that even if we define full-time work as 40 hours per week, which the reader will recall (Table 3-10) is far above the average work week in most jobs, and even if we assume that full-year means working all 52 weeks a year, this "only" amounts to 2080 hours per year of work. At the minimum wage of $3.35 this comes to only $6,968 a year--a full $4,021 below the official poverty threshold for a family of four and $13,329 below the BLS Minimum adequacy standards--both in 1985 dollars. In fact, it would take three people working full-time, full-year at the minimum wage level to earn $20,904, a mere $697 above the Minimum Adequacy standard. By 1989, as this book was going through its final editing, these gaps have widened as the poverty and low income standards have increased with inflation while the minimum wage has not.[24]

I have left to an endnote a more detailed discussion of the history and impact of the minimum wage, and the reader is referred to such studies as that in Smith and Vavrichek (1987) and Mellor (1987) for more information, as well as to the myriad of newspaper articles that are surrounding the current (1989) Congressional debate on various bills to finally raise the minimum wage; however, one critical point must be made here. Various politicians, most significantly, Ronald Reagan and George Bush, have tried to paint a picture of the typical minimum wage worker as a teenager who would otherwise be unemployed. That is a totally false picture. As of March 1985, about 5,200,000 American workers earned the minimum wage or less, and of these only 32.1 percent were teenagers, while 25.8 percent were adult women and 42.1 percent were adult men. Moreover, in 30.5 percent of the cases of such workers, they were the sole support for their families. Also, while it is true that most of those earning the minimum wage or less worked part-time, some 31 percent worked full-time at that rather pitiful wage (Smith and Vivrichek 1987). By 1986, the proportion of full-time workers being paid the minimum wage or below had increased to 34.3 percent. (Mellor 1987). Racially/ethnically, 83 percent of the workers earning the minimum wage or less (in 1986) were White, 14.6 percent were Black, and 9.2 percent were Hispanic (which adds to more than 100 percent since some of the Hispanics are also classified as White) (Mellor 1987).

Beyond the issue of the minimum wage, as we will see in more detail in the next chapter, even at the average hourly earnings (for all production and nonsupervisory workers in nonagricultural employment) of $8.53 in 1987 (again in 1985 dollars), working full-time, full-year resulted in only $17,742, or $2,465 below the BLS Minimum Adequacy standard. We will return to the issue of the effect of the pattern of wages in the U.S. on the distribution of income. But at this juncture, let us focus for a moment on the issue of the employment experience of the poor, that is, of those below even the official poverty level.

Employment Data on Those Below the Poverty Level

This subject can be approached in a number of ways and I have attempted to present enough data to give a fairly comprehensive perspective. Let us first look at the data for 1985, at the end of the quarter century which is our primary focus[25], and then we will attempt to gain a bit of a historic focus afterwards. For 1985, we first look at the data that pertain to the work experience of all individuals living below the poverty level, then we will focus on the narrower data for poor householders in general and for poor female households in particular. Then, in order to broaden our perspective, we will look at data that pertain to householders living at or below 125 percent of the poverty level and finally at data that provide some insight into the situation of those families living below the BLS Minimum Adequacy level.

The data on "all" individuals living below the poverty level pertain to all of those ages 15 or older. But, in order to avoid the impact of the very high levels of teenage unemployment and to also avoid the effects of the work patterns among the elderly, those 65 and older, I also present data restricted to those between 18 and 64, and do so for Whites and Blacks, men and women, separately, to examine the issue of differences along racial and sexual lines. Looking at Table 4-9, we find that 41.5 percent of all poor individuals ages 15 and older worked during 1985, while the figure jumps to 67.1 percent for White males between the ages of 18 and 64 and to 51.6 percent for Black males in the same age group. Among women, who in our society have the primary responsibility for child care and who often head households without the assistance of a husband, the figures for Whites in this age group is 44.2 percent and for Blacks 38.6 percent.

Thus, more than two-thirds of poor White males, a majority of poor Black males, and more than a third of poor females, all within what is normally considered the working years, were indeed working--and were poor anyhow. Amazingly, more than one-fifth (21.7 percent) of the White males in this age group were poor despite having worked full-time, full-year, and another 5.6 percent worked full-time for 40 to 49 weeks. However, for poor Black males the figure for full-time, full-year work dropped by about half to 10.3 percent. It is interesting to note that the proportions of poor White and Black females in this age group who worked full-time, full-year, while less than that of Black males, were quite similar, with the Black females having had a slightly higher rate, 6.7 percent, than their White counterparts, 6.5 percent. In Table 4-9 are also data on those who worked part-time for the full year and for 40 to 49 weeks. The overall point is that many of these poor persons worked, and a significant number of them did so for most of the year, but were still poor.

Turning to the question of why the others did not work, I have presented data concerning both those who did not work at all during the year and those who worked, but for less than 50 weeks--the two categories reported by the Bureau of the Census. Looking first at those who did not work at all, we find that from 21 percent to 40 percent, depending on the group, did not work because of illness or disability and that this was the most often cited reason among the males in the selected age group. The second most important reason for these males, both Black and White, was the inability to find work. So unemployment does play a significant role, even though it was the reason cited by only 24.5 percent of the White and 30.8 percent of the Black poor males.

Among the women in this age group, the burden of what the Bureau of the Census calls "Keeping House", which in most cases means caring for children, was cited as the most important reason for not working, 62 percent of the time by poor White women and 49.5 percent by poor Black women. While some of this may have been done by choice, the lack of low cost, high quality, publicly available child care in America leaves many of these women with no choice but to stay home and care for their kids, even though they can not provide a standard of living above the poverty level for them (The important issue of child care, and the related issues of parental leave upon the birth of a child and of health insurance for children, are discussed in a fairly lengthy endnote which the reader is urged to consult.[26]) It is interesting to note that illness and disability are cited far less frequently by the women of both races than by the men.

It is when we turn to the reasons given for not working all year, by those who did work for some portion of the year, that we really see the impact of unemployment. From a low of 30.3 percent for the White women to a high of 59.2 percent for the White men (with the Blacks of both sexes falling in between), we see that it is the inability to find work that resulted in working less than full-year. But, among the women, we see here too that the burden of "keeping house" is also a very significant factor.

Turning to Table 4-10, we narrow our focus to "family householders" (what used to be referred to as "heads of families") as a group and separately for Blacks and Whites. Then, in Table 4-11, we examine the situation among female-headed family households where no husband is present.

Looking at the data on family householders of poor families (Table 4-10), we find 50.3 percent of the poor family householders worked, that 20.5 percent of them worked for the full year, and that 16.4 percent of the householders worked full-time, full-year. If we compare that information to the data for poor persons between the ages of 18 and 64 (Table 4-9), noting that the data in Table 4-10 could only be separated by race, not sex, and keeping in mind that there are more female poor persons in absolute numbers in both racial groups than there are males, we find that the employment history of the poor family householders is quite consistent with that of poor persons between the ages of 18 and 64. The exception is that poor White family householders worked full-time, full-year somewhat less often and poor Black family householders somewhat more often than was true of the comparable group of poor persons between the ages of 18 and 64.

Turning to the reasons given by these poor family householders for either not working during the year or for working less than 50 weeks during the year, we again find a pattern of answers that is quite similar to that for poor persons between the ages of 18 and 64, except, as would be expected, (1) the proportion of those retired is higher in the householder data where the age is not limited to 64 and (2) a smaller proportion of poor family householders indicated "going to school and other." Thus, it would seem that poor family householders are neither likely to work much more or less than poor persons in general, which is to say that a very significant number of them do indeed work, or are looking for work, and that most of the rest are either ill/disabled, are taking care of their families, or are retired. This is hardly a picture of the lazy, irresponsible group of people that many politicians on the political right would have the public believe is typical.

Since the plight of single mothers, that is, in Census terminology, of female family householders where there is no husband, but where there are children present, is both a legitimate matter of some concern given the numbers of such family units in poverty and a matter of much public discussion, I have isolated the data for these folks in Table 4-11. The first column within each racial group is for all such female householders regardless of the presence of children. The next two columns, in each racial category, are for those with any children under the age of 18 and for those with children under the age of 6.

What we find, not surprisingly, is that the proportion of poor female family householders who worked full-time, full-year (6.5 percent) is less than half of the proportion of all poor family householders (16.4 percent) who so worked. However, when we focus on those women with children under the age of 18 in their families, a slightly larger proportion (6.9 percent) worked full-time, full-year. And, while there is a slight falloff from that latter figure when we isolate those women with children under the age of 6, these mothers still worked full-time, full-year in the same proportion (6.5 percent) as did poor female householders in general. It is interesting to note that Black poor female householders, *especially* those with children, were more likely to work full-time, full-year than their White counterparts. For example, 8.2 percent of poor Black mothers of kids under age 6 were working full-time, full-year, as compared to 5.2 percent of similar Whites. However, if one compares poor White female family householders aged 15 and older (Table 4-11) to all poor White women between the ages of 18 and 64 (Table 4-9), one finds a very similar level of full-time, full-year work. Thus, being a householder did not reduce the full-time, full-year work effort, on average, below that which poor White women in general made. On the other hand, poor Black female householders made even *more* of an effort, working full-time, full-year in 7.8 percent to 8.2 percent of the cases (Table 4-11) compared to 6.7 percent for all poor Black women aged 18-64 (Table 4-9). Thus, the image of female householders as less likely to work full-time, full-year than householders in general is true, though the differential is far less in the Black community.

On the other hand, as one might expect, there does seem to be a pattern of a somewhat larger proportion of poor female householders who worked part-time, than poor householders in general, if we compare the data on those who worked at all and take into account those working full-time. Thus, for poor householders generally, considering the data for All, White and Black, those who worked part-time during at least part of the year accounted for 15 percent, 14.5 percent and 16.7 percent, respectively. Whereas, among poor female householders the comparable figures were 18.5 percent, 19.5 percent and 17 percent, respectively. This is not very surprising since one might have expected that women, especially those with children, would be more likely to work part-time (U.S. Department of Commerce 1987b).

If we look at the reasons given by poor women householders for not working, we find, not surprisingly, that the major difference is that the women, especially those with children and especially those with very young children, indicate that "keeping house" is far and away the most common response. However, illness and the inability to find work are also common responses, with the inability to find work being a more common response among Black women, as it was on the earlier tables as well. Among those who worked, but less than 50 weeks, the inability to find work is, as on the earlier tables, a much more common response than for those who did not work at all. But here again, and again not surprisingly, we find that "keeping house" is also a very common response, especially for those with children and even more so for those with very young children.

Thus, the impression that is often popularized of the poor, including in particular poor female family heads, as being lazy and making little attempt to earn a living or look for work is not true. Moreover, given that the United States has made, perhaps by default, a social policy decision not to provide low cost, quality child care puts these poor families, especially those headed by a single mother, in the position of either abandoning their children in order to go to work, or staying home to care for them. The long term social and economic costs of the former course of action will be far higher than would be the short term costs of providing an adequate system of welfare support and child care for these families.

Secondary Workers in Poor Households

So far, we have focused on either poor persons as individuals or on the person with nominal responsibility, in the eyes of the Bureau of the Census, for a family household. There is another way to look at the work effort within poor families. That is, one can inquire about the overall effort of persons within a family unit to work and earn money to support that family, whether the worker(s) nominally is the "head" or "householder" or not. Using this approach, the following facts can be gleaned from the data available for 1985:[27] To begin with, in addition to the 54.7 percent of the householders who worked, 16.5 percent of them full-time, full-year, in some 21.1 percent of the poor households, there were actually 2 or more people who worked. Within married-couple poverty families, in addition to the 62.1 percent of the householders who worked, 36.4 percent of the spouses worked, with 26.8 percent of the householders and 11.7 percent of their spouses having worked full-time, full-year. In all, 34.4 percent of the married-couple poverty families had 2 or more people working, including, in 7.7 percent of these families, someone other than the householder or the spouse. Within the poverty families headed by a single adult (91.8 percent of which were headed by a single female), in addition to the 40.5 percent of the householders who worked, 7.3 percent of them full-time, full-year, in 18.7 percent some other family member also worked. Overall, 9.3 percent of the single headed poverty families had two or more persons working (U.S. Department of Commerce 1987b).

To view the matter from the reverse perspective for a moment, only 38.6 percent of all poor families in 1985 had no one working; while, within married-couple poor families, this fell to only 27.4 percent which were without someone who worked (and these figures include the 19.2 percent of poor householders who were ill, disabled or retired). Even among single-headed families, with all the pressures concerning child care, less than half, 48.6 percent, were without someone who worked.

Thus, while the problems of unemployment, part-time employment, and part-year employment are significant contributors to the problem of poverty in the U.S., it is clear that there are many other factors that are as significant and perhaps even more significant. There is a clear and urgent need either (1) to provide low cost, quality child care so that single parents and spouses who wish to work can do so or (2) to provide for an adequate level of public support to families with children, especially young children, to enable a parent to remain home with them without plunging the family into poverty. It would appear that illness and disability are significant factors in preventing many householders from working. Here again there is a need for a level of public support adequate to replace that person's potential earnings and keep the family out of poverty. However, beyond all these issues, which are often talked about, at least by progressive policymakers, there is the fact that in many poor families people, often more than one, are working, often full-time, full-year, but the wage levels are so low that the family can not escape from poverty.

In the next chapter, we will look more closely at the structure of wages in America and how they impact on the distribution of income. The above discussion should at least provide a good motivation and background to that discussion.

Employment Data on Those Below the 125 percent of Poverty Level

In order to broaden our discussion on the topic of the employment experience of the "poor," Table 4-12 provides some data on families and female headed families (female householder with no husband present) who, in 1985, lived below 125 percent of the poverty level. For a family of four, this would have amounted to $13,736 in 1985, compared to $10,989 for the poverty level and $20,207 for the adjusted BLS Minimum Adequacy level. That is, 125 percent of the poverty level amounts to only 68 percent of the Minimum Adequacy level. Nevertheless, it is the only such alternative threshold for which the Census Bureau provides adequate data and it does provide a somewhat broader perspective.

In this context, we find that the proportions of householders who worked at all are about the same as we found for poverty level householders (Table 4-10). However, not very surprisingly, the proportion who worked full-time, full-year is significantly higher, 24 percent higher on average (20.4 percent compared to 16.4 percent) and 48 percent higher for Blacks (15.5 percent compared to 10.5 percent). We also find a remarkably higher rate, in fact six times higher, of full-year, part-time workers: 24.6 percent for those below 125 percent of the poverty threshold compared to 4.1 percent (20.5 minus 16.4) for those below the poverty threshold. Among those householders below the 125 percent level who did not work during the year, we find an 11.3 percent higher level of illness or disability (26.6 percent compared to 23.9 percent) and a 13.9 percent lower rate of "keeping house" (34.7 percent compared to 40.3 percent). Unfortunately, the figures for "unable to find work" are not reported separately.

Thus, not unexpectedly, we find that even with this modest increase in the income level threshold, there is a significant increase in the work effort, and, somewhat surprisingly, a higher incidence of illness and disability keeping householders from working--while the pressures of child care keeping the householder home are a bit lessened. Overall, the general thrust of our comments about the causes of poverty are even more relevant when we look at this slightly broader group.

Employment Data on Those Below the BLS Minimum Adequacy Level

Finally, throughout the earlier portion of this book, the point was repeatedly made that the adjusted BLS Minimum Adequacy standard provided a more meaningful definition of being poor in America than did the far more restrictive Social Security official definition of poverty. While the Census Bureau does not report detailed data based upon the BLS thresholds, we can approximate that for 1985 rather closely by using the income level of $20,000, since the adjusted BLS Minimum Adequacy level for a family of four was $20,207. While, as discussed earlier, using a figure like $20,000 for all families does not take into account differences in family size or composition, it does serve to provide a very useful first approximation as to the situation in what we might call low income, if not officially poor, families. Table 4-13 provides data concerning the number of earners and the number of full-time, full-year earners for all families earning below $10,000 (recall the official poverty threshold in 1985 was $10,989), for those earning between $10,000 and $20,000, and, as a basis for comparison, for all families regardless of income level.

This table also breaks down this data by racial/ethnic groups, a process that reveals some interesting differences. I have also provided a line of data for each racial/ethnic group for the families earning less than $20,000, that is combining, via weighted averages, the data for the "poor" families earning below $10,000 and the "low income" families earning above that, but less than the Minimum Adequacy amount of $20,000, so that the potential hazards of dealing with aggregate data can be examined.

Looking first at the data for all families, regardless of racial/ethnic group, what Table 4-13 reveals rather clearly is that the percentage of low income families having one earner (as the Census Bureau calls them) is only slightly higher than for poor families, 41.1 percent compared to 38.4 percent; while the incidence of low income, as compared to poor, families having two or more earners is dramatically larger, more than twice as large, 35.2 percent compared to 16.8 percent. It would appear that it is the presence of additional earners that is one crucial factor in the family moving from being poor to being low income. The other obvious difference is a significant increase in the proportion of families having an earner working full-time, full-year (54 percent compared to 18 percent) and, of course, a decrease in the number of families with no earner present (23.7 percent compared to 44.9 percent).

A very interesting set of differences appear when one looks at the data across racial/ethnic groups, especially for those families in the $10,000 to $20,000 bracket. The figures for the families earning below $10,000 are generally quite similar, though the Black families do show a somewhat lower incidence of two or more earners and also a lower incidence of full-time, full-year earners. However, there is a remarkable difference in the employment patterns among the low income families as between the Whites on one hand and the Blacks and Hispanics on the other.

The Black and Hispanic families reveal a far lower proportion with no earners (12.0 percent and 8.8 percent, respectively) than do the White families (25.8 percent); which is reflected, across the board, in a higher incidence of one earner, of two or more earners and of full-time, full-year earners than among the White families. Thus, on average, there are .67 full-time, full-year workers in the Black families and .70 in the Hispanic families, but only .51 in the White families; 37.2 percent of the Black families and 45.9 percent of the Hispanic families have two or more earners compared to 34.9 percent of the White families.

The point of this observation is that while all of these families are in the same income bracket, the work effort within the minority low income families is *significantly greater* that among the White families. Clearly, the higher incidence of low income status among the minority families is not a result of laziness or of a failure to work as hard as their White counterparts.

If one compares the data for the poor and low income families, in any of the racial/ethnic groups, with that for all families in that group or with all families as a whole, one sees that the significant difference is that the broader group tends to have a lower incidence of one earner families and a much higher incidence of two or more earners in a family, hence a higher average number of workers per family. In addition, the broader groups are more like to have full-time, full-year earners.

This data confirms the trends noted earlier for those below the official poverty line and those below 125 percent of that

threshold. It would indeed appear to be the case that the earnings
of one worker in America are often simply insufficient to provide
a family with an income beyond the low income/minimum adequacy or
even poverty level, no matter how hard that one earner may work.[28]
Thus, a very large proportion of those at the lower end of the
income distribution are clearly not there simply because of a lack
of work effort, but rather seem to suffer from problems stemming
from low wages and part-time work.

Some Historical Perspective

Given the limitations of space, I will not attempt to reproduce
the detailed analysis of employment data on a historical basis back
to 1960. But a few comments are in order. The proportion of poor
family householders who worked rose during the 1960s, reaching a
peak of 55 percent in 1969. Then, during the 1970s, it fell slowly
and has held fairly steady during the 1980s, remaining, as reported
above, at about 50 percent. Similarly, the proportion of poor
persons age 15 and over who worked has shown a similar pattern of
rising a bit during the 1960s, dropping a bit during the 1970s, and
then holding relatively steady during the first half of the 1980s,
so that in 1980 it stood at 39.9 percent compared to the 41.5
percent reported above for 1985. There have been some fluctuations
in the proportions of poor persons giving various reasons for not
working, but the general pattern has been fairly stable. Thus, in
1985, there were 1.6 percent more reporting being ill or disabled,
1.8 percent less retired, 4.5 percent less keeping house, and 2.7
percent more unable to find work, and 1.5 percent more reporting
school attendance or other reasons, than in 1980. The significant
changes perhaps being the increase in those unable to find work
resulting from the recessions and economic changes noted earlier and
the somewhat surprising decrease in those staying home to keep
house.

THE EDUCATIONAL EXPERIENCE OF THE POOR

As with the issue of employment and the poor, there are many
common misperceptions about the educational experience of the poor.
It is certainly true that the less education one has the lower one's
income is likely to be and the more likely it is that one will live
in poverty. We will explore that general topic--the relationship
between education and the distribution of income, especially the
pattern of earned income, as it affects people of different
racial/ethnic groups and different sexes-- in the Chapter 5. Here,
we focus on a more narrow topic, the educational experience of those
considered poor. Is it true that the poor have such a lack of
educational background that the likelihood of their finding well
paying employment is minimal? The evidence is a bit surprising.
Table 4-14 presents some of the relevant facts (for 1985[29]),
with Part I of this table providing us with some numbers against
which we can compare the figures in Part II, which is our primary

focus.   Looking first at the experience of all those ages 15 and above, the broadest category for which these data are reported, we see, in the first column of Part I of Table 4-14, that it is indeed true that the incidence of poverty is higher the less education one has. Thus, the poverty rate among those with no reported education, an admittedly rather small group of about 200,000 people, is 34 percent, while for those who have at least an elementary school education (8 years) it is 21.3 percent. This drops to 9.9 percent for high school graduates and to only 5.2 percent for those with one or more years of college--the upper category for this data. (More detailed data on the impact of college and postgraduate education on earned income will be examined in the Chapter 5.)

However, in order to gain a more useful perspective, in Part II of Table 4-14, I have narrowed the focus to those poor persons ages 22 to 59. The reason for this is to look at those people who have reached an age by which one could reasonably expect them to have completed their *initial* education (by which I mean to allow for their going back to school at a later point) and have eliminated many of those who have reached the age by which most of our citizens are, at least, contemplating retirement. Also, those who are age 60 and over (in 1985) would have reached age 18 in 1943. Our focus is more on those who have at least had a postwar opportunity to go to school. Thus, focusing on those in the age 22-59 category places our attention where it belongs--on those who "should" have finished school and whom one might expect to be out working.[30]

Looking at the first column in Part II of Table 4-14, we see that only 1.3 percent of the poor persons age 22-59 had no education, and, adding the first four figures in that column, only 20.2 percent had an elementary education or less. While this latter number is hardly insignificant, especially when we compare it to the fact only 7.1 percent of the total population in this age group had such a meager amount of education (sum of the first four numbers in the second column of Part I of Table 4-14), it still reveals that almost 80 percent of these poor people had more than an elementary school education.   In fact, 57 percent of these poor persons are high school graduates, including almost one in five (19.5 percent) who had at least some college education. Again, these numbers imply that a smaller proportion of the poor are high school graduates that was true for their age cohorts as a whole (82.7 percent) and fewer had some college experience. Nevertheless, most Americans do not have the impression that more that half of all poor persons in this prime working age group have completed high school and almost one-fifth have a year or more of college. A lack of education, in and of itself, is not the cause of poverty for a substantial portion of those who are poor.[31]

When we break down the data for poor persons in this age group by race and sex, we find some interesting patterns. In general, women are less likely to have dropped out before high school than men, and more Blacks have at least finished their elementary education than have Whites.[32]   On the other hand, high school dropouts are far more typical in the poor Black population (42.9 percent for males and 31.5 percent for females) than in the poor White group (18.6 percent for males and 22.1 percent for females).

Even here though, we see an interesting difference--White males are less likely to drop out of high school than their female counter-parts, but in the Black community it is the women who are less likely to drop out. Poor Whites, both males and females, are more likely to have gone on to get at least some college education than is true among poor Blacks, and in both communities the men are more likely to have gone to college than the women.[33] Nevertheless, even among poor Black women in this age group, some 13.6 percent have had at least some college experience.

The point of this analysis is to indicate that while it is certainly true that the poor tend to have less education that the population as a whole, it is at the same time true that more than half of those in the 22-59 age group have completed high school and almost a fifth have had some college education. Moreover, while the proportions are a bit less among Blacks than Whites, it is still true that more than half of the poor Blacks in this age group have also finished high school and about a sixth have some college. Years of formal education, in and of itself, can not explain why these people are so much poorer than many of their educationally similar cohorts.

Another perspective on the educational background of those in poverty is gained by focusing on the educational achievement of the householders (heads of households) of poor families in general, and of female heads of poor households in particular. Table 4-15 presents this data for 1987. There, for comparison purposes is also presented the data for all householders and for all female householders. In addition, this perspective allows us to look at the data for Hispanic householders, as well as Whites and Blacks.[34]

What is most remarkable about this data is that it reveals a far lower amount of education among poor Hispanic householders, than for either Whites or Blacks. Thus, 6 percent of poor Hispanic householders reported having no education at all, compared to only 0.6 percent of the Blacks and 1.9 percent of the Whites. Similarly, an astounding 40.4 percent of the Hispanics had less than 8 years of elementary education, compared to 15.4 percent of Blacks and 18.6 percent of Whites. One suspects that the higher proportion of those with such little education among Whites as compared to Blacks is due to the higher concentration of poor White households in nonmetropolitan areas, which includes, of course, many very small rural areas. (We will talk more about where the poor live in the next section.)

Even given the caveats about comparability discussed in the last cited endnote, it is interesting to note that among both the Whites and Blacks, the proportion of poor householders with less than a completed grade school education is considerably higher than that reported in the earlier discussion of poor adults generally. One might suspect that this is in part due to the inclusion in the householder's data of persons age 60 and older, who are more likely to have had little education. Nevertheless, even if one compares the data for poor householders to that of all householders (in Table 4-15), one finds that the poor were about three times more likely to have had less than a full (8 years) grade school education.

Looking at the issue of high school dropouts, poor householders, in general, were about twice as likely to have started, but not completed, high school than householders generally, and this was the pattern across the racial/ethnic groups. The proportion of those who graduated from high school, but did not go on to college, is about the same for poor White and Black householders as for householders generally; but among Hispanics, the proportion is about one half of that for the other groups.

It is at the level of having attended at least one year of college (which unfortunately is the only breakdown of college attendance in this body of data) that we see a clear pattern between all of the groups. Compared to householders generally, poor White householders had attended college about 40 percent as often (15.3 percent compared to 39 percent), Blacks about one-fourth as often (10.2 percent), and Hispanics about one-sixth as often (7 percent). Overall, about half of the poor White and Black householders were high school graduates, compared to only one-fourth of poor Hispanics.

The pattern among poor female householders is similar, though in every racial/ethnic group the women were more likely to have had more a bit more education than was true of poor householders generally. Hence, they clearly had more than their male counterparts. On the other hand, female householders in general had less education that all householders as a group. These two factors taken together imply that the educational differentials between poor female householders and female householders generally, was less than the figures for male and female householders combined.

The remarkably lower level of educational achievement among Hispanic householders can be attributed to a combination of two factors: (1) the high levels of immigration of adults already past school age who had little education in their native lands from which they emigrated, and (2) the language problems they had as children in school in the U.S., since it is likely that most of these adults (all of whom are over the age of 25) did not have the benefit of bilingual teaching.

Nevertheless, having said all of this, it is still the case that the data indicate that, overall, about half of all poor householders were high school graduates and some 14.5 percent had attended at least one year of college. Even given the problems with the educational system in the U.S. today, one would think that such people have the ability to hold down jobs that should pay them enough to rise above poverty. The question is do such jobs exist for these people. Beyond that, we clearly do need to establish educational programs for these adults to enable to acquire the basic skills needed to economically survive in a modern economy.

WHERE THE POOR LIVE

The popular perception is that the poor in America are concentrated almost exclusively in the central cities of our major metropolitan areas. As Table 4-16 shows, while there is a concentration there of the Black and Hispanic poor populations, it is not true of the poor as a whole. In this regard, one needs to keep in mind, for example, that "only" 29.8 percent of the poor in 1987 were Black and 16.8 percent Hispanic. For the poor population as a whole, 42 percent lived in the central cities; 28.5 percent lived in suburban areas within a metropolitan area, but outside the central cities, and 29.6 percent lived in nonmetropolitan areas, which, given current Bureau of the Census definitions, includes small towns and villages and rural areas.

However, these overall figures obscure some important differences between where, on the one hand, the White, and, on the other hand, the Black and Hispanic poor populations live. The poor White population was, in 1987, almost evenly divided with about one-third each in the central cities, in the suburbs, and in the nonmetropolitan areas. On the other hand, the poor Black population was much more concentrated with 59.2 percent in the central cities, while only 17.7 percent lived in the suburbs, and 23.1 percent in the nonmetropolitan areas. But the most concentrated poor population was the Hispanics, with 62.9 percent in the central cities, 27.8 percent in the suburbs, and only 9.4 percent in the nonmetropolitan areas. To look at the matter from a different perspective, we find that the overall incidence of poverty was only marginally higher (1.6 percentage points) in the central cities (15.4 percent) than it was in the nonmetropolitan areas (13.8 percent). The lowest incidence, not surprisingly is in the suburbs, but even here it is a not inconsequential 6.5 percent.

The point is that if we try to address the problems associated with poverty solely by policies focused on the central cities, we would miss 58 percent of the poor population, including 66.8 percent of poor Whites, 40.8 percent of poor Blacks, and 37.2 percent of poor Hispanics. In commenting on her recent study for the Center on Budget and Policy Priorities, Kathryn Porter argued, "that poverty is just as much a problem in rural areas as in inner cities" (Hey 1989). Congressman George Miller, after a hearing on rural poverty commented that, "Poverty in America wears many faces. The poverty rate in the countryside was 17 percent in 1987 and its growing twice as fast as urban poverty" (ibid.).

CONCLUSION

As we discussed in Chapter 1, one of the primary motivations for being concerned with the distribution of income within a society is to become aware of those at the bottom of the distribution. In this chapter, I first presented data raising questions about just how we define poverty and/or low income status, and then presented a rather detailed look at the situation of those who are the less fortunate within American society. The plight of all too many women and children has been a particular concern, as has been the situation facing a large proportion of our minority population. In the course of this effort, I have attempted to break down some of the stereotypes about the work effort, educational level, and other characteristics of these people. However, the over-arching issue must not be ignored--poverty, however defined, is an economically and socially correctable problem, the question is whether we have the political will to do so. Or, to put it another way, the existence of poverty and low income may serve a variety of economic interests and political economic groups/classes, the issue is whether we as a nation have the political will to change the political economic system so as to enable us to greatly narrow the distribution of income.

In Chapter 5, we will look in more detail at the effect of education, industry, and occupation on the distribution of income, in particular earned income, and hopefully gain more insight into the nature of the problem and the source of possible avenues for solutions.

NOTES

1. Again, the reader is reminded that the bulk of the work on this book was completed at a point when 1985 was the latest year for which complete data regarding the poverty population in the U.S. were available. Since then, while the manuscript was undergoing the usual editing, complete data for 1986 and partial, preliminary data for 1987 became available. It has not been feasible to redo all of the earlier work, but wherever practical, reference to the more recent data has either been included in the text or, in most cases, in the endnotes. However, examination of the latest data does not suggest that any significant changes have occurred in the composition or nature of the poverty population. Hence, the observations and conclusion in the text stand as valid as this manuscript is undergoing final editing early in 1989.

2. The Social Security Administration poverty threshold levels also differentiate single (unrelated) individuals and two person families by whether the householder (called the head of household in earlier years) is under age 65 or 65 and older.

3. The figures for 1987 that would go into a new last column in Table 4-2 show no significant changes from 1986, in fact the figures for the poorest 20 percent, the second 20 percent and the richest 20 percent are identical to 1986. The only change is of 0.1 percentage points added to the numbers for the middle and fourth 20 percent's, which probably result from rounding, since no other brackets show a corresponding decline. Thus, the total one gets if one adds the figures for 1986 is 99.9 percent, while in the preliminary figures for 1987 it is 100.1 percent. Hence, the statements made in the text based on the comparisons to 1986 still stand, except for the very minor changes just noted, when using the 1987 preliminary data.

4. However, as discussed in Chapter 2, noncash transfers are not included in these income figures.

5. Danziger's comments are quoted in an article by Robert Samuelson in Newsweek (Samuelson 1987).

6. The data for 1987 are from the so-called "Advance Data" release (U.S. Department of Commerce 1988c). They must be viewed as preliminary and are also not as complete as that which will be

available at a latter point. So some of the remaining tables in this chapter use earlier data when those are the latest available.

7. The facts cited in this paragraph are from Part 1 of a four-part series of articles by Helmore and Laing published in *The Christian Science Monitor* (Helmore and Laing 1986a).

8. In fact, one must go back to 1966 to find higher percentages than have existed during the 1980 to 1987 period.

9. Unemployment data for Blacks, as opposed to the category "Blacks and Others," have only been reported since 1972.

10. For more detailed information concerning the plight of so-called displaced workers see Horvath 1987, Flaim and Sehgal 1985, and Kassalow 1985.

11. The supplementary data, that is, data other than that in the tables, cited here and elsewhere in our discussion of poverty are, unless otherwise footnoted, from U.S. Dept of Commerce 1987b or d and 1988c.

12. Both of these facts are from Helmore and Laing (1986d: 29-30).

13. One aspect of this set of problems was revealed in a study by Reynolds Farley of the University of Michigan who found that Blacks have less incentive to get married. He was quoted in a report about the study as saying, "Black women, when they look around and think about getting married, see that the pool of Black men with high earnings is relatively small. This gives them less of a financial incentive to get married or to remain married" (*Dayton Daily News* 1989). This is then a contributing factor to the problem of female-headed families which is discussed in more detail a bit later in this chapter. This was echoed by comments from William Julius Wilson of Chicago University, quoted in the report by Daniels (ibid.), "As Black women pull ahead of Black men, . . . 'the social distance and hostility between men and women' are likely to increase, seriously harming 'social integration within the Black community' as a whole."

14. It is to be hoped that the welfare reform legislation passed by Congress in the fall of 1988 will provide some measure of improvement since it does address some of these problems, such as the presence of an able-bodied male in the home. However, it remains to be seen how this new program will be administered and funded in the future.

15. This article by Moynihan is excerpted from a longer speech published in the *Congressional Record*, 100th Congress, 2nd Session, vol. 134, no. 4, January 28, 1988. The special issue of *Focus*, subtitled *Welfare Reform and Poverty*, in which the excerpt appears also contains the article cited earlier by Irwin Garfinkel entitled "The Evolution of Child Support Policy," as well as a number of other pieces of relevance to the discussion in the text.

16. The Luxembourg Income Study is a recent, and on-going major effort to develop a database of comparable income data that will allow for meaningful cross-country income distribution comparisons. It can be accessed via transoceanic telecommunications at low cost and is rapidly coming into widespread use. See Coder, Rainwater and Smeeding (1988) for a description of the database

which currently covers 10 nations, and which will be expanded over the next few years to cover several more.

17. Australia, Canada, Israel, the Netherlands, Norway, Sweden, Switzerland, the United Kingdom, the United States, and West Germany.

18. For other cross-country work on income distribution see Smeeding 1988, and Smeeding and Torrey 1988.

19. The statistics quoted above, including the quote, are all from (Helmore and Laing 1986b: 28), which, in turn, quoted sources from the Alan Guttmacher Institute, the U.S. Department of Health and Human Services, and an unspecified study done at Johns Hopkins University.

20. It should be noted that the proportion of poor families headed by a woman had decreased a bit in the mid-1980s so that by 1985 the proportion was 48.1 percent compared to 50.3 percent in 1978. However, in 1986 and 1987, the proportion increased again, to 51.4 percent and 51.5 percent, respectively, wiping out the very modest gains made earlier.

21. It should be noted that here again the most recent data shows that the poverty and near-poverty rates for children in White female-headed families *decreased* from 1986 to 1987, while it *increased* for similar Black and Hispanic families.

22. This is especially true in the United States where the level of unemployment benefits is quite minimal and their duration, normally 26 weeks or six months, is quite short as compared to unemployment benefits provided in most other industrialized nations. One effect of this situation is that, for example, in 1986, we averaged 8.2 million workers officially unemployed at any one time, while the average number of those receiving unemployment benefits, including all federal and state programs, was only 2.7 million, or 33 percent. In fact, this situation has been deteriorating fairly steadily for some years now. A study by James Ellenberger of the AFL-CIO, reported in the *AFL-CIO News* (1989) indicated that,

In 1975, 76 percent of jobless workers received unemployment compensation. By last year [1988], that had dropped to 32 percent. The unemployment rate averaged 8.5 percent in 1975, which meant that 8 million persons were jobless. But 6 million of them received unemployment compensation. . . . Unemployment averaged 5.5 percent in 1988, translating into 6.7 million jobless Americans. But only 2.2 million of them received benefits. The system wasn't working (ibid.: 1, 14).

23. There is a minor problem with terminology here. The Bureau of the Census has dropped the terms "head of family" and "head of household" in favor of the term "householder" and "family householder." This is, in large part, in response to the charge of sexism for singling out the husband in a married couple and labeling him as the "head," implying a dominant position. Now,

If the house is owned (or rented) jointly by a married couple, either the husband or the wife may be listed first, thereby becoming the reference person, or the householder, to whom the relationship of the other household members is recorded (U.S. Department of Commerce 1987b: 164).

24. By late 1987, the issue of the adequacy of the legal minimum wage had become a political issue of some importance. This is not very surprising. What is perhaps surprising is that it took so long. The problem is that the minimum (hourly) wage has failed badly, especially since the early 1970s, to keep up with inflation, let alone improve the real wage position of the lowest paid workers. In 1960, it stood at $1.00, which in 1985 dollars would have been $3.63. By 1968, the minimum wage stood at $1.60 at which point it reached its highest value, in real terms, of just under $5.00 (actually $4.95) in 1985 dollars. But by 1974, while it had increased in nominal value to $2.00, in 1985 dollars it amounted to only $4.36, a significant worsening in real terms. In 1981, it was set at $3.35, where it still stands as this book is being edited in the spring of 1989.

Thus, by 1985, it stood, in real terms, 8 percent below the 1960 level, 33 percent below the 1968 peak value, and more than 23 percent below the 1974 level. If one assumes that a person worked 40 hours per week, 52 weeks per year at the minimum wage, and expressed the earnings in constant 1985 dollars, this would result in annual earnings of $7,550 in 1960, $10,296 in 1968, $9,069 in 1974, and only $6,968 in 1985. By 1987, this had dropped even further to $6,559 and by the first quarter of 1988, a minimum wage annual income (again in 1985 dollars) amounted to only $6,470, more than 37 percent below its real value in 1968, 20 years earlier. This level of income in the first quarter of 1988 equaled 59 percent of the official poverty level and only 32 percent of the Minimum Adequate Budget. This is yet one more indication of the tremendously different pattern of wages between the period of the 1960s and the period since the early 1970's.

Not surprisingly, the poverty rate among those earning the minimum wage is much higher than among those earning above it. That is, for example in 1985, while about 70 percent of these persons were living in families in which there were one or more other workers bringing home earnings, it was still the case that 22.0 percent of the adult men and 22.5 percent of the adult women who earned the minimum wage or less lived in poverty, compared to only 5.5 percent and 6.3 percent, respectively, of those who earned more per hour. Among teenagers, the rates were 12.5 percent for those earning the minimum wage or less, and 9.3 percent for those earning more, implying that more of the poorest paid teenagers lived in families with other earners; while at the same time, the poverty rate for the better paid teenagers was considerably higher than for their adult counterparts (Smith and Vavrichek 1987).

25. At the time this was written, much of the detailed data developed in this section were available only through 1985. An examination of the data that have since become available for 1986 indicates that they do not differ significantly from the 1985 information. Even the partial 1987 data that have just been

released as this is being edited shows the same patterns as discussed in the text, although there has been some decreases in the proportion of poor households working. Thus, the proportion of poor householders who worked during the year decreased from 50.3 percent in 1985, to 50.1 percent in 1986, to 47.2 percent in 1987, while those working full-time, full-year increased from 16.4 percent to 16.7 percent, 1985 to 1986, but then dropped to 14.6 percent in 1987. Among poor female-headed households, the decrease was much less, with 39.6 percent working in 1985, 40.1 percent in 1986 and 39.3 percent in 1987. In fact, female-heads of poor households worked full-time, full-year a bit more in 1987 (7.8 percent) than in 1985 (6.5 percent), though the 1987 figure did represent a decrease from 1986 (8.3 percent). The decreases from 1986 to 1987 are consistent with other evidence that the economy had begun to weaken a bit, especially for the Black and Hispanic poor, although officially the expansion was still in effect throughout 1987. Nevertheless, these relatively minor changes do not alter the general thrust of the analysis and comments in the text.

26. Studies indicate that in 1987, 53 percent of the mothers in the labor force go back to work before their newborn children are even a year old, 65 percent of all mothers in the labor force have school-age children, and there are some ten million children under the age of six who have either two working parents or a single parent who supports the family. In the decade from 1978 to 1988, the proportion of women in the labor force increased by 13.8 percent (from 49.1 percent to 55.9 percent), while the proportion of working women with children increased by 22.9 percent (from 52.9 percent to 65 percent). Even more dramatic is the increase in the proportion of working women who have children under age 6, which amounted to 28.4 percent, going from 43.7 to 56.1 percent.

But this country, unlike most of the rest of the industrialized world, has, as of this writing, no legally mandated program of parental leave, even without pay. Most other industrialized, dare one say civilized, nations require that the mother or father be given as much as six months off with pay and a year or more without pay upon the birth of a child. This policy persists in American despite such testimony as that by Edward Zigler, Director of Yale University's Bush Center in Child Development, to the effect that,

> Despite what we know about bonding--it helps a child learn to trust, to feel secure, and as a result, to do better in school--neither business nor Congress can agree on a parental leave policy. Bonding takes place shortly after birth, during the time permitted by infant care leaves. Bonding gives a new mother time to recover from childbirth, and the new family a chance to develop "secure attachments.
>
> Without early secure attachments, without parental leave, without developmentally designed day care, we will raise a nation of "impoverished" children--that is, children who lack the skills, curiosities, resources, and values that will equip them for adolescence and adulthood. (Zigler and Watson 1988)

Nor does this nation have any adequately funded system of child care facilities (again, an area in which we are behind much of the rest of the industrialized world), despite the fact that by 1995 it is estimated "that two-thirds of all pre-schoolers will have mothers in the workforce" (Kantrowitz 1988). In total, in 1986, the United States had only 40,000 day-care centers, which were augmented by only 105,000 licensed day-care homes, which together provided care for some 2.1 million children. This left millions of others to be sent to unregulated day-care facilities, plus millions of yet others who were left home, often alone or with siblings too young to provide adequate, safe care, while their mothers attempted to earn enough money to feed these children and pay the rent. Then, of course there are the millions of other mothers, as noted in the body of this study, who can not work because they can not find nor afford child care.

Another issue of concern is the lack of health insurance coverage for a substantial and growing proportion of our nation's children. Recent studies indicate that, "From 1978 to 1984, the number of children in families with no medical insurance rose by 30 percent, to 24 percent of all kids." (Monmaney 1988) What may be surprising to the uninitiated is that: "More than half of these kids [without health insurance] live in homes where at least one parent works full time... [and that] Medicaid covers only half of all poor children" (Harkness 1988). One result of this is that as recently as 1984, two out of every five children in the U.S. were not immunized against polio, measles, mumps, and rubella (ibid.). Yet another outcome of our treatment of children, especially of the youngest among them, is that in 1955 the infant mortality rate (the proportion of children who live 24 hours, but die within a year) was the sixth best in the world, while Japan ranked seventeenth. As of 1987, the U.S. had fallen to nineteenth, while Japan had risen to first. To think that eighteen other nations are better able than the U.S. to care for their expecting mothers and their young children is tragic and humiliating.

The combination of the lack of parental leave, inadequate day care, and poverty is indeed impoverishing as many as half or more of the children in this country at present (recall the earlier discussion of the numbers of children living in poverty, near-poverty (125 percent of poverty level) or below the Minimum Adequacy level of family income). Aside from the human emotional and psychological costs that are being borne by these children and their families, and beyond the incredible losses in productivity this country is suffering and will suffer because of what is being done to, and what is not being done for, these children, are the vast social costs that our society will be forced to bear in the form of welfare, crime, detention and prison facilities. One study noted, "that $1 spent on preschool projects such as Head Start can save $4.75 on later social costs" (Zigler and Watson 1988). N o nation can afford to ignore and abuse its children, as the United States is doing, and expect to remain "competitive" (the key catchword of the 1980s) in a modern world. For purely pragmatic economic reasons, if not for reasons of humane moral standards, this nation simply must begin to address the urgent needs of our children and their parents.

27. The figures cited in this paragraph are a bit different from those discussed above (in Tables 4-9 to 4-12) because of the way the data are tabulated and reported by the Bureau of the Census. The earlier data, much of which were from Table 21 in U.S. Department of Commerce (1987b), pertained to the work experience of householders of poverty family households in general. The data reported just below was developed from information in Table 20 of the same source which pertains to the numbers of workers in poverty family households where the householder is a civilian. The difference relates to householders who are in the military service. Thus, the larger category included, for 1985, 7,223,000 poverty households, while the latter, smaller group included 7,165,000 poverty households. Apparently, there are some 58,000 family households in which the nominal head, or householder, is in the military and the family is officially defined as in poverty. In itself, it is a rather sad statement if the United States is not willing to pay even its military service people enough to keep all of their families at least out of poverty. A relatively cursory look at the data for 1986 which just recently became available, does not indicate any significant change in the patterns reported in the text for 1985. This sort of detailed data was not yet available for 1987 as the final editing of this manuscript took place.

28. In fact, the evidence presented above, especially in combination with the discussion of wage patterns in the Chapter 5, would seem to lend some support to the notion put forward by Karl Marx so many years ago that, in a capitalist economy:

> Wages will rise and fall according to the relation of supply and demand . . . Within these fluctuations, however, the price of labor will be determined by the cost of production . . . [of] labor power . . . [which] is the cost required for maintaining the worker as a worker and of developing him into a worker. . . . [In addition,] there must be included the costs of reproduction, whereby the race of workers is enabled to multiply and to replace worn-out workers by new ones. . . . The price of this cost of existence and reproduction constitutes wages. Wages so determined are called the wage minimum. . . . Individual workers, millions of workers, do not get enough to be able to exist and reproduce themselves; but the wages of the whole working class level down, with their fluctuations, to this minimum (Tucker 1972: 175-176).

When it was the norm for a worker's family to be supported by the labor of a single worker, then Marx would argue the worker would, on average, have to earn enough to support himself and his wife and raise the children. But, if the social norm were to change so that it became typical that both the husband and wife would work, then Marx would argue that it would only be necessary to pay each about half of the required subsistence wage for a family, which is about the situation we have arrived at in America. Of course, in this social context, a family that had only one earner would typically be unable to support itself on that single wage alone.

By the way, Marx, in discussing the subsistence wage level noted that it ". . . is formed by two elements--the one merely physical, the other historical or social." He went on to argue that,

> The ultimate [lower] limit is determined by the physical element, that is to say, to maintain and reproduce itself, to perpetuate its physical existence, the working class must receive the necessaries absolutely indispensable for living and multiplying. . . . besides this mere physical element, the value of labour is in every country determined by a traditional standard of life. It is not mere physical life, but it is the satisfaction of certain wants springing from the social conditions in which people are placed and reared up. . . . This historical or social element . . . may be expanded, or contracted, or altogether extinguished, so that nothing remains but the physical limit (Marx 1969b: 57).

Thus, one could argue that the official poverty threshold in the United States is a pretty good estimate of Marx's physical subsistence level, while the BLS Minimum Adequacy standard could be argued to be a reasonable estimate of his historical or social subsistence level.

29. The data recently available for 1986 show no significant changes from the 1985 data in this regard, and these types of detailed data for 1987 were not yet available as this was being edited. The 1987 data that are available, for householders age 25 and older, of poor households and of households in general, are discussed in the context of Table 4-15.

30. If some of the folks in this category are continuing their college education or postgraduate education, they "should," by the age of 22, at least have completed one year of college and would therefore be lumped together in the category "one or more years of college" with those who have finished college or dropped out.

31. I hasten to add that this book is not the place to rehash the many studies that have been made in recent years of the American educational system and its failings. I would quite agree that merely measuring years of education, rather than the quality of that education, is a problem in this or any similar analysis. A high school education completed at an outstanding suburban or central city magnet school can hardly be compared to the educational results one is likely to have obtained from surviving four years at many of our lower quality schools. Nevertheless, this quantitative measure is the only data available to a study such as mine, and it does provide at least a useful starting point.

32. This may, in part, be a reflection of the fact that a larger proportion of the poor Black population lives within metropolitan areas (77.5 percent) compared to poor Whites (67.4 percent).

33. However, recall the earlier discussion, for example, in the cited article by Marshall (1987), indicating that in recent years Black women are far more likely to attend and remain in college than Black males.

34. The data in Table 4-14 and 4-15 are not directly comparable for reasons beyond the narrower focus of Table 4-15 on householders. In Table 4-14, we are looking only at those in the 22-59 age group; whereas, in Table 4-15 we are looking at those ages 25 and older. Also, Table 4-14 reflected data for 1985; whereas, Table 4-15 contains 1987 data. In this latter regard it might be noted that there is not a lot of difference between the 1985 and 1987 data for Table 4-15. For example, the percentage of poor householders who were high school graduates in 1985 and 1987, respectively, was 49.2 percent and 48.9 percent. This reflected a decrease in the proportion of poor Black householders who were high school graduates (48.1 percent to 47.0 percent) and an increase in the proportion of Hispanic high school graduates (23.3 percent to 25.2 percent), while there was no change at all in this proportion among poor White householders.

Table 4-1
Percentage of Families Living Below Poverty Level by Size of Family
and Comparative Data on Persons and Families Living Below Other Related Thresholds
1985

Size of Family	Distrib. of Families by Size	Income Requirement % Equiv. of Family of 4	Income Requirement Poverty Threshold Level	Percentage of such Families Living Below the Poverty Level — All	White	Black	Hispanic
Two Persons	40.1%	64%	$6,998	9.1%	7.6%	24.6%	18.8%
Three Persons	24.2%	78%	$8,578	11.1%	8.9%	27.5%	26.0%
Four Persons	21.0%	100%	$10,989	11.3%	9.1%	29.0%	24.2%
Five Persons	9.6%	118%	$13,007	14.9%	11.9%	30.0%	28.7%
Six Persons	3.2%	134%	$14,696	19.0%	15.2%	35.6%	30.3%
Seven or More	1.9%	152%	$16,656	32.1%	25.0%	49.7%	46.2%
Total	100.0%			11.4%	9.1%	28.7%	25.5%
Percentage of Families, Undifferentiated by Size, Living Below the Four Person Family Poverty Level of $10,989				15.4%	13.1%	33.8%	28.5%
Percentage of Persons Living in Families, Adjusted for Size, Below the Poverty Threshold				12.6%	9.9%	30.5%	28.3%
Percentage of Unrelated Individuals Living Below the Poverty Level				21.5%	19.6%	34.7%	33.2%
Percentage of All Persons Living Below the Poverty Threshold (with Familes/Households Adjusted for Size)				14.0%	11.4%	31.3%	29.0%
Percentage of All Persons Living Below 125% of the Poverty Level (with Families/Households Adjusted for Size)				18.7%	15.7%	38.8%	36.8%
Percentage of Families, Undifferentiated by Size, Living Below the Adjusted B.L.S. Low (or Minimum Adequate) Budget				34.4%	31.6%	58.3%	52.8%
Percentage of Families, Undifferentiated by Size, Living Below the Adjusted B.L.S. Moderate, But Adequate Budget				53.9%	51.5%	74.3%	71.9%
Mean Size of Families in Poverty				3.56	3.45	3.75	4.22
Mean Size of Families Regardless of Income				3.21	3.15	3.55	3.87
Mean # of Children per Poverty Family with Children				2.23	2.14	2.39	2.57
Mean # of Children per Family with Children				1.85	1.82	2.01	2.17

Source: U.S. Department of Commerce 1986a and 1987a.

TABLE 4-2
Percentage Share of Aggregate Income
Received by Each Fifth and Top 5% of Families
1947-1986

Quintile	1947	1960	1965	1970	1975	1980	1985	1986	Comparison of 1986 to Earlier Figures
The Poorest 20%	5.0%	5.0%	5.2%	5.4%	5.4%	5.1%	4.6%	4.6%	Lowest since 1954*
The Second 20%	11.8%	12.1%	12.2%	12.2%	11.8%	11.6%	10.9%	10.8%	Lowest on Record**
The Middle 20%	17.0%	17.7%	17.8%	17.6%	17.6%	17.5%	16.9%	16.8%	Lowest on Record***
The Fourth 20%	23.1%	23.7%	23.9%	23.8%	24.1%	24.3%	24.2%	24.0%	Lowest since 1974#
The Richest 20%	43.0%	41.4%	40.9%	40.9%	41.1%	41.6%	43.5%	43.7%	Highest on Record##
The Richest 5%	17.2%	16.3%	15.5%	15.6%	15.5%	15.3%	16.7%	17.0%	Highest on Record###
The Poorest 40%	16.8%	17.1%	17.4%	16.6%	17.2%	16.7%	15.5%	15.4%	Lowest on Record
The Richest 40%	66.1%	65.1%	64.8%	64.7%	65.2%	65.9%	67.7%	67.7%	Highest on Record

Notes:
* Fluctuated between 5.0% and 5.6% from 1962 to 1981. Been at 4.7 or below since 1982. Lowest on record was 4.5% in 1949,'50, and '54.
** Fluctuated between 12.0% and 12.7% from 1950 to 1971.
*** Fluctuated between 17.6% and 18.1% from 1951 to 1971.
# Fluctuated between 24.2% and 24.4% from 1975 to 1985; however, fluctuated between 23.1% and 24.0% from 1947-1974.
Fluctuated between 40.4% and 41.9% from 1951 to 1981.
Fluctuated between 15.2% and 15.9% from 1962 to 1981.

Source: U.S. Department of Commerce 1987a and 1987d.

Table 4-3
Changes in the Gap Between Rich and Poor Families
1947-1987
(All figures in constant 1985 dollars)

	1947	1960	1973	1982	1987
Income Level at 95th Percentile	$38,829	$49,133	$72,684	$71,328	$81,879
Income Level at 80th Percentile	23,657	31,942	46,623	44,571	50,199
Income Level at 20th Percentile	7,620	10,105	14,726	12,482	13,710
The Gap Between the 20th & 95th	$31,209	$39,028	$57,958	$58,846	$68,169
The Gap Between the 20th & 80th	16,037	21,837	31,897	32,089	36,489
The 20th as a % of the 95th	19.6%	20.6%	20.3%	17.5%	16.7%
The 20th as a % of the 80th	32.2%	31.6%	31.6%	28.0%	27.3%

	Percentage Changes in Income Levels				
	1947-60	1960-73	1973-82	1982-87	1973-87
95th Percentile	26.5%	47.9%	-1.9%	14.8%	12.2%
80th Percentile	35.0	46.0	-4.4	12.6	7.7
20th Percentile	32.6	45.7	-15.2	9.8	-6.9

Note: The 95th percentile can be interpreted as the median income of the richest 10% of the population, while the 80th percentile can be interpreted as the median of the richest 40% of the population, and the 20th percentile as the median of the poorest 40% of the population. The population refers to all families.

Source: U.S. Department of Commerce 1987a,d and 1988c.

Table 4-4
The Changes in Median Family Income: 1960-1987
(In constant 1985 dollars)

| | 1960* | 1973 | 1982 | 1987 | Percentage Changes | | | |
					'60-'73	'73-'82	'82-'87	'73-'87
All Families	$20,421	$29,172	$26,116	$29,272	42.9%	-10.5%	12.1%	0.3%
White Families	$21,202	$30,484	$27,420	$30,620	43.8%	-10.1%	11.7%	0.4%
Black Familes*	$11,737	$17,596	$15,155	$17,171	49.9%	-13.9%	13.3%	-2.4%
Hispanic Families	n/a	$21,097	$18,085	$19,266	n/a	-14.3%	6.5%	-8.7%

Note: * In 1960, the figure for Black families is actually for "Black and other
         Races." 1967 is the first year separate data is reported for Blacks
         alone. In 1967, Blacks were 91% of the "Blacks and other Races" category.

Source: U.S. Department of Commerce 1987a,d and 1988c.

Table 4.5
Comparative Data on Persons and Children in Households, Families and Female-Headed Families Living Below The "Official" Poverty Level
1960-1987

All Persons

	1960	1965	1970	1975	1980	Peak Year*	1987
All Persons	22.2%	17.3%	12.6%	12.3%	13.0%	15.2% ('83)	13.5%
Whites	17.8%	13.3%	9.9%	9.7%	10.2%	12.1% ('83)	10.5%
Blacks***	55.1%	41.8%	33.5%	31.3%	32.5%	35.7% ('83)	33.1%
Hispanics**	n/a	n/a	21.9%	26.9%	25.7%	29.9% ('82)	28.2%

All Persons Living in Families

	1960	1965	1970	1975	1980	Peak Year*	1987
All Persons	20.7%	15.8%	10.9%	10.9%	11.5%	13.9% ('83)	12.1%
Whites	16.2%	11.7%	8.1%	8.3%	8.6%	10.7% ('83)	9.1%
Blacks***	54.9%	40.9%	32.2%	30.1%	31.1%	34.7% ('82)	31.8%
Hispanics**	n/a	n/a	21.5%	26.3%	25.1%	29.2% ('82)	27.7%

Unrelated Individuals

	1960	1965	1970	1975	1980	Peak Year*	1987
All Persons	45.2%	39.8%	32.9%	25.1%	22.9%	23.4% ('81)	20.8%
Whites	43.0%	38.1%	30.8%	22.7%	22.4%	21.2% ('81)	18.2%
Blacks***	57.0%	54.4%	48.3%	42.1%	41.0%	41.0% ('80)	38.3%
Hispanics**	n/a	n/a	29.9%	36.6%	32.2%	36.8% ('84)	30.5%

All Related Children Under 18 Living in Families

	1960	1965	1970	1975	1980	Peak Year*	1987
All Persons	26.5%	20.7%	14.9%	16.8%	17.9%	21.8% ('83)	20.0%
Whites	20.0%	14.4%	10.5%	12.5%	13.4%	17.0% ('83)	15.0%
Blacks***	65.5%	50.6%	41.5%	41.4%	42.1%	47.3% ('82)	45.1%
Hispanics**	n/a	n/a	27.8%	33.1%	33.0%	39.6% ('85)	39.3%

All Persons Age 65 and Older****

	1960	1965	1970	1975	1980	Peak Year*	1987
All Persons	35.2%	28.5%	24.6%	15.3%	15.7%	15.3% ('81)	12.2%
Whites	33.1%	26.4%	22.6%	13.4%	13.6%	13.1% ('81)	10.1%
Blacks***	62.5%	55.1%	48.0%	36.3%	38.1%	39.0% ('81)	33.9%
Hispanics**	n/a	n/a	24.9%	32.6%	30.8%	27.4% ('87)	27.4%

All Persons in Female-Headed Families

	1960	1965	1970	1975	1980	Peak Year*	1987
All Persons	48.9%	46.0%	38.1%	37.5%	36.7%	40.6% ('82)	38.3%
Whites	39.0%	35.4%	28.4%	29.4%	28.0%	31.2% ('83)	29.5%
Blacks***	70.6%	65.3%	58.7%	54.3%	53.4%	58.8% ('82)	54.8%
Hispanics**	n/a	n/a	57.4%	57.2%	54.5%	60.1% ('82)	55.0%

All Persons in Female-Headed Households (incl. unrel. indiv)

	1960	1965	1970	1975	1980	Peak Year*	1987
All Persons	49.5%	46.0%	38.2%	34.6%	33.8%	36.2% ('82)	33.6%
Whites	42.3%	38.5%	31.4%	28.1%	27.1%	28.7% ('82)	26.4%
Blacks***	70.0%	65.1%	58.8%	53.6%	53.1%	54.7% ('82)	53.8%
Hispanics**	n/a	n/a	55.5%	55.6%	52.5%	57.4% ('82)	53.0%

Related Children under 18 in Female-Headed Families

	1960	1965	1970	1975	1980	Peak Year*	1987
All Persons	68.4%	64.2%	53.0%	52.7%	50.8%	56.0% ('82)	54.7%
Whites	59.9%	52.9%	43.1%	44.2%	41.6%	47.1% ('83)	45.8%
Blacks***	81.6%	76.6%	67.7%	66.0%	64.8%	70.7% ('82)	68.3%
Hispanics**	n/a	n/a	66.7%	68.4%	65.0%	72.4% ('85)	70.1%

Notes:
* Peak Year refers to highest year in 1981-1987 period.
** Data for "1970" is actually for 1973, the earliest year for which this data is available.
*** Data for "1960" is actually for 1959 and data for "1965" is actually for 1966 due to anomalies in the way such data is published
**** Data for "1960" is actually for 1959 and data for "1965" is actually for 1966, again due to anomalies in reporting.

Source: U.S. Department of Commerce 1987d, 1988c and earlier numbers in this series.

Table 4-6
Comparative Data on Persons and Children in Households, Families and
Female-Headed Families Living Below 125% of the "Official" Poverty Level
1970-1987

	All Persons including Unrelated Individuals				All Persons Living in Families				Related Children Under 18 Living in Families			
	1970	1980	Peak Year*	1987	1970	1980	Peak Year*	1986	1970	1980	Peak Year*	1987
All Persons	17.6%	18.3%	20.3% (81/82)	18.1%	15.7%	16.0%	18.6% ('83)	16.0%	20.8%	23.7%	27.9% ('83)	25.1%
Whites	14.3%	14.9%	16.9% (81/82)	14.7%	12.2%	12.7%	15.0% ('83)	12.6%	15.5%	18.7%	22.7% ('83)	19.6%
Blacks	42.9%	40.2%	43.8% ('82)	40.2%	41.9%	38.8%	43.2% ('82)	38.6%	52.3%	49.8%	56.1% ('82)	52.8%
Hispanics	n/a	35.3%	38.5% ('82)	36.0%	n/a	34.7%	37.8% ('82)	35.3%	n/a	44.5%	48.2% (82/83)	47.6%

	All Persons (incl. unrel. indiv.) Living in Female-Headed Households				All Persons Living in Female-Headed Families				Related Children Under 18 Living in Female-Headed Families			
	1970	1980	Peak Year*	1987	1970	1980	Peak Year*	1986	1970	1980	Peak Year*	1987
All Persons	47.0%	42.6%	44.9% ('82)	41.4%	46.4%	44.6%	48.1% ('82)	44.8%	62.9%	59.3%	64.0% ('82)	61.9%
Whites	40.2%	35.9%	37.7% ('82)	34.4%	36.3%	35.2%	38.7% ('83)	35.7%	53.4%	50.2%	55.3% ('83)	53.3%
Blacks	67.9%	62.0%	65.6% ('82)	61.3%	68.0%	62.4%	67.0% ('82)	62.0%	77.0%	72.8%	78.6% ('82)	75.2%
Hispanics	n/a	62.2%	66.6% ('82)	60.6%	n/a	63.8%	69.0% ('82)	62.1%	n/a	74.1%	79.5% ('82)	76.6%

Note: * Peak Year refers to highest year in 1981-1987 period.

Source: U.S. Department of Commerce 1987d, 1988c and earlier numbers in this series.

108

Table 4-7
Children Living Below the Poverty Level as a Percentage of All Similarly Aged Children of that Racial/Ethnic Group: 1966-1987

	1966	1970	1975	1980	1987
Under Age 6					
All	18.1%	16.6%	18.2%	20.7%	22.7%
White	12.4%	11.8%	14.0%	16.0%	17.6%
Black	50.3%	42.2%	40.8%	45.8%	49.0%
Hispanic	n/a	n/a	n/a	34.6%	41.8%
Age 6 to 15					
All	17.6%	14.9%	16.8%	17.8%	20.2%
White	12.3%	10.5%	12.4%	13.4%	15.3%
Black	51.9%	41.5%	33.6%	41.2%	45.2%
Hispanic	n/a	n/a	n/a	33.0%	39.8%

Note: * 1966 is the earliest year for which this detailed data is available.

Source: U.S. Department of Commerce 1987d and 1988c and earlier numbers in this series.

Table 4-8
Percentage of Families in Poverty by Type of Family and Race/Ethnic Origin 1987

Race/Ethnic Origin	All Families	Married Couple Families	Male-Headed No Wife	Female-Headed No Husband
All	10.8%	6.0%	12.5%	34.3%
White	8.2	5.2	10.3	26.7
Black	29.9	12.3	24.3	51.8
Hispanic	25.8	18.1	15.7	51.8

Source: U.S. Department of Commerce 1988c.

Table 4-9
Work Experience of Working-Age Adults in Poverty, by Race: 1985*

Work Experience	All Age 15+	White:Age 18-64 Male	White:Age 18-64 Female	Black:Age 18-64 Male	Black:Age 18-64 Female
Ave. Weeks Wked	31.5				
Worked during Yr	41.5%	67.1%	44.2%	51.6%	38.6%
Worked FT/FY	9.0%	21.7%	6.5%	10.3%	6.7%
Wked FT/40-49 wks	2.4	5.6	4.1	1.6	1.9
Worked PT/FY	4.6%	4.9%	6.3%	5.2%	5.5%
Wked PT/40-49 wks	1.6	1.8	2.6	2.6	0.9
Did Not Work due to:					
Ill/Disabled	21.9%	40.8%	15.3%	39.7%	21.0%
Retired	16.8	9.3	4.6	5.1	1.4
Not Find Work	9.8	24.5	7.6	30.8	16.7
Keeping House	31.2	2.1	62.0	0.2	49.5
School/Other	20.2	23.1	10.4	24.3	11.4
Worked < 50 Weeks due to:					
Ill/Disabled	6.8%	7.0%	6.4%	7.8%	9.0%
Not Find Work	42.0	59.2	30.3	57.1	42.9
Keeping House	15.8	1.5	33.0	1.0	22.8
School/Other	35.4	32.1	30.6	34.2	25.1

Note: * Percentages in the upper part of the table refer to the
          proportion of poor persons having the given
          characteristics specified in the column's title who had
          the work experience specified to the left; whereas, the
          percentages in the bottom part of the table indicate what
          proportion of such heads of households "Who Did Not Work"
          during the year gave the indicated reason, and,
          similarly, for those who "Worked Less Than 50 Weeks"
          during the year.

Source: U.S. Department of Commerce 1987b.

Table 4-10
Work Experience of Head of Households in Poverty, by Race: 1985*

Work Experience	All Races	White	Black
Worked during Yr	50.3%	54.6%	39.9%
Worked Full-Year	20.5	23.0	14.8
Worked 40-49 wks	5.6	6.2	4.1
Worked FT/FY	16.4	18.9	10.5
Wked FT/40-49 wks	3.8	4.4	2.3
Did Not Work			
Ill/Disabled	23.9	23.7	25.6
Retired	15.2	18.7	9.0
Not Find Work	14.5	12.9	16.5
Keeping House	40.3	38.2	44.9
School/Other	6.1	6.4	4.1
Worked < 50 Weeks			
Ill/Disabled	9.4	9.5	9.9
Not Find Work	54.4	55.9	49.5
Keeping House	17.7	15.9	23.5
School/Other	18.5	18.8	17.1

Note: * See note below Table 4-9.

Source: U.S.Department of Commerce 1987b.

111

Table 4-11
Work Experience of Female Head of Households in Poverty, With No Husband Present, by Presence of Children and by Race: 1985*

Work Experience	Female All Races with or without children	w/children under age 18	w/children under age 6	White Female with or without children	w/children under age 18	w/children under age 6	Black Female with or without children	w/children under age 18	w/children under age 6
Worked during Yr	39.6%	40.2%	37.6%	40.9%	42.2%	37.7%	38.0%	37.9%	37.6%
Worked Full-Year	11.1	11.5	9.8	10.4	10.9	7.9	12.2	12.4	11.9
Worked 40-49 wks	4.3	4.2	4.6	5.2	4.9	5.5	3.3	3.5	3.8
Worked FT/FY	6.5%	6.9%	6.5%	5.6	5.8%	5.2%	7.8%	8.2%	8.2%
Wked FT/40-49 wks	2.4	2.4	2.8	2.5	2.5	3.1	2.3	2.5	2.8
Did Not Work									
Ill/Disabled	17.1%	14.3%	9.8%	14.9%	11.2%	6.1%	20.7%	18.4%	14.3%
Retired	4.0	1.7	1.3	4.9	2.0	1.4	3.0	1.4	1.2
Not Find Work	12.1	12.9	10.8	9.1	10.4	7.8	15.9	16.3	14.1
Keeping House	61.5	65.3	72.7	65.3	69.8	78.2	56.3	59.5	66.2
School/Other	5.4	5.8	5.5	6.0	6.7	6.4	4.1	4.3	4.2
Worked < 50 Weeks									
Ill/Disabled	10.4%	9.6%	9.7%	10.1%	9.0%	9.3%	10.6%	10.0%	10.8%
Not Find Work	37.4	36.4	31.0	33.8	32.7	25.9	44.1	43.7	38.2
Keeping House	33.2	34.9	41.1	36.1	38.2	43.4	27.9	28.7	36.8
School/Other	19.0	19.2	18.0	20.0	20.1	21.4	17.3	17.6	14.2

Note: * See note below Table 4-9.

Source: U.S.Department of Commerce 1987b.

112

Table 4-12
Work Experience of All Head of Households
and of Female Head of Households
Below 125% of Poverty, by Race:
1985*

Work Experience	All Head of Households		
	All Races	White	Black
Worked during Yr	53.2%	56.4%	44.4%
Worked FT\FY	20.4	22.3	15.5
Worked PT\FY	4.2	4.1	4.4
Mean # Wks Worked	37.5 wks	38.0 wks	36.3 wks
Did Not Work:			
Ill/Disabled	26.6%	26.6%	28.2%
Keeping House	34.7	31.6	41.6
Other	38.7	41.8	30.3

Work Experience	Female Head of Households		
	All Races	White	Black
Worked during Yr	43.4%	45.0%	41.2%
Worked FT\FY	10.2	9.3	11.4
Worked PT\FY	4.9	5.2	4.5
Mean # Wks Worked	33.0 wks	33.1 wks	33.3 wks
Did Not Work:			
Ill/Disabled	19.3	16.8	23.2
Keeping House	58.7	61.5	54.4
School/Other	22.1	21.7	22.4

Note: * See note below Table 4-9.

Source: U.S.Department of Commerce 1987b.

Table 4-13
Number of Earners per Low Income Family
and per Family Regardless of Income,
by Race/Ethnic Group: 1985

Race/ Ethnic Group	Family Income	Percentage with:			Mean # of Earners per Family	Mean # of FT/FY Earners per Family
		No Earners	One Earner	Two or More Earners		
All	Below $10,000	44.9%	38.4%	16.8%	0.76	.18
	$10,000-20,000	23.7	41.1	35.2	1.19	.54
	Zero - $20,000	32.1	40.0	20.6	1.02	.40
	All Incomes	14.6	29.1	56.3	1.64	.94
White	Below $10,000	43.8	37.8	18.5	0.78	.20
	$10,000-20,000	25.8	39.2	34.9	1.16	.51
	Zero - $20,000	32.3	38.7	29.0	1.02	.40
	All Incomes	14.2	28.5	57.3	1.65	.95
Black	Below $10,000	49.0	39.9	11.0	0.66	.12
	$10,000-20,000	12.0	51.7	37.2	1.38	.67
	Zero - $20,000	31.9	45.3	23.1	0.99	.38
	All Incomes	19.2	34.0	46.7	1.51	.84
Hispanic	Below $10,000	44.6	39.9	15.4	0.74	.19
	$10,000-20,000	8.8	45.5	45.9	1.50	.70
	Zero - $20,000	26.3	42.8	31.0	1.13	.45
	All Incomes	14.5	33.8	51.7	1.62	.89

Source: U.S. Department of Commerce 1987a.

Table 4-14
The Educational Experience of the Poor
and of the General Population:
1985

Part I

Years of Education Completed	Percentage of All Persons Age 15 and Over with Given Education Living in Poverty	Percentage of All Persons Age 22-59
No years completed	34.0%	0.5%
Elementary: 1 to 5	32.7%	1.4
6 to 7	28.4%	2.2
8	21.3%	3.0
High School:1 to 3	19.3%	10.5
4	9.9%	40.7
College: 1 or more	5.2%	41.7
Total		100.0
High School Graduates		82.7%

Part II

Years of Education Completed	Percentage of Poor Persons Age 22 to 59				
	All	White		Black	
		Male	Female	Male	Female
No years completed	1.3%	1.5%	0.9%	1.2%	0.6%
Elementary: 1 to 5	4.8	5.3	4.9	5.6	2.8
6 to 7	6.7	7.7	6.9	8.2	3.9
8	7.4	9.1	7.2	5.9	6.0
High School:1 to 3	22.8	18.6	22.1	42.9	31.5
4	37.5	34.3	39.4	33.2	41.5
College: 1 or more	19.5	23.4	18.5	17.0	13.6
Total	100.0	100.0	100.0	100.0	100.0
High School Graduates	57.0%	57.7%	57.9%	50.2%	55.1%

Source: Calculated from U.S. Department of Commerce 1987b.

Table 4-15
The Educational Experience of Poor Householders
and of Poor Female Householders by
Race/Ethnic Group
1987

Part I

Years of Education Completed	Percentage of Poor Householders Age 25 and Older				Percentage of All Householders Age 25 and Older
	All	White	Black	Hispanic	
No years completed	1.9%	1.9%	0.6%	6.0%	0.5%
Elementary: 1 to 7	17.6	18.6	15.4	40.4	6.4
8	8.9	10.0	7.1	8.7	5.2
High School:1 to 3	22.7	20.1	29.8	19.8	12.0
4	34.4	34.1	36.7	18.2	36.9
College: 1 or more	14.5	15.3	10.2	7.0	39.0
Total	100.0	100.0	100.0	100.0	100.0
High School Graduates	48.9%	49.4%	47.0%	25.2%	75.9%

Part II

Years of Education Completed	Percentage of Poor Female Householders Age 25 and Older				Percentage of All Female Householders 25 and Older
	All	White	Black	Hispanic	
No years completed	1.5%	1.7%	0.4%	5.2%	0.9%
Elementary: 1 to 7	13.0	15.3	10.9	35.0	8.5
8	8.0	8.3	7.7	10.4	6.0
High School:1 to 3	25.7	19.6	33.2	20.9	16.5
4	38.6	38.8	38.7	22.6	40.5
College: 1 or more	13.2	16.3	9.2	5.7	27.6
Total	100.0	100.0	100.0	100.0	100.0
High School Graduates	51.8%	55.2%	47.9%	28.4%	68.1%

Source: U.S. Department of Commerce 1988c.

116

Table 4-16
Where the Poor Live
1987

Location	Percentage of the Poor by Race/Ethnic Group				Incidence of Poverty (Percent of Total Pop. in Given area)
	All	White	Black	Hispanic	
Metropolitan Area	70.4	67.2	76.9	90.7	10.0%
Central City	42.0	33.2	59.2	62.9	15.4
Suburbs	28.5	34.0	17.7	27.8	6.5
Non-Metropolitan	29.6	32.8	23.1	9.4	13.8

Source: U.S. Department of Commerce 1988c.

117

The Effects of Race, Sex, Education, Industry, and Occupation on the Distribution of Income Among Those Working Full-Time, Full-Year

RACIAL AND SEXUAL DISCRIMINATION PATTERNS AMONG FULL-TIME, FULL-YEAR WORKERS

The media, many conservative politicians, and even many naive progressives would have us believe that the major cause of the wide differences we see in the earnings of Americans, especially the differences we observe when we view the data in racial/ethnic or sexual categories, is unemployment or the incidence of part-time work. While these factors certainly do have more of an impact upon minorities and women in the U.S., as we have seen, they are not the major cause of the wide differences in income. Table 5-1 reveals a plethora of interesting observations on this point.

First, it is important to note that this table deals only with persons who have worked full-time, full-year[1] for the duration of the year in question. By looking at differences in earnings by race/ethnic group and sex in this setting, we are able to ignore, for the moment, the effects of unemployment and part-time labor, and, hence, are able to make a most conservative evaluation of the differentials in income that exist even in the best of circumstances --when the individuals involved are working at full-time jobs throughout the year. Second, it is interesting to observe that this table lets us consider the longer historical period stretching back to 1939, and extending to preliminary figures for 1987.

Income Differentials by Race/Ethnic Group

Focusing first on the summary in the middle portion of Table 5-1 which deals with Black/White differentials, and particularly on columns 1 and 2 there, one can examine the pattern of racial discrimination in income among full-time workers. What is found is that from 1939 through 1975 the gap between Blacks and Whites who worked full-time, full-year, narrowed significantly. However, during the decade, from 1975 through 1985, the gap between Black and

White males (column 1), and that between Black and White females (column 2), again widened. Once again, we see the evidence of a significant change in the pattern of the distribution of income occurring in the early to mid-1970s. The figures for 1986 (not shown) and 1987 indicate some improvement in relative terms,[2] but it remains to be seen whether this is a short term aberration or not. In any event, despite this modest improvement, by 1987, both Black males and females who worked full-time, full-year, still stood further behind their White counterparts, in relative terms, than had been true 12 years earlier in 1975.

However, in absolute terms, if one converts the incomes in 1975 and 1987 into constant dollars of the same value, one finds that the gap in real purchasing power has narrowed, in the case of Black and White males from $12,329 dollars in 1975 (in 1987 dollars) to $8,078 in 1987, an improvement of some 34.5 percent. Between Black and White females, the gap in purchasing power has narrowed slower, by 5.9 percent, but was always much smaller, standing at only $1,564 in 1987.

If one looks at Hispanic-White income differentials, the lower part of the ratios in Table 5-1 is relevant. Here, in columns 1 and 2, we see a steady deterioration in the relative incomes of Hispanic full-time, full-year workers, compared to Whites of the same sex, with no indication of a turnaround.[3] In fact, since 1985, there has been a *decrease* among Hispanic males even in current dollar income, let alone constant dollar income, while every other group has seen at least a modest increase. Thus, in terms of constant dollar purchasing power, there was a rather modest improvement of some $246 (in 1987 dollars--3,584 to 3,830) from 1975 to 1987 between the two female groups, but a widening of the gap between Hispanic and White men from $8,165 to $10,455.

Among both males and females, the gap between Hispanic and White full-time, full-year workers is wider than between Blacks and Whites. There is little doubt that among full-time, full-year workers, Hispanics fall below Blacks in income. Although the gap is not large (see columns 5 and 6 in the bottom portion of Table 5-1), there has been some widening of the gap between Hispanic and Black males since 1980, while the relative position of Hispanic females, compared to Black females, fluctuated within a narrow range.

Income Differentials by Sex

If one focuses upon the issue of discrimination based on sex within the White community, one sees exactly the opposite pattern. Column 4 reveals that, after reaching a post-war peak of 65.4 percent, the gap between the income of White women and White men steadily widened until 1975 (57.4 percent), at which point it began to narrow. However, it took until 1987 to surpass, slightly, the 1955 level, and it had still not reached the 1949 level of 65.4 percent. Nevertheless, after more than a quarter century in which the relative position of White women deteriorated, the improvement since 1975 has been quite substantial in both relative and absolute terms. On the other hand, it is still quite disturbing to find that after all the education women have pursued, after all the talk of opening up the economic marketplace to them, and despite the advances of the last decade or so, in 1987, full-time, full-year White women workers still earned only 64.7 percent of the income of White men, leaving a gap of $9,688 at the medians.

Thus, we begin to get a picture of the trade-off that often seemed to exist between improvements in the racial gap versus improvements in the sexual gap. One further indication of this is that through the 1950s, the order of income was White male, White female, Black male, Black female; but since 1960 the median income of full-time employed Black males has exceeded that of similarly employed White females. While White women have been catching up to Black men since 1975, in 1985 and 1987, the percentage gap between them was the same as it had been back in 1960.

Thus, from World War II through the immediate post-war period, and then continuing through the time of the civil rights movement, the gap between Black and White earnings narrowed, while the sexual gap among Whites widened. But then, with the rise of the women's liberation movement, a movement largely run by White women, and the growing weakness of the civil rights movement, the pattern is reversed and the sexual gap narrows while the racial one widens. Only in the two most recent years, 1986 and 1987, have both gaps narrowed a bit. We will have to see whether this is a new, positive trend, or a short-term aberration.

A special case is that of Black and Hispanic women, who feel the impact of both forms of discrimination. Here, columns 2, 3, and 6 in the middle portion of the Table 5-1 and columns 2, 3, 4, and 6 in the lower portion are relevant. Looking first at the situation for Black women, in the middle portion of the table, in column 3, one can see that Black women have steadily closed the gap with Black men. When compared to Whites, either male or female (columns 6 and 2, respectively), the position of Black women improves through 1975, but since then they have lost ground to White women, while continuing to make some progress compared to White men. How can this be explained?

Black women seem to be primarily affected in the wage market by their race. During the earlier period, they improved their relative situation considerably with regard to all the other groups, but especially as compared to White women. By the mid 1970s, the market almost seems to be saying (with the figure of 95.5 percent in column 2), if you are going to hire a woman, it might as well be a Black as a White. But then, with a new focus on the issue of sex and a lessening of a focus on race, Black woman, given their gender, managed to continue to make some modest progress compared to White men; but given their race, lost considerable ground to White women (through 1986, see endnote 2). However, we need to remain clear that the dual forces of racial and sexual discrimination continue to exert their effects, with Black women workers earning less than any other group, except Hispanic women.

Hispanic women have moved to close the gap with Hispanic men (column 3 in the bottom portion of the table), much the way Black women did with Black men, such that, by 1987, the gap of 83.3

percent between Hispanics, was almost identical to the 83.6 percent between Blacks. We also find that while Hispanic females lost ground to White females (column 2, bottom) from 1975 through 1987, they gained ground compared to White males (column 4, bottom), again following the same basic pattern we found with Black females.

Some Conclusions Concerning the Pattern of Income Differentials

Thus, over all, if one compares the respectively similar columns in the two lower portions of table 5-1, one finds that the same patterns emerge between Hispanics and Whites as was true between Blacks and Whites; that is, (1) the racial/ethnic discrimination (columns 1 and 2) increased over the decade from 1975 to 1985, (2) the sexual discrimination was reduced (columns 3 and 4/6), and (3) the racial/ethnic effects are more powerful than those related to gender so that (columns 2) the gap between White women and Hispanic, as well as Black, women widened.

Overall, the data in Table 5-1 support, but do not prove, a number of contentions, including: (1) social movements do effect the pattern of wages paid in the U.S.; (2) the U.S. seems unable to simultaneously address the matters of racial and sexual discrimination, instead it appears to alternately play-off one form of discrimination against the other; (3) the growth of a predominately White-led women's movement was to be expected in the mid-1970s given the economic pressures on those women; (4) sexual discrimination among both Black and Hispanic workers has steadily continued to lessen, while racial discrimination among female workers (as well as among male workers) increased over the decade 1975-85, which poses some serious questions for the women's movement (there was some sign of improvement in the racial differentials among Blacks and Whites, though not Hispanics and Whites in the 1985-87 period); and (5) the wide gaps in income between men and women, between Blacks and Whites, and between Hispanics and Whites are not primarily a function of unemployment or part-time work, since the patterns are still all too vivid when these factors are taken into account.

Looking at the Differentials in Earnings Instead of Income

It should be noted that in order to test the robustness of these trends, I also constructed, in-so-far as possible given the limitations of the available data, tables similar to 5-1, but using total earnings, rather than total income; that is, omitting so called unearned, or property related income, but including self-employed earnings, both farm and non-farm. Table 5-2 reports this data for 1975-86.[4]

As this table indicates, the basic patterns reported above (for the period since 1975) are still evident in this data. One difference is that when one looks at earnings instead of total income, Hispanic females steadily close the gap with Black females, and for 1986 at least, begin to do so with regard to White females, though this latter fact may well be a one year aberration. The small declines between 1985 and 1986 in the ratios between Blacks and Whites in columns 5 and 6 in the middle portion of the table are one-year deviations for 1986 that showed up in the income data as well, but were (in terms of income) reversed in 1987. One suspects that the same will be true of the earnings data.

In virtually every category the ratios between earnings and between incomes in 1986 were within a percentage point, or at most two, of each other. This is not surprising given that, at the median in 1985 for example, the difference between earnings and total income, that is, the income from property as opposed to wages and salaries, was in the rather narrow and low range of $282 (Black females) to $686 (White females), and amounted to only 4.2 percent of the latter's total income.

In addition to the work reported in the tables, examination was also made of series consisting of only wage and salary earnings to eliminate the effects of earnings from farm and non-farm self-employment. Finally, to test for the possible bias due to the inclusion of younger workers, data was also examined for those 18 years and older and 25 years and older. With a few very minor variations, the pattern of the trends in income/earnings between the various groups remained as reported above.

One interesting figure to emerge from these alternative formulations is that when one examines the total earnings for those full-time, full-year workers who are age 25 and older, the relative improvement in the income of White women between 1980 and 1985, as compared to that of Black men, is such that in 1985, for the first time since the mid-1950s, the income of White women exceeded that of Black men.

An Alternative Analysis of Male-Female Income Differentials

In contrast, a more pessimistic view of what has been happening in recent years to the relative economic position of women is developed in a recent study by Albelda, Lapidus, and McCrate (1988), a summary of which is available in the journal *Dollars and Sense* (Albelda 1988b). Here, Albelda reports on the development of what is described as the Per capita Access to Resources (PAR) index. The purpose of this measurement is to try to capture what has been happening to the stream of actual economic resources available to women, compared to that available to men, since 1967.

In particular, the creators of this index wanted a measurement that reflected the changing family structure and the growing presence of female-headed households, households in which the woman does not have access to the resources brought in by a male worker. This measurement, which is built on household income, does not isolate the earnings of full-time, full-year workers, but includes income from part-time and/or part-year work, as well as from welfare and other transfer payments.

The results of this effort to develop a more global measurement of the per capita income of women compared to that of men demonstrates that the gap between the two has, with some short-lived exceptions, been steadily widening from 1967 to 1985, the latter being the latest available figure. In 1967, the PAR index shows that the per capita income of women is 92 percent of that of men; but, by 1985, it had dropped to only 87 percent. Thus, Albelda concludes that while "Over the last 10 years, the gap between men's and women's wages has narrowed. . . . In fact, women's per capita income relative to that of men's has declined" (Albelda 1988b: 6).

THE IMPACT OF EDUCATION UPON INCOME

The Data for 1986

This analysis begins by examining the data for 1986, the latest available as of this writing. Table 5-3 extends the work in Table 5-1 even further by considering the issue of the number of years of school completed. Here again, in order to make the most conservative comparisons, we first look at the median income of full-time, full-year workers. In order to allow for a reasonable period of time for workers to complete their education and secure employment, we further limit ourselves to an examination of those age 25 or older. What becomes clear is that gaining an education does not significantly alter the patterns of discrimination in earnings based upon either sex or race.

Looking first at the issue of racial discrimination, one finds that the ratio of Black male to White male income shows no significant improvement as the amount of education increases. In fact, the highest such ratio, 96.7 percent, occurs among those with the least education. Even for those completing four years of college (16 total years of schooling), the ratio is no better than that among high school dropouts or those with an elementary education or less. Those completing 1 to 3 years of college exhibit a higher ratio than among those with 4 years of college. Only those with some post-graduate education (17 plus years) even get close to the level of those with the least education. Consistently, regardless of education (beyond the lowest level), Black males, even though they work full-time, full-year, earn 11 percent to almost 27 percent less than White males who are similarly educated, even when both work full-time, full-year.

Among women, the first relevant point is that, as we saw in the earlier data, there is far less racial discrimination than among the men, to the extent that the *lowest* ratio of Black to White female income (83.5 percent) is better than all but the *highest* such ratios among males. In general, the differential between Black and White women runs in the range of 4.5 percent to 16.5 percent. But, having said that, it must quickly be pointed out that there is no clear pattern of reduced discrimination as the amount of education increases, except that the highest ratios are found among those with 4 or more years of college.

When one looks at discrimination based upon sex, within either the Black or White communities of fully employed persons age 25 and older, there is, again, little indication of any pattern of reduced discrimination as education increases. Thus, one finds that the ratio between White female and male earnings fluctuates within the relatively narrow range of about 60 to 71 percent, regardless of educational achievement with the two highest ratios occurring among those with the most and the least education. Among Black men and women there is also not a clear pattern of improvement as education increases, although, again as in the data in the preceding section, we see percentage differentials that, except at the two lowest levels of education, are consistently smaller (the ratios higher) between Black men and women than between White men and women.

One should not misinterpret the evidence as to the effect of education. In an absolute sense, education certainly is positively related to higher earnings for every group. In general, regardless of race or sex, those with a completed college education (16 years) tend to earn about twice as much as those with only a grade school education and about 50 percent more than those with a high school diploma. Moreover, for those in every group, postgraduate education pays off with earnings 13 to 36 percent higher than that received by college graduates. But, there is little evidence that increased levels of education reduces the degree of racial or sexual economic discrimination, except perhaps for post-graduate training.

To view the matter from a slightly different perspective, getting an education does improve the likelihood that one will escape from poverty, at least if one works full-time all year. However, given the discrimination practiced against Blacks (as well as other minorities) and women, the amount of education that one must complete to stand a reasonable chance of living an economically acceptable life, even if one works full-time all year, varies greatly. We can use the BLS adjusted Minimum Adequacy and Modest but Adequate standards developed earlier (see Table 2-1), which, expressed in 1986 dollars, amount to $20,605 and $30,771, respectively, together with the 1986 poverty level of $11,203, as the bases for comparison. In this way, we see that in 1986, White male high school dropouts (11 to 13 years of school) earned a median income only $216 above the Minimum Adequacy level. But even White males require a 4 year college education (16 years of education) to reach an income above the Modest But Adequate BLS level. For Black males, it requires at least some college education to surpass even the Minimum Adequacy threshold, and it takes postgraduate work to exceed the Modest But Adequate standard.

For women, the picture is even more severe. Unless they complete high school, they are unlikely to exceed by more than a few dollars the level of poverty. White women, even when they work full-time, full-year, surpass the Minimum Adequacy level only if they complete a 4 year college education. But even with that amount of education, White women earn a median income some $3,728 less than Black males, a differential of almost 17 percent. Black women with that same 4 years of college education fall $544 below White women, and also require four years of college to exceed the very modest Minimum Adequacy standard. The achievement of the Modest but Adequate level exceeds, by $3,529 and $4,481, the average (median) reach of fully employed White and Black women, respectively, even when they have a postgraduate education.[5] Is it any wonder that female-headed households have such a high incidence of poverty or that so many households require two earners, even if one is a White male?

An Historical Perspective

Up to this point our discussion has been limited to data from 1986, the latest detailed data available at the time this was written. However, I have examined similar data for past years and the basic conclusion that there is no significant decrease in the racial or sexual discrimination in income among full-time, full-year workers as their education increases has been a consistent pattern. Table 5-4 presents the ratios of median income by sex and race for such workers for 1975, 1980, 1985, and 1986 to provide some feel for this historical data. The general lack of any consistent pattern of the ratios rising with income is quite clear. It is also clear from the fairly substantial changes in some of the ratios between 1985 and 1986, that the data are not overly stable in the short run. Nevertheless, a couple of interesting patterns do emerge from these historical observations, patterns that warrant further study elsewhere.

The ratio of Black male to White male income fell from 1975 to 1985, but then increased in 1986, for those with 8, 12, or 13 to 15 years of education, while it increased among those with 4 years of college (16 years of education) from 1975 to 1985, but then fell in 1986. We will have to see if 1986 is really the start of some new trends, or simply an aberration. From the overall data discussed earlier for full-time, full-year incomes, I suspect that the latter is true. The ratio has also fallen between Black females and White females with either 12 or 13 to 15 years of education, again except for, in this case, a very small reversal in 1986. But perhaps the most troubling pattern is the widening gap (decreasing ratios) between the income of Whites and Blacks, both male and female, who complete high school, where even the increase among women in 1986 still leaves that ratio below both the 1975 and 1980 levels. Even among those with the highest two levels of education, there has been a good deal of fluctuations in the ratios between Blacks and Whites, but certainly not any clear pattern of improvement. These patterns are yet another reflection of the stubborn, and even growing, racial inequalities in our society during the late 1970s and the 1980s.

On the other hand, the ratios between the median incomes of White women and White men show a rather clear pattern of increases at every level of education over the period from 1975 to 1986, such that virtually every ratio was higher in 1986 than it had been in 1975. The ratios between the incomes of Black women and Black men also tended to increase from 1975 to 1985, although there was a good deal more fluctuations along the way and some soft spots in 1986 that alert us to possible problems. Nevertheless, overall, these figures tend to confirm that during the same period when racial inequalities were often widening, sexual inequalities were narrowing at most educational levels, especially between White women and White

men. These results are also consistent with the trends discussed
earlier.

The Impact of Education upon Income, Regardless of Employment
Condition: A Comparison to those Working Full-Time, Full-Year

Tables 5-3 and 5-4, and the discussion above, were limited to
those working full-time, full-year so as to enable us to examine the
situation in which the maximum positive effects of education upon
earnings could be viewed; that is, to allow us to view the effects
of education upon earnings apart from the problems of unemployment
and part-time employment. However, we know that education also
impacts upon the likelihood of one being unemployed or of being
forced to accept part-time work. We also know that some people,
regardless of education may either choose not to work or to work
part-time (for example, to raise children), or may simply drop out
or be forced out of the labor market by the costs of child care or
other considerations. So, for comparison, Table 5-5 displays the
median income of all persons age 25 and older, regardless of their
employment condition. That is, it includes those persons who had
worked part-time or part-year or had been unemployed or out of the
labor force.

In Table 5-5, as one would expect, the absolute (median) amount
of income is considerably less for every group at every level of
education. Moreover, the pattern of how income increases as
education increases reflects not just one's earnings, but the
proportion of persons in that category not working or working part-
time and/or part-year. In this context it is interesting to note
that the more education, the closer the median income (in Table 5-
5) is to that of those fully employed. Thus, even for White males,
the figure in Table 5-5 for those with 7 years or less of education
is only about 59 percent of that in Table 5-3, while for those with
17 or more years of education it is almost 92 percent as much. This
pattern is true regardless of race or sex and reflects the fact that
the more education one has the less likely one is to be out of the
labor force, unemployed, or working part-time or part-year.

The general pattern of income and education for Black and White
males is about the same in Table 5-5 as it is in Table 5-3; however,
the ratios of Black male to White male incomes are consistently much
lower (except among high school dropouts) in Table 5-5, indicating
that Blacks are more likely either to be working part-time or part-
year or be working at such part-time or part-year jobs at lower pay
or not be employed or not in the labor force.

However, among the women the patterns are quite different.
Within the broader labor market covered in Table 5-5, Black women
with a 4 year high school education have about the same income as
White women (98.3 percent) and Black women with any education beyond
high school have a higher median income than White women with a
similar amount of education. While a number of different factors
are involved, it would seem that the main cause of this is that the
White women with these educational levels are more likely not to be
in the labor force or to be voluntarily working part-time or part-

year, primarily to raise children, than is the case with their Black counterparts.

Not unexpectedly, it would also seem that White women are more likely to be in one of these situations than their White male educational cohorts, as demonstrated by the lower values of every ratio on the White Female/White male row in Table 5-5 compared to Table 5-3. This also seems to be true of Black women compared to Black men, but only when both have less than four full years of college--and even for those with 1 to 3 years of college the figures are much closer within the Black community than among Whites. Not surprising given this perspective, the ratios comparing Black female to White male incomes are far lower across the board on Table 5-5 than on Table 5-3.

Thus, in examining the data in Tables 5-3 and 5-5, the point is driven home that in looking at the effect of education on income, taking into account work/labor market experience is essential to avoid confusing the different factors involved. It is also quite clear, as I suggested at the beginning of this section, that the differentials in income at the various educational levels between the racial/ethnic groups and between the sexes, generally tend to be considerably lower when one focuses upon those working full-time, full-year, with the notable exception of the differentials between Black and White women and between Black women and Black men, when they have had some college education or, in the case of the women, have even completed high school.

THE PATTERN OF EARNINGS AMONG OCCUPATIONS

Some Introductory Comments

Some have argued that it is not just education that is crucial to one's earnings, but also the industry and the occupation to which one applies that education. This is certainly true. Indeed, there are many other factors such as region of the country, and urban-rural differentials that are also relevant to understanding the causes for and the pattern of the distribution of income in the U.S. Perhaps the single most important factor is the earnings and class background of the family into which one is born. However, these other matters lie beyond the purview of this book. So, this study of the distribution of income will end with a short examination of the effects of occupation and, then in the next section, of industry, leaving the other matters for a later time.

As we begin the examination of the pattern of earnings among a variety of occupational categories, it should be noted that as we have (for the most part) been doing throughout this chapter, we will limit ourselves to those who worked full-time, full-year during the year in question so as to avoid distortions in those patterns that are due to part-time and/or part-year employment. This analysis begins with a detailed examination of the data for 1985. However, once that analysis is completed, we will look at the available data for the historical period back to 1960, and to preliminary figures through the first quarter of 1988.

In looking at occupational data, one must first address the issue of how narrow or detailed a set of occupational categories to explore. In this study, for 1985, I have grouped the data into some 13 Bureau of Labor Statistics occupational categories which are then grouped again into four areas: white collar, blue collar, service, and farming, forestry and fishing. There are published annual data available with about sixty occupations identified and even more detailed data, with more than 200 categories, that can also be obtained. However, the exploration of this degree of detail is beyond the scope of this book.

The Data for 1985

The detailed data for 1985 is presented in Table 5-6. A number of points must initially be made. The data by sex and race/ethnic group are only published in terms of means, rather than the medians which I would prefer to use. However, median data are available by sex and those are also reported. As is expected, the mean figures are considerably higher (by $1,000 to more than $5,000) than the medians due to the presence of some "extreme" high values. Thus, when looking at these figures, it should be kept in mind that they may considered as overly conservative or optimistically high measurements. It should also be observed that the occupational categories used in 1985 were relatively new, having only been employed by the BLS since 1982--more will be said about this matter when we look at the historical data. Finally, it should be noted that the dollar figures reported are for total money earnings, rather than total income or merely wage and salary earnings. That is, the figures do include earnings from self employment, not just wages and salaries, but do not include so-called unearned income such as from dividends or other property income. Then, to place these figures in some meaningful context, it should be recalled that the official poverty level for a family of four in 1985 was $10,989, while the adjusted BLS Low or Minimum Adequacy threshold was $20,207 and the BLS Moderate or Modest but Adequate threshold was $30,177.

Keeping these figures in mind and looking at the earnings reported in Table 5-6, the first thing that one notes is that only White males in three occupational groups (Executive- Administrative- Managerial, Professional Specialties, and Sales) within the white collar category earned more, on average, than the amount defined for the Modest but Adequate, or Moderate, budget standard and that even in the case of those in Sales, this level is exceeded by only a few hundred dollars. No women of any race/ethnic origin and neither Blacks nor Hispanics of either sex, no matter what their occupation, earned, on average, enough in 1985 to reach the Modest but Adequate budget level.

White males, except in the three lowest paying of the reported occupational categories (Handlers-Helpers-Laborers, Services other than Protective or Household, and Farming *et al*), did earn enough, on average, to surpass the Minimum Adequacy standard. However, for Black and Hispanic males, only those in three top paying white collar occupations (Executives, *et al*, Professionals, and

Technicians) plus Hispanics in Sales[6] earned enough to reach the level of Minimum Adequacy. For women in all racial/ethnic groups, only those in the top two white collar occupations (Executives and Professionals) achieved, on average, the Minimum Adequacy earnings necessary to support a family in 1985; but, except for those in Private Household Service and in Farming, they did escape, on average, the poverty level.

Looking at the overall means (the All Occupations line), which are weighted by the numbers of workers in each occupational category, we find that no group averaged above the Moderate level and only White males surpassed, again on average, the Minimum Adequacy level. To put it slightly differently, one finds that the average Black man, working full-time, full-year, earned only $19,949, which was more than $350 below the Minimum Adequacy budget level, while the average White woman had earnings almost $3,000 below this standard. The average Black woman's earnings were a remarkable $4,748 less than Minimum Adequacy, while the average Hispanic woman's earnings were even lower at $5,631 below Minimum Adequacy. Even the average White man earned only $28,159, which while above the Minimum Adequacy level, is still more than $2,000 below the Moderate level. All of which is yet further evidence that regardless of occupation, most Blacks and women and even many White males, do not earn an income above the BLS Low or Minimum Adequacy budget, even when they work full-time all year.

And, again, it should be pointed out that these are the conservative mean (arithmetic average) figures, not the more typical median (middle) figures. The latter, as one can see by examining the last two columns, are consistently even lower. Thus, for example, the median income for all Males in the Sales occupations is $25,445, more than $4,700 *below* the Moderate level; whereas, the mean figure was $30,103, which is almost exactly at that level. In general, those occupational categories in which extremely high earnings are likely to be achieved by a few workers, namely the highest paying white collar jobs, are the ones where the mean most distorts the results from that which would be presented by the use of the median.

Racial/Ethnic and Sexual Patterns in 1985

To examine the racial/ethnic and gender patterns present in the occupational data for 1985, the key ratios are presented in Table 5-7. Here one finds (columns 1 and 4 in the upper portion) that racial discrimination among men was worse in the white collar occupations than in the blue collar and service positions, with the widest differentials (lowest ratios) between males in the different racial/ethnic groups having occurred among those in the Sales and Executive occupations, and for Blacks in the Professional jobs. Moving up the occupational ladder to the Executive, Administrative, Managerial level, while increasing a Black or Hispanic male's absolute level of income, does little or nothing to improve his position (on average) relative to that of White males.

Among women the pattern of racial/ethnic differentials is not quite so clear. Black women in the Executive, Administrative Support, and Other (than Household and Protective) Services occupations actually earned, on average, more than their White female counterparts. For both Black and Hispanic women, the lowest ratios with their White female occupational counterparts occurred in the Sales area. Overall, as we have seen with data presented earlier, the racial/ethnic differentials among women is considerable less than among men, but that in large part reflects the much lower earnings of White women (as compared to White men).

It should be noted that the racial/ethnic ratios for all occupations taken as a whole are considerably lower (the differentials wider) than would be obtained by merely averaging the ratios for each occupation. This reflects the fact that a higher proportion of the White workers are in the better paying occupations, while a higher proportion of the Black and Hispanic workers are in the lowest paid.

Sexual discrimination, at least as it affects White women (column 1 in the lower portion of Table 5-7), seems also to be worst in many of the white collar occupations, especially in the Sales, Executive, and Professional jobs, and also in the rural (Farming, etc.) occupations. The sexual discrimination imposed on Black and Hispanic women when their earnings are compared to their male racial/ethnic counterparts, is consistently less than the differentials between White women and White men. However, this is largely the result of the discrimination already visited upon Black and Hispanic males as compared to White males. Thus, overall, the earnings of Hispanic and Black women are the lowest. Again, as with the racial/ethnic data, the overall sexual ratios for the "All Occupations" category are considerable lower than would be found by simply averaging the figures for the separate occupations due to the greater presence of women in many of the lowest paid occupations.

Thus, one sees that the pattern of racial and sexual discrimination spans the occupational spectrum. When looking at these data, and remembering again that they pertain to full-time, full-year workers, one sees once more that the problem of relatively low income and poverty for American workers as a whole, and especially for women, Blacks, and Hispanics, is caused by low earnings in many occupations, compounded by the discriminatory pattern of wages even within occupational groups, not just by unemployment or part-time work.

The Trends in Occupational Earnings Data Since 1960

Consistency Problems in the Data
Obtaining and presenting consistent occupational earnings data over the period since 1960 is an almost impossible task. The problems are manifold. Separate occupational data for Black workers are not available until 1967, and for Hispanic workers not until 1975. The data by sex are available, both as mean and median figures for the entire period, but the racial/ethnic data are reported as medians from 1967 to 1974, and only as means since 1975.

Then, in 1982, the Bureau of Labor Statistics began to present occupational data according to a totally new set of occupational definitions which, in the words of one of the economists with primary responsibility in the BLS for analyzing and reporting this data, presents us with the problem that ". . . the new classification system is vastly different from the previous one . . . [such that recent] data are not compatible with those available [earlier]" (Mellor 1986: 28). Or, as the BLS puts it in their official publications: ". . . the new system is so radically different in concepts and nomenclature from the [old] 1970 system that comparisons of historical data are not possible without major adjustments" (U.S. Department of Labor 1988: 160). Thus, presenting complete data that are consistent over the period from 1960 to 1985 or later is simply not possible.

However, it is possible to examine the trends by making comparisons between sets of data that are comparable, though of necessity there are breaks in the picture thus presented. What I have done in Tables 5-8 and 5-9 is the following. Using the old occupational categories, data is presented showing the trends from 1960 to 1967 by sex, then from 1967 to 1973 by sex and for Whites and Blacks. The year 1973 is displayed because that was the peak year, in real inflation adjusted terms, for earnings in most occupations. Then, the changes from 1973 to 1975 by sex are presented. All of these data are developed in terms of the median earnings for each occupation.

Then the trends from 1975 to 1981 are shown by sex and for Whites, Blacks, and Hispanics using the mean earnings and by sex using the medians. At this point I switch, of necessity, to the new occupational classifications, and report the trends by sex and race/ethnic group again using the means and also by sex using the median, for the period from 1982 to 1985. All of this employs published annual data. Finally, in order to display some more recent information and since some data are published in a more timely fashion that the general income data or even the annual earnings data, I switch to annual estimates based upon weekly earnings (again of full-time workers), to indicate, at least on a preliminary basis, the trends from 1985 to the first quarter of 1988 by sex using medians.

Thus, while it is not appropriate to make comparisons across, for example, the whole period from 1975 to 1985, it is possible to look at the trends from 1975 to 1981 and from 1982 to 1985. In every case, I first adjusted the earnings to express them in terms of real 1985 dollars of purchasing power to render them comparable to each other and to the data already presented in earlier sections, at least on that basis. In this manner, I think the reader will be able to obtain a rather clear and correct impression of what has been happening to occupational earnings across the time period that is the focus of this book.

The Trends from 1960 to 1981
Looking first at Table 5-8, we see that from 1960 to 1967 and from then to 1973, earnings increased fairly substantially in virtually every occupational category and for men and women, Whites,

Blacks, and Hispanics. On a percentage basis--and we must be quick to recognize that these percentages apply to different initial starting positions--we also see that from 1967 to 1973 the earnings of Blacks tended to increase at a faster rate than did that of Whites, while those of White women, especially those in the white collar occupations, increased at a slower pace than that of White males.

This impression is confirmed when one examines the detailed data involving the ratios between the sexes and between Blacks and Whites for each occupation in each of the given years. Due to space limitations these data are not shown, but they indicate that median female earnings as a percentage of those of males across the occupational spectrum decreased from 60.4 percent in 1960, to 57.8 percent in 1967, to 56.6 percent in 1973. There was a modest increase of 1.7 percentage points in the Managerial, et al. occupations and of 2.0 percentage points among Professionals over the full 13 year period; but the ratio in even these two white collar occupational categories were lower in 1973 than they had been in 1967--that is, most of the improvement in the relative position of women in the white collar occupations occurred between 1960 and 1967. Indeed, the overall deterioration in the position of women from 1967 to 1973 would have been even more severe if there had not been some modest improvement in the blue collar and service sectors during this period.

On the other hand, the detailed data indicate that there was substantial improvement in the relative position of Blacks, both male and female, across the entire occupational spectrum during the 1967-73 period. Some examples make this clear: as between Black and White males there was an improvement of 15.1 percentage points among Managers, et al., 5.7 points among Professionals, 7.5 points among Craftsmen, and 9.1 points among (non-farm) Laborers. Thus, overall, across the full range of occupations, Black male median earnings as a percentage of that of White males increased from 64.6 percent in 1967 to 68.4 percent in 1973; while that of Black women compared to White women increased even more dramatically from 74.6 percent to 85.3 percent.

However, from 1973 to 1981 there was a major shift in direction. Table 5-8 makes this quite clear. Beginning in the period 1973-75 and continuing until 1981, real median and mean earnings begin to fall in virtually every occupational category. Among Black males the decrease is dramatic--reaching to as much as 12 to over 16 percent in the six short years from 1975 to 1981. However, the situation for White women is rather different. Over the full occupational range, their mean earnings drop only 1.8 percent in the 1975-81 period, in part due to substantial increases in the Sales (and also in the poorly paid Personal Household Service) occupations and due to smaller decreases (than their White male counterparts) in the Managerial and (non-household) Service occupations. Overall, the position of White women, relative to that of White men, improves during this period, albeit to only 59.2 percent (in terms of median earnings), which is still below the 60.4 percent figure for 1960.

The Trends Since 1982

Turning to the data that is organized in terms of the new occupational classifications, that is the data since 1982, in Table 5-9 we can observe an overview of what has occurred from 1982 to 1985, with some preliminary figures for the period from 1985 to early 1988. Following the inflation of the late 1970s and early 1980s and the Reagan recession of 1981-82, we see that real earnings began to increase in most occupational categories. However, within this general pattern, again, there are some important variations.

Looking at the white collar occupations, we see that the mean earnings of White males increased at a considerably faster pace (and, of course, on top of an already higher basis) than did those of Black or Hispanic males. The result (documented in detailed work that, again, is not shown due to space limitations) is that Black mean earnings in virtually every white collar occupational category we are examining fell as a percentage of that of White males. However, the relative position of Black males improved in virtually every blue collar field and in the protective services (while worsening in the other service occupations and in farming), with the net result that the overall mean position of Black males improved a modest 0.7 percentage points from 70.1 percent in 1982 to 70.8 percent in 1985.

Hispanic males fared far worse than did their Black counterparts when the relative position of Hispanic males is compared to that of White males during this period. With the exception of a very modest (0.4 percentage point) improvement in the Administrative Support/Clerical occupations, Hispanic males fell farther behind their White counterparts in every other white collar occupation, as well as in occupations across the blue collar and service areas. The net result was that the relative position of the mean earnings of Hispanic males fell 4.1 percentage points, from 74.0 percent to 69.9 percent of that of White males, in just these three years.[7]

Among women, Blacks lost ground to Whites in every white collar occupation except for Administrative Support/Clerical, although the mean earnings of Black women in the managerial fields remained slightly (1.2 percent) above that of the White women. They also lost ground throughout the blue collar and service occupations, with the net result that Black female mean earnings fell from 91.6 percent (in 1982) to 89.6 percent (in 1985) of that of White females across all occupations.

Unlike their male counterparts, Hispanic women held their own compared to White women, led by relatively larger improvements in their mean earnings in the managerial and professional occupations, as well as in the Administrative Support/Clerical and (Other) Service occupational categories. These gains largely offset slippage in the Sales and blue collar areas, such that their overall position held just about constant (84.6 percent in 1982 and 84.5 percent in 1985).

Turning to the issue of female/male earnings ratios and in particular to the situation of White women, we find that the period since 1982, on average, continued the pattern begun in 1973 of relative improvement of White female earnings compared to those of

White males, but with considerable unevenness. In the white collar area, white women saw their relative mean position improve among Professionals, Technicians, and Sales occupations, while slipping a bit among Managers and among Administrative Support/Clerical positions. In the blue collar and service area the results were also mixed, but the net result was an improvement from 59.8 percent of mean White male earnings in 1982 to 61.3 percent in 1985. Black women saw their position relative to Black men deteriorate, but very slightly (from 78.1 percent to 77.5 percent), while Hispanic women saw an even smaller increase (from 68.4 percent to 68.6 percent) compared to Hispanic men.

Overall, looking at median female to male earnings across the full occupational spectrum, which is one of the few ways that allows us to make some long-term comparisons, we find that in 1982 women achieved a major benchmark--at 60.6 percent of median male earnings they had finally surpassed the point (60.4 percent) they had reached twenty two years earlier in 1960. By 1985, that figure had increased further to 62.1 percent. Looking at the preliminary data for the period 1985 to early 1988, it would seem that this pattern is continuing, though, as before, with some unevenness.[8] Their relative position appears to have improved by 1 to 3 percentage points in most of the white collar occupations--to as much as 72.6 percent in the Professional Specialties. However, among the executives and managers, it slipped by .5 percentage points to 64.1 percent in early 1988. There was considerable improvement for women in the Protective Services occupations, reaching 84.8 percent in the preliminary 1988 figures, but significant deterioration among the "Other" services (from 81.7 percent to 75.1 percent). The picture is also quite mixed in the blue collar area, with improvement in the Precision Production, etc. and in the Machine Operators, etc. groups, but serious deterioration in the Transportation, etc. and Handlers, etc. occupational areas where the median weekly earnings of women actually fell by 11.6 percent and 13.8 percent, respectively (see Table 5-9).

Thus, when we look at the data by occupational categories, on the one hand, the period since 1982 would appear to generally be consistent with that from 1973 to 1981 in that women, especially White women, have continued to improve their position relative to White males; whereas Blacks have at best about maintained their position on average, while suffering serious deterioration in the white collar occupations, and whereas Hispanics males saw their relative position worsen across the occupational spectrum. (However, it should not be forgotten that, as the figures in Table 5-6 for 1985 demonstrated, both Black and Hispanic males, as well as White males, continue, on average, to earn more than women of any race/ethnic group, across the full range of occupations.) Overall, the analysis of the earnings data broken down by major occupational categories is consistent with the picture painted in the first section of this chapter of the changing patterns of sexual and racial/ethnic discrimination in earnings, especially since the early 1970s.

On the other hand, the period since 1982 is quite different from the period between 1973 and 1981 in that the mean earnings in most occupational categories have been increasing in the most recent period; whereas, they had been falling during the earlier one. However, as Table 5-9 and our earlier discussion points out, there have been a scattering of occupations that have seen average earnings continue to fall, especially for some groups of workers, especially within the blue collar area and within Private Household Service and agriculture.

One question which is impossible to answer definitively is whether the increases since 1982 have restored occupational earnings to the peaks first reached in 1973. The difficulty is, of course, the changed occupational classification system and the lack of compatibility between the data since 1982 and that in 1973. However, as a very rough comparison, one can look at the 1973 median earnings by sex expressed in 1985 dollars, comparing occupational groupings that seem generally comparable to other groupings in 1985. Such an effort suggests that by 1985 the median earnings, especially of males, in most of the higher paying occupations had surpassed by a small margin (5 to 10 percent) those of 1973, but that in some of the lower paying occupations median real earnings in 1985 were little higher, and in some cases considerably lower, than in 1973. Even in some of the fairly well paying white collar occupations there would appear to have been little or no improvement compared to 1973.

While these are somewhat impressionistic observations, they are supported by the further observation that the median real (1985 dollars) income across all the occupations of fully employed males and females in 1973 was $27,081 and $15,337, respectively; while the comparable figures across all occupations in 1985 was $24,195 for males and $15,624 for females, leaving men about 11 percent below and women about 2 percent above the 1973 peaks (which, by the way, further supports the finding that fully employed women, on average, have been narrowing the gender gap during this period). Thus, the improved occupational earnings since 1982 which are so often touted, especially by politicians associated with the Reagan and Bush administrations, do not appear so glorious when we realize how far those earning fell, in real terms, during the period from 1973 to 1981. Here again it would appear that many Americans are living no better in the mid to late 1980s than they had been back in the early 1970s.

THE PATTERN OF EARNINGS AMONG INDUSTRIES

Detailed data concerning average (mean) hourly earnings and hours worked by major industrial area are available on a much more timely basis than much of the other data that I have been examining. As of this writing, data are already available for the full year 1987, which I will use, and there are even preliminary data for the first quarter of 1988 to which I will make reference. This time we will begin by looking first at the historical pattern from 1960 through the first quarter of 1988, highlighting 1972, which was the peak year for average hourly earnings. Then we will examine in more detail the picture painted by the 1987 data as to the level and distribution of purchasing power implicit in these earnings figures.

The Historical Pattern from 1960 to 1987

We start by looking at Table 5-10, and noting that these figures are for what are referred to as "production and nonsupervisory workers in private nonagricultural employment," who constituted, in 1987, some 85 percent of all private, non-agricultural employment.[9] These figures are broken down by major industry so that we can look for significant variations in the pattern of earnings between industries over time and in any given year.

Looking first at the upper portion of Table 5-10, and focusing initially on the historical pattern, one finds that from 1960 to 1972 there were substantial increases in the average hourly earnings (measured in real, inflation adjusted, 1985 dollars) in virtually every industrial category--with an overall average increase of 25.3 percent over the 12 year period, or about 2.1 percent per year. When one looks at weekly earnings over this same period (see Table 5-11), one again finds increases in every industrial category, but, except in Mining, the increases in weekly earnings are less, in many cases considerably less, than the increases in hourly earnings due to the shortening of the work week. Overall, weekly wages increased by only 20.1 percent over the 12 year period, for an average of 1.7 percent per year.

However, for the 15 year period from 1972 to 1987, a very different picture emerges. Looking again first at hourly earnings (Table 5-10), one finds that in only one industry, Mining, was there any increase at all, and then only 3.5 percent over a decade and a half. In all of the others, the real hourly earnings actually *fell*, by more than 22 percent in the Construction industry, and by 10.3 percent overall. In fact, if one looks at the overall average hourly earnings in real terms, year by year (not shown) since the peak in 1972, one finds that except for modest increases for three years in the late 1970s and for one year following the recession of 1981-82, there has been a steady deterioration. Preliminary data for the first quarter of 1988, shows that this downward spiral is continuing.[10]

But this hides the even worse picture that emerges when one turns to the weekly earnings data. Here one finds that on average, weekly earnings fell by more than 15 percent over this 15-year period, led by an astounding 27.9 percent fall in the Retail Trade industry. Due to a slight increases in weekly hours worked, the Construction and Manufacturing industries demonstrated a bit slower decrease in terms of weekly earnings than hourly earnings, but all of the other industries had poorer performances in terms of weekly earnings due to the reduction in hours worked per week. This evidence makes it quite clear that the problems discussed earlier of the fall in median family income and of the growing numbers of families and individuals living at poverty or low income levels were not caused simply by growing unemployment and layoffs due to the short-term effects of the recession in the early 1980s. A much more fundamental restructuring of the American economy has been underway since the early 1970s.

The changes over the entire 27-year period, reported in both tables, demonstrate (Table 5-10) that the increases in hourly earnings from 1960-1972 were not quite annulled by the decreases since then. Thus, the 1987 hourly figures stand 12.4 percent above those for 1960, for an average rate of growth of less than 0.4 percent. This is hardly a sterling picture of increased real earning over a 27-year period.

However, the even more relevant weekly figures (Table 5-11) paint an even starker picture. Here, the combination of falling hourly earnings (since 1972) and falling hours of work (since 1960, as shown in Table 3-10) result in real weekly earnings in 1987 that are only 1.3 percent above those in 1960, on average, across the entire spectrum of industries in America. This is equivalent to a pitiful 0.05 percent average annual increase in weekly earnings over a period of more than a quarter of a century. Is it any wonder that so many families have seen little or no improvement in their standard of living, unless they have increased the number of persons working to support that family, or that so many families with only one earner are in such economic difficulty?

It should be noted that the average figure for the 27-year period quoted just above was heavily influenced by the two fastest growing industrial sectors in the American economy, Retail Trade and Other Services. Retail Trade saw its average weekly earnings *fall* by 24.6 percent. This is the industry which has been growing rapidly in employment over this entire period (see Table 3-7) to stand at 18.1 percent of total nonagricultural employment (21.7 percent of private nonagricultural employment) in 1987. The Other Services sector did experience an increase in real weekly wages, but only of 2.9 percent over the 27-years; and this in what by 1987 was by far the largest of the listed sectors, standing at 28.4 percent of private and 23.6 percent of total nonagricultural employment. These figures could only be partially offset by the unusually good performance of the Mining industry (a not so glorious 30.6 percent higher weekly wages over the 27-year period) in which employment has been stagnant in absolute terms and steadily falling in relative terms, such that by 1987 it stood at only 0.8 percent of private and 0.7 percent of total nonagricultural employment. All of the other industries also displayed weekly wages in 1987 that were higher in 1987 than in 1960, by 3.7 percent to 18.4 percent.

A Closer Look at the Data for 1987

Looking more closely at the data for 1987 in the lower part of Table 5-10, we see the impact of these hourly and weekly earnings on the distribution of annual income. Here, I have constructed two columns, one showing the annual equivalent earnings given the actual average hours actually worked per week in each industry, and the other showing the potential annual income if someone had worked a full 40 hours per week, in both cases for 52 weeks. The 52-week assumption avoids the issue of part-year employment. Both of these figures are expressed in 1985 constant dollars of purchasing power, so as to enable us to compare them to the rest of the data presented in this book.

With the exception of the Manufacturing and Mining industries, where the actual average hours per week exceed the 40 hour standard by an hour or two due to overtime, the annual equivalent based upon 40 hours of work per week *exceeds* the annual equivalent based upon the *actual* hours worked per week by as much as 36 percent (in Retail Trade). For all industries taken as a whole, the 40-hour per week annual figure of $17,742 stands some 15 percent above the annual figure of $15,436 built upon the *actual* average hours worked per week. This is yet another measure of the effect of the declining average work week in the U.S. (recall Table 3-10), which has remained below the cutoff for full-time work, 35 hours, since 1985.

Finally, the last two columns in the lower part of Table 5-10 express the *highest* of these two annual equivalents as percentages of the BLS Low or Minimum Adequacy standard for 1985 (discussed earlier) of $20,207 and of their Modest but Adequate (or Moderate) standard of $30,177. Thus, the percentages in these last two columns are extremely conservative and generous in that they assume hours of work of either 40 or the actual number, whichever is more, and in that they assume that these earnings were received for all 52 weeks of the year. Even so, the picture they paint is quite disturbing to say the least.

In these last two columns, one finds that, on average, workers in only three industries: Mining, Construction, and Transportation/ Public Utilities were even potentially able to exceed the Minimum Adequacy Budget and none were likely, on average, to be able to reach the Moderate level, even if they did work full-time, full-year in the very generous sense in which that was defined. To be sure, since these are averages, some workers did earn more. On the other hand, these earnings figures are means, not medians; hence, they are already high due to the few workers who earn a great deal, compared to the figures that could be developed if one were able to use data on median earnings. In light of these results, which are very conservative and optimistic, is it any wonder that most families need two breadwinners in order to have any hope of living at all comfortably.?[11]

CONCLUSION

Thus, overall, earnings by industry show a pattern quite consistent with that found when we examined the earnings on an occupational basis. Together, these figures demonstrate that the problems of low wages, low earnings, and low income discussed throughout the earlier portions of this book are not the artifacts of something that occurred primarily in certain industries or occupations within our economy. Rather they demonstrate the widespread, systemic nature of the factors that have caused this deterioration in the relative position of a growing proportion of our population.

Moreover, the material in this chapter, taken as a whole, indicate that even when we look at full-time, full-year workers, abstracting from the problems of unemployment and of part-time and part-year employment, the importance of the changes in the U.S. economy since the early 1970s that became so obvious in the first few chapters remain. We also see that the relatively poor positions of women in general, and of Blacks and Hispanics, continue to be evident when we look at the experience of those who are fully employed, regardless of their level of education and across the full spectrum of industries and occupations. Again, this is not to minimize the burdens of unemployment and underemployment that are disproportionately borne by women and minorities in America. Rather, the point is to again emphasize that the problems facing this nationthat result from the distribution of income are far more fundamental and more deeply systemic and structural than can be addressed by simple make-work projects or job training efforts aimed at the unemployed. What the analyses in this chapter demonstrate is that even if we somehow overcame the problems of unemployment and underemployment,

--we would still have considerable poverty and low income populations,

--we would still have vast differences in income between men and women and especially between White men and everybody else,

--we would still find that education did not close the gender or racial/ethnic gaps in income,

--we would still find that families with one earner could, on average, live above the low income level only if that earner were a White male, and that, on average, even such families could not live at the moderate level, and

--we would still face the problem of the need to reverse a number of destructive trends within the American economy: the falling hourly earnings, the shrinking workweek (unless we are willing to pay more for less work), the growing disparity in the income and earnings of minorities.

Merely moving things along a bit faster in the same direction our economy has been going in recent years and with the same policies will simply not solve these problems.

Thus, if this nation is seriously going to go about the business of addressing these problems in income distribution, we are going to have to undertake the rather complete restructuring of the manner in which wages and salaries are determined, across the full range of occupations and industries, and with particular attention to the earnings of women and minorities. This is no small undertaking. But if we are to avoid the movement toward two societies--one quite affluent, mostly White, and typified by two earners or more per family, and the other consistently living below a reasonably defined low income level or even in abject poverty, and often, but by no means always, supported by a single breadwinner, we must make the effort.

NOTES

1. This is also referred to by the Census Bureau as "Year-round, full-time workers."

2. Actually, the ratio of Black female to White female income continued to fall in 1986, reaching 87.5 percent, but then rebounded almost four percentage points to 91.2 percent in 1987. It remains to be seen whether the results for 1987 are the start of a new trend or but a short, one year aberration along a continuing path of deterioration.

3. There was a modest improvement in the ratios (for both males and females) from 1985 to 1986, but the deterioration from 1986 to 1987 more than wiped out the gains in 1986. Thus, the 1987 figures stand well below those for 1985 and conform to the trend that has occurred rather steadily since 1975.

4. Data for 1987 broken down by race/ethnic group and sex were not yet available as this was being edited.

5. The data do not allow for distinctions between, for example, a one year masters degree program and a full Ph.D., although this clearly would need to be done in a study that focused more on this topic.

6. There were not enough Hispanic male Technicians to report meaningful averages, but the patterns suggest that those in that group probably earned as much, if not more, than Blacks in that occupation.

7. I have not made any attempt in this work to differentiate between the earnings patterns of Hispanics that have been in the United States during the whole period in question, and those that are recent immigrants. At various points in this book it is quite likely that part of the cause of the changing income figures for Hispanics may be the fluctuations in immigration flows.

8. It should be noted that the two sets of figures for 1985 are not directly comparable. The ones used in the 1982-85 comparisons are for mean and median annual earnings of workers who actually worked full-time, full-year. The figures used in the 1985-88 comparisons are median weekly earnings of workers who *typically* work full-time, but who may or may not have actually worked full-year.

9. This broad category is defined by the Bureau of Labor Statistics to include (1) all "production and related workers in the manufacturing and mining" industries, (2) all "construction workers in the construction" industry and (3) all "nonsupervisory employees in private service producing industries." The first group includes "working supervisors and all nonsupervisory workers [including group leaders and trainees] engaged in fabricating, processing, assembling, inspecting, receiving, storing, handling, packing, warehousing, shipping, trucking, hauling, maintenance, repair, janitorial, guard service, product development, recordkeeping and other services closely associated [with production]." The construction workers include all "working supervisors, qualified craft workers, mechanics, apprentices, helpers, laborers. . . ." The third group is perhaps the broadest. "Nonsupervisory employees

include employees (not above the working supervisory level) such as office and clerical workers, repairers, salespersons, operators, drivers, physicians, lawyers, accountants, nurses, social workers, research aides, teachers, drafters, photographers, beauticians, musicians, restaurant workers, custodial workers, attendants, line installers and repairers, laborers, janitors, guards and other employees at similar occupational levels . . ." (U.S. Department of Labor 1988: pp. 170-171). The anomaly in this last classification is that, for example, it would not include a purely clerical person in the construction industry, but would include clerical persons in service industries. That is, the classification is both industry and occupation specific. Nevertheless, it is the basis for one of the broadest and most commonly used barometers of industrial earnings.

    10. Om fact data available during the final editing of this book make it clear that this pattern continued into 1989.

    11. I can not help but to urge the reader to again reread the discussion of Marx's argument as to the determination of wages which was outlined in Endnote 28 to Chapter 4. It seems sadly prophetic in light of much of the data presented in this chapter.

Table 5-1
Table 5-1
Median Income by Race/Ethnic Group and Sex
of Full-Year, Full-Time Workers
and Ratios Between Incomes:
1939-1987 (in current dollars)

	White	Black			White	Black	Hispanic
1939				**1970**			
Male	$1,419	$639		Male	$9,447	$6,435	n/a
Female	863	327		Female	5,536	4,536	n/a
1949				**1975**			
Male	3,160	1,829		Male	13,459	9,848	$9,588
Female	2,068	1,049		Female	7,737	7,392	6,577
1955				**1980**			
Male	4,458	2,831		Male	19,720	13,875	13,790
Female	2,870	1,637		Female	11,703	10,915	9,887
1960				**1985**			
Male	5,572	3,683		Male	25,693	17,971	17,344
Female	3,377	2,289		Female	16,482	14,590	13,522
1965				**1987**			
Male	6,693	4,172		Male	27,463	19,385	17,008
Female	3,995	2,793		Female	17,775	16,211	14,191

Income Ratios

	1	2	3	4	5	6
Year	Black Male/ White Male	Black Female/ White Female	Black Female/ Black Male	White Female/ White Male	White Female/ Black Male	Black Female/ White Male
1939	45.0%	37.9%	51.2%	60.8%	135.1%	23.0%
1949	57.9	50.7	57.4	65.4	113.1	33.1
1955	62.3	57.0	57.8	64.4	101.4	36.7
1960	66.1	67.8	62.2	60.6	91.7	41.1
1965	62.3	69.9	67.0	59.7	95.8	41.7
1970	68.1	81.9	70.5	58.6	86.0	48.0
1975	73.2	95.5	75.1	57.4	78.6	54.9
1980	70.4	93.3	78.7	59.3	84.3	55.3
1985	69.9	88.5	81.2	64.1	91.7	56.8
1987	70.6	91.2	83.6	64.7	91.7	59.0

Income Ratios

	1	2	3	4	5	6
Year	Hisp Male/ White Male	Hisp Female/ White Female	Hisp Female/ Hisp Male	Hisp Female/ White Male	Hisp Male/ Black Male	Hisp Female/ Black Female
1975	71.2%	85.0%	68.6%	48.9%	97.4%	89.0%
1980	69.6	84.5	71.7	40.1	99.4	90.6
1985	67.5	82.0	78.0	52.6	96.5	92.7
1987	65.1	79.8	83.3	54.2	92.2	91.9

Notes: For 1939-65, "Blacks" is actually "Nonwhites." The dollar figures for 1939 & 1949
are median wage and salary income, not total income. For 1939-75, age is 14 and
over, since then is 15 and over. Figures for 1987 are preliminary.

Source: U.S. Department of Commerce 1988c and 1987a,d and earlier numbers in the
P-60 series.

Table 5-2
Median Earnings by Race/Ethnic Group and Sex
and Ratios Between Earnings
for Full-Year, Full-Time Workers:
1975-1986 (in current dollars)

	White	Black	Hispanic
1975			
Male	$13,054	$9,707	$9,413
Female	7,513	7,237	6,431
1980			
Male	19,157	13,547	13,558
Female	11,277	10,672	9,679
1985			
Male	25,062	17,479	17,051
Female	15,796	14,308	13,066
1986			
Male	25,927	18,339	16,815
	16,442	14,734	13,836

Earnings Ratios

Year	1 Black Male/ White Male	2 Black Female/ White Female	3 Black Female/ Black Male	4 White Female/ White Male	5 White Female/ Black Male	6 Black Female/ White Male
1975	74.4%	96.3%	74.6%	57.6%	77.4%	55.4%
1980	70.7	94.6	78.8	58.9	83.2	55.7
1985	69.7	90.6	81.9	63.0	90.4	57.1
1986	70.7	89.6	80.3	63.4	90.0	56.8

Earnings Ratios

Year	1 Hisp Male/ White Male	2 Hisp Female/ White Female	3 Hisp Female/ Hisp Male	4 Hisp Female/ White Male	5 Hisp Male/ Black Male	6 Hisp Female/ Black Female
1975	72.1%	85.6%	68.3%	49.3%	97.0%	88.9%
1980	70.8	85.8	71.4	50.5	100.0	90.7
1985	68.0	82.7	76.6	52.1	97.6	91.3
1986	64.9	84.3	82.3	53.4	91.7	93.9

Notes: For 1975, figures are for age 14 and older; since 1980, they are for age 15 and
older. These figures are for Total Earnings, not Total Income, the difference
being that unearned (property) income must be added to earnings to get income.

Source: U.S. Department of Commerce 1988c and 1987a and earlier numbers in the P-60 series.

144

Table 5-3
Median Income by Sex, Race, and Education
for Full-Year, Full-Time Workers
Age 25 and Older:
1986 (in current dollars)

| | Years of School Completed | | | | | | |
| | Elementary | | High School | | College | | |
	7 or Less	8	9 - 11	12	13 - 15	16	17 or More
White Male	$14,603	$18,847	$20,821	$25,390	$28,634	$35,201	$39,857
Black Male	14,125	16,470	15,716	18,700	23,317	26,156	35,457
Gap (WM-BM)	$478	$2,377	$5,105	$6,690	$5,317	$9,045	$4,400
Black Male/ White Male	96.7%	87.4%	75.5%	73.7%	81.4%	74.3%	89.0%
White Female	$10,399	$11,463	$12,632	$16,148	$19,064	$22,428	$27,242
Black Female	9,260	9,839	11,423	14,869	15,916	21,884	26,290
Gap (WF-BF)	$1,139	$1,624	$1,209	$1,279	$3,148	$544	$952
Black Female/ White Female	89.0%	85.8%	90.4%	92.1%	83.5%	97.6%	96.5%
White Female/ White Male	71.2%	60.8%	60.7%	63.6%	66.6%	63.7%	68.3%
Black Female/ Black Male	65.6	59.7	72.7	79.5	68.3	83.7	74.1
Black Female/ White Male	63.4	52.2	54.9	58.6	55.6	62.2	66.0

Source: U.S. Department of Commerce 1988a.

145

Table 5-4
Ratios of Median Income by Sex, Race, and Education
for Full-Year, Full-Time Workers
Age 25 and Older:
1975, 1980, 1985, and 1986

Ratio	Year	Elementary		High School		College		
		7 or Less	8	9 - 11	12	13 - 15	16	17 or More
BM/WM	1975*	85.9%	90.2%	75.2%	82.8%	84.3%	70.2%	79.4%
	1980	84.7	78.1	69.9	78.9	78.7	72.0	85.3
	1985	85.4	74.4	79.2	74.3	71.0	79.2	78.2
	1986	96.7	87.4	75.5	73.7	81.4	74.3	89.0
BF/WF	1975	87.6	80.8	93.6	102.3	102.7	94.5	87.8
	1980	105.1	n/a	93.0	94.6	89.7	97.9	102.2
	1985	87.1	105.6	93.7	87.9	87.1	91.6	95.1
	1986	89.0	85.8	90.4	92.1	83.5	97.6	96.5
WF/WM	1975	58.5	55.3	55.6	56.4	59.3	57.8	66.6
	1980	62.6	60.4	58.0	58.6	62.0	61.4	65.1
	1985	66.4	59.5	61.0	63.3	66.4	64.8	65.3
	1986	71.2	60.8	60.7	63.6	66.6	63.7	68.3
BF/BM	1975	59.7	49.5	69.2	73.3	72.4	77.8	73.6
	1980	77.7	n/a	77.3	70.3	70.7	83.5	77.9
	1985	67.4	84.5	72.2	74.8	81.4	75.0	79.4
	1986	65.6	59.7	72.7	79.5	68.3	83.7	74.1

Notes: * 1975 data are for those age 18 and older, data since 1980 are for
age 25 and older. BM = Black Male, WM = White Male, BF = Black
Female, WF = White Female, n/a = not available due to the small
numbers of persons (Black females) with this amount of education
working full-time, full-year.

Source: U.S. Department of Commerce 1988a, 1987a and earlier numbers in
the P-60 series.

Table 5-5
Median Income by Sex, Race, and Education
for All Persons Age 25 and Older:
1986 (in current dollars)

	Elementary		High School		College		
	7 or Less	8	9 - 11	12	13 - 15	16	17 or More
White Male	$8,639	$11,468	$14,000	$20,468	$24,536	$31,815	$36,625
Black Male	6,030	7,138	11,318	14,465	18,917	21,827	29,019
Gap (WM-BM)	$2,609	$4,330	$2,682	$6,003	$5,619	$9,988	$7,606
Black Male/ White Male	69.8%	62.2%	80.8%	70.7%	77.1%	68.6%	79.2%
White Female	$4,840	$5,349	$5,938	$8,388	$11,408	$15,865	$21,376
Black Female	4,303	4,572	5,190	8,244	12,520	18,845	23,595
Gap (WF-BF)	$537	$777	$748	$144	($1,112)	($2,980)	($2,219)
Black Female/ White Female	88.9%	85.5%	87.4%	98.3%	109.7%	118.8%	110.4%
White Female/ White Male	56.0%	46.6%	42.4%	41.0%	46.5%	49.9%	58.4%
Black Female/ Black Male	71.4%	64.1%	45.9%	57.0%	66.2%	86.3%	81.3%
Black Female/ White Male	49.8%	39.9%	37.1%	40.3%	51.0%	59.2%	64.4%

Header span: *Years of School Completed*

Source: U.S. Department of Commerce 1988a.

Table 5-6
Mean Earnings by Occupation, Sex,
and Race/Ethnic Group and
Median Earnings by Occupation and Sex
for Full-Year, Full-Time Workers
1985

Occupation	Male Means White	Black	Hispanic	All	Male Median All
White Collar					
Executive, Administrative & Managerial	$38,777	$28.073	$28,435	$38,167	$32,872
Professional Specialties	37,992	29,174	31,719	37,657	32,688
Technicians & Related Support	28,626	23,709	NA	28,165	(*)
Sales	30,586	18,984	22,205	30,103	25,445
Admin. Support, incl Clerical	24,924	19,730	19,186	24,064	22,997
Blue Collar					
Precision Production, Craft & Repair	24,653	20,790	20,364	24,396	23,269
Machine Oper. and Assemblers	22,215	19,752	16,906	21,867	(*)
Transp. and Material Moving	23,312	19,026	18,453	22,672	(*)
Handlers, Helpers & Laborers	17,221	15,002	14,266	16,764	15,755
Service					
Private Household Services	NA	NA	NA	NA	NA
Protective Services	24,872	20,271	25,615	24,218	23,877
Other Services	15,679	14,207	13,534	15,265	13,628
Farming, Forestry & Fishing	11,195	9,438	11,220	11,230	10,361
All Occupations	28,159	19,949	19,692	27,430	24,195

Occupation	Female Means White	Black	Hispanic	All	Female Median All
White Collar					
Executive, Administrative & Managerial	$22,254	$22,529	$20,687	$22,246	$20,565
Professional Specialties	22,984	20,644	22,158	22,838	21,781
Technicians & Related Support	19,473	17,168	NA	19,196	(*)
Sales	15,627	12,500	12,038	15,368	12,682
Admin. Support, incl Clerical	15,704	16,163	15,345	15,790	15,157
Blue Collar					
Precision Production, Craft & Repair	17,885	14,469	15,177	17,329	15,093
Machine Oper. and Assemblers	13,939	13,595	11,175	13,807	(*)
Transp. and Material Moving	14,339	NA	NA	14,269	(*)
Handlers, Helpers & Laborers	13,260	NA	NA	13,248	12,704
Service					
Private Household Services	5,993	NA	NA	5,926	5,888
Protective Services	19,102	NA	NA	19,097	18,030
Other Services	10,841	10,992	10,501	10,894	10,291
Farming, Forestry & Fishing	6,157	NA	NA	6,275	6,783
All Occupations	17,253	15,459	14,576	17,033	15,624

Notes: NA - Data not available due to small number of persons in this category.
(*) - Data not reported in this category. However, for all Technicians, Sales, and Admin. Support combined: Median was Male: $24,957, Female: $15,117. Similarly, for Machine Oper., Transp., and Handlers combined: Median was Male: $19,648, Female: $12,309.
Source: U.S. Department of Commerce 1987a.

148

Table 5-7
Ratios of Occupational Earnings
by Sex and Race/Ethnic Group
for Full-Year, Full-Time Workers
1985

Occupation	Ratios Between Racial/Ethnic Groups by Sex					
	BM/WM	BF/WF	BF/WM	HM/WM	HF/WF	HF/WM
White Collar						
Executive, Administrative						
& Managerial	72.4%	101.2%	58.1%	73.3%	93.0%	53.3%
Professional Specialties	76.8	89.8	54.3	83.5	96.4	58.3
Technicians & Related Support	82.8	88.2	60.0	NA	NA	NA
Sales	62.1	80.0	40.9	72.6	77.0	39.4
Admin. Support, incl Clerical	79.2	102.9	64.8	77.0	97.4	61.6
Blue Collar						
Precision Production, Craft						
& Repair	84.3	80.9	58.7	82.6	84.6	61.6
Machine Oper. and Assemblers	88.9	97.5	61.2	76.1	80.2	50.3
Transp. and Material Moving	81.6	NA	NA	79.2	NA	NA
Handlers, Helpers & Laborers	87.1	NA	NA	82.8	NA	NA
Service						
Private Household Services	NA	NA	NA	NA	NA	NA
Protective Services	81.5	NA	NA	103.0	NA	NA
Other Services	90.6	1014	70.1	86.3	96.9	67.0
Farming, Forestry & Fishing	84.3	NA	NA	100.2	NA	NA
All Occupations	70.8	89.6	54.6	69.9	84.5	51.8

Occupation	Ratios Between Sexes by Race/Ethnic Group				Median Earn
	Mean Earnings				
	WF/WM	BF/BM	HF/HM	All F/M	All F/M
White Collar					
Executive, Administrative					
& Managerial	57.4%	80.3%	72.8%	58.3%	62.6%
Professional Specialties	60.5	70.8	69.9	60.6	66.6
Technicians & Related Support	68.0	72.4	NA	68.2	(*)
Sales	51.1	65.8	54.2	51.1	49.8
Admin. Support, incl Clerical	63.0	81.9	80.0	65.6	65.9
Blue Collar					
Precision Production, Craft					
& Repair	72.5	69.6	74.5	71.0	64.9
Machine Oper. and Assemblers	62.7	68.8	66.1	63.1	(*)
Transp. and Material Moving	61.5	NA	NA	64.5	(*)
Handlers, Helpers & Laborers	77.0	NA	NA	79.0	80.6
Service					
Private Household Services	NA	NA	NA	NA	NA
Protective Services	76.8	NA	NA	78.9	75.5
Other Services	69.1	77.4	77.6	71.4	75.5
Farming, Forestry & Fishing	55.0	NA	NA	55.9	65.5
All Occupations	61.3	77.5	74.0	62.1	64.6

Notes: WM = White Male, WF = White Female, BM = Black Male, BF = Black Female,
HM = Hispanic Male, HF = Hispanic Female. NA = Data not available due
to small number of persons in one or both categories involved in the
ratio. All ratios are between mean earnings figures unless otherwise
noted. (*) Data not reported in this category. However, for all
Technicians, Sales, and Admin. support the ratio is 60.6% and similarly
for Machine Oper., Transp., and Handlers it is 62.6%.

Source: All ratios are computed from earnings figures reported in Table 5-6.

149

Table 5-8

Percentage Changes in Constant 1985 Dollar Occupational Earnings, by Sex and Race/Ethnic Group

1960-67, 1967-73, 1973-75, 1975-81

| | 1960-1967 | | 1967-1973 | | | | | |
| | Male | Female | Male | | | Female | | |
Occupation	All	All	All	White	Black	All	White	Black
White Collar								
Managers, Officials								
& Proprietors	18.2%	23.8%	17.3%	17.6%	45.7%	15.9%	13.7%	NA
Professionals								
& Technical Wkers	19.1	25.1	9.9	9.5	18.6	8.1	7.3	12.8%
Sales Workers	14.9	19.1	19.2	19.4	NA	7.7	6.9	NA
Clerical Workers	11.5	8.6	18.3	18.7	21.8	8.1	7.9	10.9
Blue Collar								
Craftsmen & Foremen	11.2	NA	13.3	13.2	25.2	22.8	21.6	NA
Operatives	10.4	5.8	13.2	13.4	19.8	10.9	11.2	7.9
Laborers (non-farm)	18.6	NA	15.0	11.0	25.8	17.0	NA	NA
Service								
Private Household	NA	-6.5	NA	NA	NA	19.6	13.8	26.9
Other Service	14.4	3.5	9.0	11.4	17.4	18.8	16.5	26.1
Farm								
Farmers and Farm Mng	30.0	NA	54.2	53.0	NA	NA	NA	NA
Farm Laborers	23.1	NA	37.9	27.3	NA	NA	NA	NA
All Employed Civilians	15.9	10.8	17.1	17.0	24.0	14.7	13.0	29.1

| | 1973-1975 | | 1975-1981 - Males | | | | Median |
| | Male | Female | Mean Earnings | | | | |
Occupation	All	All	All	White	Black	Hispanic	All
White Collar							
Managers, Officials							
& Proprietors	-8.5%	-1.7%	-7.3%	-6.4%	-16.4%	-4.9%	-6.5%
Professionals							
& Technical Wkers	-6.9	-3.4	-6.2	-5.7	-13.7	-4.0	-5.9
Sales Workers	-5.8	-3.0	-3.7	-3.7	NA	NA	-5.8
Clerical Workers	-5.6	-3.5	-8.1	-6.6	-16.4	-25.1	-7.8
Blue Collar							
Craftsmen & Foremen	-6.1	-2.3	-7.1	-7.1	-3.6	-4.3	-7.0
Operatives	-3.2	-3.7	-5.6	-5.8	-3.2	-5.5	-10.0
Laborers (non-farm)	-8.3	-15.6	-4.0	-4.7	-3.3	-6.1	-5.6
Service							
Private Household	NA	-3.7	NA	NA	NA	NA	NA
Other Service	-1.3	-2.6	-13.5	-13.7	-12.9	-16.7	-12.6
Farm							
Farmers and Farm Mng	-18.3	NA	-48.0	-48.0	NA	NA	-50.2
Farm Laborers	-7.6	NA	-4.5	-1.4	NA	NA	-0.5
All Employed Civilians	-5.8	-2.2	-6.4	-6.2	-6.9	-5.9	-6.0

Table 5-8 (continued)
Percentage Changes in Constant 1985 dollar Occupational Earnings, by Sex and Race/Ethnic Group
1960-67, 1967-73, 1973-75, 1975-81

	1975-1981 - Females				Median
	Mean Earnings				
Occupation	All	White	Black	Hispanic	All
White Collar					
Managers, Officials					
& Proprietors	-4.0%	-4.1%	NA	NA	-3.9%
Professionals					
& Technical Wkers	-6.0	-5.9	-4.9	NA	-8.2
Sales Workers	19.0	19.2	NA	NA	21.8
Clerical Workers	-5.0	-4.3	-11.3	-6.3	-8.0
Blue Collar					
Craftsmen & Foremen	-7.4	-7.8	NA	NA	-5.1
Operatives	-0.2	-0.3	5.0	-4.5	-2.5
Laborers (non-farm)	-7.3	-7.0	NA	NA	-12.0
Service					
Private Household	20.1	19.2	NA	NA	25.9
Other Service	-5.5	-4.3	-11.1	-1.7	-9.2
Farm					
Farmers and Farm Mng	NA	NA	NA	NA	NA
Farm Laborers	NA	NA	NA	NA	NA
All Employed Civilians	-2.2	-1.8	-3.5	1.1	-5.4

	1960-1973		1973-1981		1960-1981	
	Male	Female	Male	Female	Male	Female
Occupation	All	All	All	All	All	All
White Collar						
Managers, Officials						
& Proprietors	38.7%	43.5%	-14.4%	-5.5%	18.7%	35.5%
Professionals						
& Technical Wkers	30.9	35.2	-12.4	-11.3	14.7	19.9
Sales Workers	37.0	28.3	-11.3	18.1	21.6	51.5
Clerical Workers	31.9	17.4	-12.9	-11.2	14.9	4.2
Blue Collar						
Craftsmen & Foremen	26.0	NA	-12.7	2.6	10.0	NA
Operatives	25.0	17.3	-12.9	-6.1	8.9	10.2
Laborers (non-farm)	36.4	NA	-13.5	1.8	18.1	NA
Service						
Private Household	NA	11.8	NA	21.3	NA	35.6
Other Service	24.7	23.0	-13.7	-11.5	7.6	8.8
Farm						
Farmers and Farm Mng	100.4	NA	-59.3	NA	-18.4	NA
Farm Laborers	69.7	NA	-8.0	NA	56.1	NA
All Employed Civilians	35.6	27.1	-11.5	-7.4	20.0	17.7

Notes: Except where noted, all figures are comparison of median
earnings converted to constant 1985 dollars. NA = Data not
available due to the small number of persons in this category.

Source: Original earnings figures are from the U.S. Department of
Commerce 1983 and earlier editions in this series.

Table 5-9

**Percentage Changes in Constant 1985 Dollar Occupational
Earnings, by Sex and Race/Ethnic Group
1982-85, 1985-88-I**

		1982-1985 – Male			
		Mean Earnings			Median
Occupation	White	Black	Hispanic	All	All
White Collar					
Executive, Administrative					
& Managerial	7.7%	7.4%	4.9%	7.7%	2.4%
Professional Specialties	5.4	4.1	-22.3	4.9	5.0
Technicians & Related Support	5.1	NA	NA	4.4	(*)
Sales	8.1	3.9	1.9	7.4	4.3
Admin. Support, incl Clerical	5.8	-1.1	6.4	4.3	0.7
Blue Collar					
Precision Production, Craft					
& Repair	0.4	7.2	0.2	0.7	-0.14
Machine Oper. and Assemblers	6.8	7.5	-1.2	6.6	(*)
Transp. and Material Moving	3.5	4.9	-3.1	3.5	(*)
Handlers, Helpers & Laborers	-3.5	0.9	-7.9	-3.1	-1.0
Service					
Private Household Services	NA	NA	NA	NA	NA
Protective Services	3.5	10.4	NA	3.9	4.4
Other Services	7.4	3.4	-3.4	5.8	1.9
Farming, Forestry & Fishing	-3.4	-4.0	-8.1	-2.8	2.3
All Occupations	4.5	5.6	-1.2	4.1	3.0

		1982-1985 – Female			
		Mean Earnings			Median
Occupation	White	Black	Hispanic	All	All
White Collar					
Executive, Administrative					
& Managerial	6.4%	4.6%	8.0%	6.4%	6.5%
Professional Specialties	6.5	4.2	20.0	6.1	6.1
Technicians & Related Support	9.3	5.2	NA	7.4	(*)
Sales	9.9	-3.3	3.8	8.8	3.5
Admin. Support, incl Clerical	3.9	8.1	4.9	4.6	7.2
Blue Collar					
Precision Production, Craft					
& Repair	9.1	NA	NA	5.6	-0.3
Machine Oper. and Assemblers	9.5	3.1	4.9	7.7	(*)
Transp. and Material Moving	14.3	NA	NA	-13.8	(*)
Handlers, Helpers & Laborers	2.1	NA	NA	-2.9	0.3
Service					
Private Household Services	-8.8	NA	NA	-9.66	-1.5
Protective Services	NA	NA	NA	9.9	7.8
Other Services	6.2	-0.4	8.4	4.9	6.5
Farming, Forestry & Fishing	15.0	NA	NA	15.3	13.9
All Occupations	7.0	4.7	6.9	6.7	7.8

Table 5-9 (continued)
Percentage Changes in Constant 1985 Dollar Occupational Earnings, by Sex and Race/Ethnic Group
1982-85, 1985-88-I

	1985 - 1988-I	
	Male	Female
Occupation	All	All
White Collar		
Executive, Administrative		
& Managerial	5.1%	4.2%
Professional Specialties	5.5	7.2
Technicians & Related Support	0.5	4.9
Sales	3.2	7.6
Admin. Support, incl Clerical	-0.5	4.2
Blue Collar		
Precision Production, Craft		
& Repair	0.6	5.3
Machine Oper. and Assemblers	-1.4	23.4
Transp. and Material Moving	-0.9	-11.6
Handlers, Helpers & Laborers	1.7	-13.8
Service		
Private Household Services	NA	0.7
Protective Services	5.9	26.2
Other Services	11.8	2.7
Farming, Forestry & Fishing	3.2	-2.6
All Occupations	(*)	(*)

Notes: NA = Data not available due to the small number of persons in
this category. (*) Data not reported in this category in one
or both periods involved in the calculation of the ratio.
However, for males and females, respectively, in all Technical,
Sales, and Admin. Support occupations, 1982-85 changes were
4.7% and 7.9%. Similarly, for males and females, respectively,
in any of the last three listed blue collar occupations, the
1982-85 changes were 2.4% and 0.2%.
The large (22.3%) drop in earnings among Hispanic males in the
Professional Specialities during the 1982-85 period is the
result of atypically high mean earnings reported in 1982,
rather than unusually low mean earnings in 1985.

Sources: The underlying data used in the 1982-85 calculations are from
U.S. Department of Commerce 1987a and earlier numbers in this
series. The data used in the 1985-88 calculations are median
weekly earnings of full-time workers during 1985 from Mellor
(1986) and during the first quarter of 1988 from the U.S.
Department of Labor (1988). These latter figures are for
only one quarter and are subject to adjustment; hence, the
1985-88 percentages must be viewed as preliminary.

Table 5-10
Average Gross Hourly Earnings of
All Production and Nonsupervisory Workers in
Private Nonagricultural Employment, by Industry, with
Annual Equivalent Earnings: 1960, 1972, 1987
(all in constant 1985 dollars)

Industry	Average Hourly Earnings			Percentage Change		
	1960	1972	1987	'60-'72	'72-'87	'60'-'87
Mining	$ 9.47	$11.42	$11.82	20.6%	3.5%	24.8%
Construction	11.18	15.58	12.02	39.4	-22.8	7.5
Manufacturing	8.20	9.82	9.41	19.8	-4.2	14.8
Transportation						
& Public Utilities	10.45	11.96	11.41	14.4	-4.6	9.2
Wholesale Trade	8.17	9.90	9.13	21.2	-7.8	11.8
Retail Trade	5.88	7.07	5.81	20.2	-17.8	-1.2
Finance, Insurance						
& Real Estate	7.33	8.64	8.32	17.9	-3.7	13.5
Other Services	7.04	8.41	8.04	19.5	-4.4	14.2
All Private Industry	7.59	9.51	8.53	25.3	-10.3	12.4

Industry	Average Hours per Week	1987 Annual Equivalent in 1985 Dollars*		Highest Annual Equivalent** Earnings as a Percent of:	
	1987	Actual Hr/Wk	40 Hr/Wk	Minimum Adequacy	Moderate
Mining	42.3	$25,999	$24,586	128.7%	86.2%
Construction	37.7	23,564	25,002	123.7	82.8
Manufacturing	41.0	20.062	19,573	99.3	66.5
Transportation***					
& Public Utilities	39.1	23,199	23,733	117.4	78.6
Wholesale Trade	38.2	18,136	18,990	94.0	62.9
Retail Trade	29.3	8,852	12,085	59.8	40.0
Finance, Insurance					
& Real Estate	36.2	15,662	17,306	85.6	57.3
Other Services***	32.5	13,588	16,723	82.8	55.4
All Private Industry	34.8	15,486	17,742	87.8	58.8

Notes: * Actual Hours/Week Annual Equivalent computed from 1987 Hourly Earnings times
Average Weekly Hours in 1987 times 52--to estimate full-year employment.
40 Hour/Week Annual Equivalent computed from 1987 Hourly Earnings times 40
hours times 52 weeks--to estimate annual earnings if worked full 40 hrs/wk
all year.

** Computed from the larger of the Actual vs the 40 hour annual equivalents
divided by the 1985 (all figures are expressed in 1985 dollars) BLS Low or
Minimum Adequacy Budget ($20,207) and by their Moderate or Modest but
Adequate Budget ($30,177).

*** For the industry categories Transportation and Public Utilities and Other
Services the "1960" data are actually for 1966 which is the first year for
which aggregate data in that category are avialable. Data for sub-
industries are available for earlier years.

Source: Calculated from data from U.S. Department of Labor 1988.

Table 5-11
Average Gross Weekly Earnings of
All Production and Nonsupervisory Workers in
Private Nonagricultural Employment, by Industry:
1960, 1972, 1987
(all in constant 1985 dollars)

Industry	Average Weekly Earnings			Percentage Change		
	1960	1972	1987	'60-'72	'72-'87	'60-'87
Mining	$383	$486	$500	27.0%	2.8%	30.6%
Construction	410	569	453	38.7	-20.3	10.6
Manufacturing	326	398	386	22.0	-3.0	18.4
Transportation						
& Public Utilities	430	483	446	12.3	-7.7	3.7
Wholesale Trade	331	390	349	17.8	-10.6	5.3
Retail Trade	226	236	170	4.5	-27.9	-24.6
Finance, Insurance						
& Real Estate	273	316	301	15.8	-4.8	10.3
Other Services	254	285	261	12.2	-8.3	2.9
All Private Industry	293	352	297	20.1	-15.7	1.3

Note: For the industry categories Transportation and Public Utilities
and Other Services the "1960" data is actually for 1966 which is
the first year for which aggregate data in that category are
avialable. Data for sub-industries are available for earlier years.

Source: U.S. Department of Labor 1988 and earlier numbers in this series.

PART II

*THE CHANGING
DISTRIBUTION OF WEALTH
IN THE UNITED STATES*

6

The Sources of Data Concerning
Wealth Holdings

WEALTH AS THE DEFINITION OF RICH AND POOR

Throughout this book, the focus has been on the current earnings of individuals and families. Rich and poor have been defined in terms of income. However, in many ways, it is more appropriate to recognize that it is wealth, more than income, that is the hallmark of the rich. For with great wealth, a stream of income is assured, regardless of the current work effort. Only wealth protects one from a prolonged interruption in income generation. Moreover, while a temporarily large stream of income will gain a certain measure of status and power, real social status and political power typically depend upon the influence guaranteed only by substantial wealth. Conversely, a lack of wealth can make even a temporary period of low income an economic disaster for a family.

Indeed, as was discussed in Chapter 1, throughout much of history, being rich was synonymous with the owning and controlling of great wealth, and it was only in the last century that rich and poor became defined in terms of current income. In large part, the more recent focus on income was the result of empirical convenience--with the advent of the income tax and the ever widening scope of census questioning, the government began to accumulate vast stores of data concerning the incomes of individuals and families in America. However, information concerning the ownership of wealth has largely escaped close government scrutiny. The well understood facts are that wealth holdings are quite concentrated, as we shall see, and that those with the wealth go to great lengths to obscure the details of those holdings from public knowledge , for example, from the taxing authorities.

Indeed, comprehensive studies of wealth holdings have not been done on a regular basis by the government, and private studies have been sporadic and often not compatible with one another. A further problem has been that studies of household wealth must somehow obtain an adequate sample of data from the relatively small and rather secretive portion of American families who possess most of it. Many of the usual sampling techniques simply did not encompass a sufficient proportion of members of this elite group to provide statistically accurate and significant data.

ESTATE TAX ESTIMATES OF WEALTH HOLDINGS

One sequence of nongovernmental studies that were done employed data published by the Internal Revenue Service from federal estate tax returns. These began with the ground-breaking work by Robert Lampman (1962) who studied the wealth holdings of the rich from 1922 to 1956, and was followed by the work of Smith and Franklin (1974) who attempted to update Lampman's work through 1969. Later, in lesser known work, Schwartz (1983) continued the same methodology for the period 1976-81, and, on a preliminary basis, for 1982 (Schwartz 1985). However, the common weakness in all of these is that reliable demographic characteristics of the population being surveyed by these federal estate tax returns are simply not available. Hence, we know almost nothing about the people/families about which the data refer, nor do we know how they compare to the general population. Thus, these estimates, while useful as a first source of data on the wealth holdings of what are presumably the wealthiest members of our society, are of questionable validity in and of themselves and provide little information on the broader issue of the overall distribution of wealth among American families.

THE EFFORTS OF THE FEDERAL RESERVE SYSTEM

Until recently it was widely agreed that the most comprehensive and accurate source of information ever obtained on private wealth holdings, that is, on the size and composition of the financial portfolios of American families was done as part of the Federal Reserve System's 1962 Survey of Financial Characteristics of Consumers. This survey very purposefully included a supplementary sample of high income families drawn from federal income tax files to ensure a large enough sample of such families to give validity to the study of wealth holdings. The results of this study were published by the Federal Reserve under the authorship of the primary researchers, Projector and Weiss (1966). The problem, of course, is that that study is now more than 25 years out of date.

However, in 1986, two new studies were published that provided much more current, detailed, and reliable data on wealth holdings. The first represented the efforts of the Board of Governors of the Federal Reserve System (FRS), in cooperation with six other governmental agencies, to have the earlier 1962 study updated. The second study was conducted by the Bureau of the Census and will be discussed in the next section. The FRS study was done in conjunction with what is known as the 1983 Survey of Consumer Finances (SCF) and indeed, at the time it was done, it provided the most comprehensive data on wealth holdings since 1962. However, the purpose of the survey was far broader:

The overriding common interest among the sponsors was the
estimation of the debt obligations and asset holdings of
a nationally representative sample of American families.
Such a balance sheet approach allows analysis of the net
financial position of families, their use of financial
institutions, their holdings of various types of assets,
and the structure and sources of their debt obligations.
. . . [In addition,] the 1983 survey sought the attitudes
of consumers toward credit use, their reactions to new
financial instruments and to consumer credit regulations,
and detailed information on consumer pension rights and
benefits. (Avery, Canner and Gustafson 1984: 679).

As in 1962, the base sample was augmented by a special
subsample of high income families identified from tax files. All
of these latter families were (as of 1980) in the top 0.5 percent
of families ranked by income, and hence provided an exceptional
opportunity to examine the financial behavior of that portion of the
population which controls so much of the nation's wealth. Moreover,
the compatibility of the methodology allowed for meaningful
comparisons to be made with the 1962 data.[1]
Subsequently, the FRS's Board of Governor's Division of
Research and Statistics was authorized to establish the Survey of
Consumer Finances as a more regular, albeit not annual, project.
The next such survey was conducted in 1986. However, the 1986
Survey of Consumer Finances actually consisted of re-interviews with
a selected group of those covered in the 1983 survey and

was designed primarily to update essential information in
the 1983 SCF--the household balance sheet and employment
data. Sufficient information was collected that household
net worth could be estimated, although more aggregated
asset and debt categories were used--roughly 25 categories
versus 85 in 1983 (Avery, Elliehausen and Kennickell
1988).

Just as the results of the 1983 survey were not compiled and
published until 1986, the results of the 1986 survey have not yet
been published as this book is being written. However, preliminary
data were presented at a conference in May 1988 (Avery and
Kennickell 1988), and full publication of the results will begin to
appear in late 1988 or early 1989. Thus, in what follows, I will
analyze data that flowed from the 1983 survey, and will augment that
from the preliminary (unpublished) 1986 data which were made
available to me by Arthur Kennickell of the Federal Reserve Board's
Division of Research and Statistics in the form of the conference
paper cited above.
In this paper, the authors explain why, given the fact that
the 1986 SCF was a reinterview of persons in the 1983 sample and
that, therefore, persons aged 18 to 21 would not be represented in
the new sample, and given the fact that:

> a significant proportion of younger adults are in school
> or the military, or live with their parents, [and hence
> that] the younger people living independently at the time
> of the 1983 SCF are unlikely to be representative of the
> population of their cohorts three years later (Avery and
> Kennickell 1988: 8),

a decision was made not to weigh the data to represent households
with heads aged 18 to 24. Hence, the data reported for 1986, and
the data that are used for 1983-86 comparisons are limited to those
households headed by those aged 25 and older. This does not appear
to bias the data in a significant manner.[2]

In analyzing the changes that occurred between 1963 and 1983
in the distribution of wealth, I benefitted greatly from access to
another as yet unpublished research paper, this one by Avery,
Elliehausen, and Kennickell (1988). This work updates the published
material relating to the 1963-83 comparative data and expands upon
work presented at conferences in 1986 and 1987. My thanks are due
to Mr. Arthur Kennickell for enabling me to build upon this material
in order to render this book as up-to-date as possible.

THE BUREAU OF THE CENSUS'S NEW SURVEY AND DATA ON WEALTH

The second new source of data concerning the wealth holdings
of American families was published in July 1986, when the Bureau of
the Census released a new study entitled *Household Wealth and Asset
Ownership: 1984* (U.S. Department of Commerce 1986c). This study
was based on data from what is entitled the Survey of Income and
Program Participation (SIPP).   This new survey represents the
culmination of some eight to ten years of research development
(after a hiatus of two years, 1981-82, due to Reagan administration
budget cuts) and is intended by the sponsoring agencies as an
on-going research and data collection tool the results of which will
be published in a new series (P-70) in the Current Population
Reports. This new survey, the SIPP, involves in-depth interviews,
with periodic reinterviews, each with a somewhat different focus.
In all, each household included in the survey is interviewed eight
or nine times at four month intervals. This is designed to provide
greater reliability of the data generally and also provide, through
planned overlapping in the sample groups, for reliability and
validity of longitudinal data.
The interviews consist of three major elements, two of which
are repeated at each interview, with the third being supplemental
and included only "during selected household visits." The first
element consists of "basic social and demographic characteristics
of each person in the household." The second focuses upon "labor
force activity, the types and amounts of income received during the
4-month reference period, and participation status in various
programs." The third, supplementary element, deals with various
"topical modules [which] cover areas that need not be examined every
4 months." Information on assets and liabilities, from which the
data on net wealth are developed, was only included in the "fourth

wave topical module" of the six waves of interviews that constituted the initial set of interviews of what is referred to as the "1984 panel" of interviewees. (All quotes are from U.S. Department of Commerce 1986c: 27-28.)

Conversations with Enrique Lamas of the Poverty and Wealth Statistics Branch, Population Division of the Bureau of the Census, indicates that current plans are to develop and publish data concerning the distribution of wealth every other year, with less detailed, unpublished data available to researchers for in-between years. According to Lamas, the data for 1986 will be published during the first quarter of 1989. This is a slightly longer lag than previously, since the 1984 data on wealth were published in July 1986. Hence, the analysis I will be presenting will be based upon the 1984 data, which are the latest available at the time of this writing.

WEAKNESSES AND COMPATIBILITY PROBLEMS IN THE WEALTH DATA

There are some interesting questions as to differences in the results produced by these two new studies--the Federal Reserve's Survey of Consumer Finances (SCF) and the Bureau of Census's SIPP--as compared to each other, to the earlier work by nongovernmental researchers, and to aggregate totals produced from the Flow of Funds Accounts of the Federal Reserve System. These differences, while certainly not at all insignificant, are covered in sufficient detail elsewhere as to not warrant a complete rehash of them here.[3] However, a few comments are necessary.

The SCF vs. the SIPP Net Worth Figures

The SIPP, which interviewed about 21,000 households in the 1984 panel, is a far broader survey than the 1983 SCF, which included 3,824 households in the basic sample, plus 438 in the high income supplementary sample. Moreover, the 1986 SCF only included reinterviews with 2,822 of the households included in the 1983 full sample. On the other hand, only the SCF conducted a focused extra effort on any high income households.

While this may seem like a small extra effort, "This sample oversamples the number of households in the top half percent of the income distribution at a rate fifteen times greater than a simple random cross-section of households" (Avery, Elliehausen and Kennickell 1988: 1). To understand the effects of these differences, after adjustments to develop comparable categories, etc., Avery, Elliehausen and Kennickell estimate that the initial (1984) SIPP results in aggregate net worth of $7,740 billion, while the basic 1983 SCF yields $8,293 billion and the full (that is, including the high-income supplementary sample) SCF yields $9,615 billion. Avery et al. argue that the difference between the SIPP and basic SCF figures is due to a smaller estimate of small business assets in the SIPP and that "the major difference between the two surveys arises from the inclusion of the high income sample in the SCF" (Avery, Elliehausen and Kennickell 1988: 9).

They argue that the inclusion of the high income subsample is crucial if we are to gain a good understanding of just who holds what types of wealth in the U.S., and is also essential if we are to understand the causes and nature of savings, especially nonhousing capital formation, in the U.S. In fact, Avery and Kennickell point out that "In light of our low national saving rate, it is astounding that we have had to wait so long" to begin to acquire the data that are beginning to allow us to build models that describe this savings behavior (Avery and Kennickell 1988: 31).

However, there is serious reason to worry about the adequacy of even the full SCF data. Avery, Elliehousen, and Kennickell (1988) point out that in the 1983 high income sample, the largest wealth holder reported holding only $87 million (in 1983 dollars), while the largest holding in the 1963 survey was only $76 million (in 1983 dollars). Assuming the honesty of these responses, a large number of far wealthier households were not surveyed at all. For example, according to their best estimate, in 1983 there were some 6,010 "missing" households with wealth between $60 and $125 million, representing a total of $499 billion in unreported wealth (in 1983 dollars). In 1963, they estimate 2,200 such "missing" households with $186 billion (in 1983 dollars) of unreported wealth (Avery, Elliehausen, and Kennickell 1988: 25-26).

Even beyond that, they cite a *Forbes* magazine special issue (The *Forbes* Four Hundred, Fall 1983) that reported that 400 individuals, each of whom held at least $125 million, held a total of $118 billion in 1983. The *Forbes* article included within its "Richest 400," 15 individuals with over $1 billion and 44 others with between $500 million and $1 billion dollars in net wealth. Apparently none of these 400 individuals were included in even the high income supplementary sample of the 1983 SCF. In a footnote, they point out that an alternative estimation method which was "quite robust" indicated that "there should have been 3,000 individuals with over $125 million [each] in wealth holding, in aggregate over $750 billion [in 1983 dollars] (ibid.: fn. 32, 26). If we combine the $499 billion from the paragraph above with this $750 billion, there is good reason to believe that the total net worth of the wealthiest households, and the overall total net worth, may be understated in the official SCF figures by about $1,249 billion in 1983, in that year's dollars. This amounts to some 12.4 percent of the $10,054.4 billion in total net worth for that year.

One might suspect that the failure to include representatives of those richest individuals or adequate representatives of those between $60 and $125 million in wealth is no accident. The high income supplementary sample was based upon the Internal Revenue Service's Statistics and Income Division having selected a presumably random group of some 5,000 high income households. Avery, Elliehausen, and Kennickell comment that, "The drawn sample appears to roughly coincide with individuals with an "extended" income of $100,000 or more in 1980 (1988: fn. 5) However, only 459 of these 5000 household agreed to participate in the survey and only 438 actually completed the interviews. Moreover, the survey was blind in that the surveyors did not have access to the tax returns of those surveyed, nor did they have any data at all on those who refused to participate.

Is it not reasonable to suspect that among the 91 percent of the high income sample who chose not to participate might lurk a more representative sample of the richest of the rich and that their failure to volunteer was hardly an oversight on their part? It is also quite possible that some of those who did participate might indeed hold far more wealth than they reported in the interviews. One is reminded of the comment by the editors of *Forbes* in the introduction to the special issue on the "Richest 400" that, "The most common response to the all-important net worth question remained "no comment . . ." (*Forbes* 1983: 86).

If one tries to account for the results of these omissions and adds to the total net worth in 1983 and to the holdings that year of the richest one-half percent, the $499 billion thought to have been missed from those having between $60 and $125 million and the $750 billion that is likely to have been the holdings of those with wealth in excess of $125 million, the result is that this richest one-half percent of the households should have their overall proportion of the total wealth increased 8.2 percentage points, from 24.3 percent to 32.5 percent. I will make reference to these estimated adjustment figures when analyzing the concentration of wealth in the next chapter.

The SCF vs. the Flow of Funds Net Worth Figures

Another issue that is often of concern is the comparison of the results of a survey such as the SCF with the aggregate figures reported in the Federal Reserve's Flow of Funds (FOF) accounts. It is usually assumed that survey data will result in a significant degree of underreporting of net wealth as compared to the aggregate figures available from various institutional and other sources that are used in constructing the FOF. On the other hand, many of the sources used in FOF accounting are not specifically designed for that purpose and the FOF does include trust and nonprofit organizational net worth that is not part of household net worth as usually defined. Moreover, while the FOF, in principle, includes a measure of all corporate equities,

> in practice, only publicly traded equities are captured in the data used to construct this figure. Almost all holdings of small, closely-held corporations, except those allocated to other categories such as real estate, are missed (Avery, Elliehausen and Kennickell 1988: 16).

There are many other problems of definition and categorization. There are even possible problems regarding the timing of the sampling of some very volatile forms of wealth and debt. Thus, it is not surprising that there are wide disparities for many classes of assets and debts between the FOF figures, even after some adjustment, and the as comparable as possible SCF figures.

In an initial effort at such a comparison, Avery and Elliehausen report that after adjustments, an examination of four broad categories of assets and two broad categories of debts results in a net SCF figure for the full (that is, including the high income subgroup) sample in 1983 that is 79.4 percent of the comparable FOF figure (Avery and Elliehausen 1986: 174). In later, much more detailed and complete work, Avery, Elliehausen and Kennickell report that the 1983 SCF full sample results in aggregate net worth for all "real" households that is 110.5 percent of the FOF figure (Avery, Elliehausen, and Kennickell 1988: 12). However, there remains a very great deal of variation in the asset by asset, debt by debt category comparisons.

The SCF vs. Estate Tax Based Estimates of the Concentration of Wealth

I mentioned earlier that there had been a series of studies of the distribution of wealth, in particular of the concentration of wealth, based upon figures obtained from the IRS from estate tax returns. One issue of some interest is how these figures compare to those that result from the SCF or from the SIPP. I do not know of any attempt to compare the estate tax results to the SIPP figures, but Avery, Elliehausen, and Kennickell did make an effort to develop a set of adjustments that would allow for a comparison of the 1963 and 1983 SCF figures and those from comparable estate tax based studies.[4]

For 1963, they were able to get figures that were roughly comparable. Looking at those individuals with gross assets of $500 million or more, the SCF showed an aggregate net worth of $1,562.2 billion compared to $1,704.5 billion based upon the estate tax method (all in 1983 dollars). Thus, the SCF figure was about 92 percent of the estate tax based estimate for these individuals for 1963. However, for 1983, the SCF aggregate was 168 percent of the estate tax figure, using the same pattern of adjustments as for the 1963 data. Even using an alternative set of adjustment rules, the SCF figure was still 156 percent of the estate tax-based figure.

In trying to account for this difference, Avery et all., argue that, "This discrepancy does not appear to stem from the number of large wealth-holders so much as the values these households report, particularly for corporate stock and real estate holdings" (ibid.: 28). That is, they do not feel that the problem is the sampling technique or sampling weights that are used, so much as the actual figures reported by those who are sampled under either method. Part of the problem may be that the estate tax-based estimates use "pre-audit" figures that may undervalue certain assets. But this does not appear to be an adequate explanation and there is agreement that more work needs to be done to understand this type of discrepancy.

Nevertheless, the implications of these rather different results for 1983 are quite significant on our estimates of the degree of concentration of wealth. For example, using the estate tax based figures results in an estimate that 19.7 percent of all U.S. household wealth was held by the richest 1 percent of individuals in 1983, while the full SCF survey figures support an estimate of 27.1 percent, using the more conservative adjustment mentioned above (Avery, Elliehausen, and Kennickell 1988). Especially given our earlier discussion of the underrepresentation of the very wealthiest households even in the full SCF and what I would consider to be the better sampling techniques used in the SCF, I would tend to accept the SCF figures as the more accurate.

Other Issues in the Wealth Data

This discussion of the data on wealth, its limitations and problems, and the issue of the compatibility between different sources of data is hardly complete or thorough. It is not meant to be. As was pointed out, there are many studies that have focused explicitly on these matters and many more will be published in the near future. Some of the issues which I have not discussed are such matters as the techniques used to choose the samples, the selection of sample weights used to develop population estimates, the handling of extreme values and the problems associated with the truncating of distributions, the problems of dealing with missing data on responses within the sample and with possible biases causes by selected nonresponses to a survey. It is not that these matters are unimportant, it is simply that an examination of them is beyond the scope of this book. My purpose in raising these issues is to alert the reader to them, so that a certain degree of caution is maintained when looking at the data that will be presented later.[5]

However, it should also be understood, that with all its weaknesses, the data concerning the distribution and amount of wealth in the U.S. that are now available and that will be emerging in the years to come are far better and more complete than any that were available a few short years ago. So, while all of the wealth figures must be viewed as preliminary estimates, they are still very valuable tools in providing important information about this topic which is, as we discussed in the first chapter, so essential to our understanding of our society and how it functions economically, socially, and politically.

NOTES

1. The results of this study have appeared in a series of articles in *The Federal Reserve Bulletin*. However, the first two articles, which appeared in September and December, 1984, reported results from only the base sample, and not from the expanded subsample of high income families. The first, and as of this writing, only widely available article to report comprehensive data, including that from this subsample, appeared under the authorship of Avery and Elliehausen (1986). A further, more detailed look at the full 1983 study will be published later this year by Avery, Elliehausen, and Kennickell (1988), who were good enough to share a draft of that paper with me.

2.   To quote from a footnote in Avery and Kennickell (1988: fn. 13: 11):

Data from the 1983 survey, which sampled the entire age distribution of households with heads aged 18 and over, indicates that little wealth is missed by ignoring the population under age 25. Asset, debt, and net worth totals would be estimated to be only 0.9 percent, 3 percent, and 0.6 percent higher respectively, if the under 25 year olds were included. These households, however, would have added 4.2 percent to income and would have increased the number of households by 8.7 percent.

3. Among the sources relevant to understanding these problems of compatibility and validity are those by Avery and Elliehousen 1986, Avery, Elliehausen and Kennickell 1988, Avery and Kennickell 1988, Broida 1962, Curtin, Juster and Morgan 1987, a series of articles by Ferber 1965, 1966a, 1966b, Ferber, Forsythe, Guthrie and Maynes 1969, Mandell and Lundsten 1978, McNeil and Lamas 1987, and Wolff and Marley 1987. For other ancillary articles see the references and bibliographies, especially in the various articles on which Avery worked.

4.   The first major study of wealth using the estate tax approach was done by Robert Lampman (1962) and covered the period from 1922 to 1956. James Smith and Stephen Franklin (1974) followed up on Lampman's path-breaking work, extending the analysis to 1969. More recently, in much less widely known work, Marvin Schwartz (1983 and 1985) continued this methodology, first addressing the period of 1976-81, and then developing preliminary data for 1982.

5.   It should be noted that many of these same statistical problems, problems associated with sampling techniques and populations estimation, also exist with regard to the income data generated by the Bureau of the Census. There have also been serious questions raised about the possible underreporting of income by the wealthy and of the underrepresentation of the poor in the Census generally, as well as in the surveys upon which the detailed income statistics are based.

For example, most of the income data that have been presented in the first part of this book are based upon the annual March Current Population Survey, which is probably the most detailed and comprehensive economic survey of American households that is conducted, encompassing, for example in 1984, a sample of some 59,000 households. When the Federal Reserve's Survey of Consumer Finances' data on income are compared to that of the Current Population Survey for the same year, 1983 for example, one finds that the SCF data is about 10 percent above that of the CPS, mostly due to differences in reported business income, and income from dividends, trusts and real estate--according to Avery, Elliehausen and Kennickell.   However, as those authors point out, "Interestingly, in a comparison of data with an 'independent source' in 1983, the Census Bureau concluded that the CPS data "under-reported by about 10 percent." (1988). Their reference for the Census Bureau quote is to the U.S. Department of Commerce (1985:

218). Thus, when dealing with income data, as with wealth data, one must make use of the best information available, while remaining aware and cautious of its limitations.

The Changing Distribution
of Wealth Since 1962

THE DISTRIBUTION OF NET WORTH IN 1983 COMPARED TO THAT IN 1962

We begin to examine the changing distribution of wealth in the United States by first turning to the Federal Reserve Board's Surveys of Consumer Finances for 1962 and 1983 which, due to their consistent methodology allow us to make a meaningful comparison over this 21 year period. Table 7-1 presents this data.

Before looking at that data, it should be noted that in order to render the presentation of data on the distribution of wealth as comparable as possible to the data presented earlier in the book on the distribution of income, wherever feasible the dollar figures have been converted into 1985 constant dollars of value. Thus, in Table 7-1 are presented figures showing the distribution of net worth, that is, of assets owned less liabilities owed, all converted to 1985 dollars. It should also be noted that this study (the Fed's SCF) included in the definition of assets the value of a family's home and other properties, the net value of any nonpublic businesses, all liquid assets (checking, savings and money market accounts, mutual funds, and certificates of deposit), individual retirement accounts (IRAs) and Keogh accounts, the cash value of life insurance and employer-sponsored profit sharing and stock-option plans, all other financial assets such as private and public bonds, stocks, trust accounts, and also notes owed to the family. It did not include one's equity in a pension plan nor the value of motor vehicles. Liabilities included all mortgages, credit card, installment and noninstallment debts, and outstanding balances owed on credit lines.

Looking at the distribution of wealth in 1983 as presented in Table 7-1, one should initially note that 13 percent of families had a negative net worth, that is, they owed more than they owned, and that this was up two percentage points from 1962. An additional 4 percent had no net worth at all in 1983. On top of this, there were 10 percent of American families with at most $3,536 (in 1985 dollars). When one remembers that this includes the equity in their home plus their checking and savings accounts, etc., it is clear that these families were in the precarious position where even a month or two without salary would leave them with absolutely no financial resources. Even those in the next couple of brackets, with total net worth up to $35,369, had the vast majority of their wealth tied up in their homes (as we shall see in more detail at a later point), not in liquid assets that could easily substitute for lost current income.[1] Those owning substantial amounts of net worth are clearly the top 15 to 30 percent of the families.

Comparing 1983 to 1962, the pattern is clear. As with the income data, the proportion of those in the middle area had decreased, while the proportion on either extreme increased. Here, one finds that the greatest decrease had occurred among those families having about $3,500 to $35,000 in constant 1985 dollars of net worth, with a smaller decrease for those with net worth from zero to about $3,500 or with about $35,000-$88,000; while those with negative net worth or those with net worth in excess of $88,000 increased as a proportion of the population. This is yet another indication of the shrinkage in the middle class (and even among those somewhat below the middle), while there was an expansion in the proportions among the poorest and among the wealthiest families.[2]

THE DISTRIBUTION OF NET WORTH AMONG DIFFERENT RACIAL/ETHNIC GROUPS AND DIFFERENT TYPES OF FAMILIES

Turning to Table 7-2, which is drawn from the Census Bureau's 1984 S.I.P.P. study, one can gain further insights into the distribution of net worth in the U.S., particularly as it is distributed among families of different racial/ethnic origin and of different types. Since this study was done only a year later than that by the Federal Reserve staff, the results should be reasonably comparable to those in the Fed's 1983 study, given the caveats discussed in the preceding chapter, and given that, again, all figures are in 1985 dollars to help make meaningful comparisons. Among the few differences in the definitions of assets by the Census Bureau, as compared to the Federal Reserve, is that the former counts the value of motor vehicles, but does not count the cash value of life insurance policies. Given that poorer families in the U.S. are far more likely to have cars than to have cash value life insurance, and that those cars are likely to constitute a significant portion of their net worth, one would expect to see the median net wealth of the poorer and lower middle income families a bit higher in this study.

In looking at Table 7-2, what is particular striking is the differences in the distribution of wealth along racial/ethnic origin lines. Thus, while only 8.4 percent of White families had a zero or negative amount of net wealth, an astoundingly high 30.5 percent of Black families and 23.9 percent of Hispanic families share that fate. Overall, this study shows 11 percent of all families with negative or zero net worth, compared to the 17 percent reported by the Federal Reserve a year earlier. It is quite possible that the inclusion of the value of motor vehicles, plus a bit of improvement over the course of the year, accounts for a significant part of the difference.

Returning to Table 7-2, when one adds the proportion of families in the lowest positive net worth bracket ($1 to $5,180), one finds that some 22.4 percent of White families are accounted for, but 54.4 percent of Black and 50.2 percent of Hispanic families. Again, one sees in very vivid terms how incredibly vulnerable a large proportion of families are to any interruption in income, especially among Blacks and Hispanics. When one looks at the middle groups, very broadly those with about $5,000 to $50,000 of net worth, and one notes, from looking ahead at Table 7-5, that 75.8 percent of the net worth of Black families, 58.4 percent of the wealth of Hispanics and 46.4 percent of that even of White families is tied up in their homes and cars, and, on average, another 13.4 percent in other nonbusiness related real estate. When one recognizes that these assets tend to play a bigger role in the "portfolios" of the middle and lower classes than in the upper classes, one again sees an indication of the illiquidity and vulnerability of a very large proportion of American families.

Table 7-2 also reveals some important information about the relative wealth positions of different types of families, in particular those characterized by having a married couple, those headed by a single female, and those headed by a single male. One finds that female-headed households are more than three times more likely (19.3 percent compared to 6 percent in 1984) to have a zero or negative net worth position than are married-couple families. Even single-male headed household (15.5 percent) are more than two and a half times more likely to be in this desperate situation. By the time one takes into account those in the lowest positive net worth position, one has accounted for a total of 39.6 percent of female-headed and 40.6 percent of male-headed families. In would appear, that families with a single primary breadwinner, whether female or male, are far less likely to be able to accumulate any significant amount of wealth--not a very surprising result given the earlier statistics on wages and earnings.

Table 7-3 reveals that, when discussing the relative positions of different types of families, it is again essential to disaggregate by the racial/ethnic origins of the families. Thus, while it is true that all female-headed families have a median net worth position considerable poorer than that for married-couple families, something that was revealed initially in Table 7-2, the differences between the positions of Whites, on one hand, and Blacks and Hispanics, on the other, is vast. Thus, while White female-headed families had a net worth that was only 42 percent of that of White married-couple families, their net worth was nevertheless more than 33 times higher than that enjoyed by Black female-headed families and more than 47 times higher than that of Hispanic female-headed families. Even among male-headed families, the differences between the racial/ethnic origin groups is quite significant with White families having had a net worth almost 4 times that of Blacks and more than 4.3 times than of Hispanics.

As the summary statistics in the lower portion of Table 7-3 indicate, the distribution of wealth across the racial/ ethnic groups is far less equal than the distribution of income, using this survey's statistics for both income and wealth. Thus, while Black median family income was only 61.8 percent of that for White families, Black median family net worth was an astoundingly small 6.2 percent of that of Whites. That is, wealth, on average, was 10 times less equally distributed. For Hispanic families the differential is about 6 times (12.6 percent of White net worth compared to 76.4 percent of income).

THE DISTRIBUTION OF NET WORTH COMPARED TO THE DISTRIBUTION OF INCOME

The section on the far right in Table 7-2 provides some interesting data on the distribution of net worth within various income brackets.[3] As one would expect, there is a strong correlation between income and wealth, with a larger proportion of those families having low incomes also having little if any wealth as compared to those families with more income and, not surprising, more wealth. Thus, for example, 49.8 percent of the families in the lowest income bracket had negative or zero wealth, while only 4 percent of those in the highest income bracket were in that situation. At the other extreme, the proportion of families with large wealth holdings increased as income increased.

What is perhaps more surprising is that there were families with very low reported incomes, for example, in the lowest income bracket, who nevertheless reported net worth in excess of $103,000, in fact, some 7.5 percent of the families in that income bracket indicated that pattern. Given that the S.I.P.P. counts all income actually received during the interview periods,[4] including earnings from employment, income from assets (interest, dividends, rents, etc.) and from other sources such as public or private retirement programs, welfare and social security programs, and even money from relatives or friends and lump sum payments (except capital gains or losses from the sale of assets or monies received from loans), it is, at first, hard to understand how someone with large wealth holdings would have such a small income.

The explanation apparently lies in a family holding wealth that was not income generating during the survey period. Such wealth was most likely in the form of either valuable real estate holdings, including, but not limited to, the family's own home or the holding of equity in a business (either in the form of stock or otherwise) during a period when neither dividends nor other payments were made. In some cases, the small amount of reported income may be an artifact of the four-month survey period and would be considerably greater were a full year's actual income evaluated. In other cases, it may actually reflect the current financial situation of the family.

At the other extreme, it is perhaps not so surprising to see that there are some families with substantial earnings ($49,700 or more) who reported a zero or negative net worth (2.2 percent). Nevertheless, the pattern between income and wealth is certainly along the general lines one would expect. Overall, looking at the upper right section of Table 7-3, one finds that the 25.7 percent of the families which are designated as poor in terms of income, shared among themselves only 9.7 percent of the total net worth of American families, while the 12.4 percent with the highest income shared among themselves 38 percent of the net worth. Thus, the median net worth of the richest (in terms of income) families ($127,919) was more than 24 times that of the poorest. There is little doubt that wealth in American is far more unequally distributed than is income.

Comparative Wealth vs. Income Distributions Among Different Racial/Ethnic Groups and Different Types of Families

Table 7-3 also reports some summary statistics from Table 7-2, including the median net worth by income brackets for families in the different racial/ethnic origin groups. What one finds is that the phenomenon just discussed of low income combined with substantial wealth was limited almost entirely to White families. Thus, the median net worth of White families in the lowest income bracket was $8,747, while that of Black families was a mere $91 (a ratio of almost 100 to 1) and that of Hispanic families was the not much more substantial amount of $453 (a ratio of almost 20 to 1). When one sees a reference to the median net wealth for all families in this low income bracket ($5,263), it is essential to understand that due to the differences between the racial/ethnic origin groups, this overall figure is truly meaningless. The overall figure is a full 40 percent below the actual amount for White families and is almost 60 times higher than that for Black families and almost 12 times higher than that for Hispanic families. The experience of these various groups with regard to wealth is so very different that to cite averages that cover up these differences is to misrepresent the actual facts for all of them.

Moreover, this is not true only among the poorest families. Among what has been labeled in Table 7-3 as "Low Income", those receiving between $11,185 and $24,184, one finds that the median net wealth of White families was 7.3 times that of Black families and 8.4 times that of Hispanic families. One interesting phenomenon is that Hispanic families with a middle to high income had much higher median net worth positions than did Black families. Among those families with $49,700 or more of income, Hispanic median net worth was 77.6 percent of that of Whites, while Black median net worth was only 45.8 percent. The Hispanic upper middle and upper class tended to have a far more secure financial position than their Black counterparts, though of course, neither, on average, enjoyed the security of Whites with similar incomes.

The Distribution of Net Worth by Family Income in 1983 and 1986

Before moving on to examine the composition of the net wealth of America's families, we turn back to the data from the Federal Reserve Board of Governors to look at the distribution of net worth they report among families of different income levels in both 1983 and 1986. This allows us to make some comparisons between the two sources of data, and also allows us to look at the pattern of changes from 1983 to 1986 which provides some initial indication of more current trends (than that in the 1962 to 1983 comparisons in Table 7-1). These data are reported in Table 7-4.

If one compares the data for 1983 in Table 7-4 with those for 1984 in Table 7-3, it would seem that the figures are roughly comparable given the different income brackets used in the two studies and the slightly different definitions of wealth, and remembering that, of course, the figures in both tables are presented in constant 1985 dollars. For, example, among all families earning less than $11,185 in the 1984 SIPP data the median net worth is $5,263 and the mean is $30,727, while in the 1983 SCF data the figures for those earning less than $10,799 are $5,732 and $30,701, respectively. One advantage of the SCF data is that six income brackets are used there, including the division of those earning above $54,000 into two groups. On the other hand the data from the SCF that have been made available as of this writing do not allow the detailed breakdown within racial/ethnic groups.

Looking more closely at Table 7-4, we see once again that wealth increases at a far faster rate than does income and that White families enjoyed a far better net wealth position than that of "non-White" and Hispanic families taken together.[5] If one looks at the pattern of changes from 1983 to 1986, even keeping in mind the limitations in the data discussed in the preceding chapter, one finds some surprising results. Among those in the lowest income bracket, the median net wealth almost doubled from $5,732 to $10,225 (again all in constant 1985 dollars), while the mean net wealth held virtually constant. When one notes that the population was slightly larger in 1986 than in 1983 and that a larger proportion of that larger population was in the lowest income group, 24 percent compared to 22.6 percent, one notes that it is quite likely that some of those falling into this low income group in 1986 brought with them a few thousand dollars more in net worth than had been the case, but that there were fewer with considerably higher net worth positions. This may well reflect the slippage of previously middle income families into the low income category due to layoffs in the industrial sectors--previously middle-income families who brought with them a few thousand dollars more in equity in their homes; while, at the same time, some of those who did have more net worth in 1983 converted some of that wealth into current income.

Among those in the next two income brackets, those with $10,800 to $32,399 in income, we find some decrease in the median net worth, but some increase in the mean net worth. That is, overall, more of these families had lower net worth positions in 1986, while a few had higher net worth, indicating some slippage among a significant portion of these lower and lower middle income families. Among those in the upper three income brackets, both median and mean net worth increased, except, surprisingly, the median net worth position of those in the highest income bracket. It is also surprising to note that the SCF study shows a slightly lower proportion of the population in this highest income group. However, as noted in the last chapter, these results for those in the highest income group may primarily reflect the fact that the very wealthiest families in the U.S. were not sampled at all in the SCF.

Looking at the differentials between White families and "Non-White and Hispanic" families, Table 7-4 indicates that the median net worth of White families actually decreased about 3.3 percent (from $52,811 to $51,069), during the period from 1983 to 1986, while that of Non-White and Hispanic families increased by more than 18 percent, from $7,414 to $8,806. However, despite some modest closing of this gap, the median net worth of White families in 1986 still stood 5.7 times more than that of the Non-White and Hispanic families. On the other hand, the mean incomes of these two groups moved in the opposite directions, with that of the Whites increasing and that of the Non-Whites and Hispanics decreasing. Again, this indicates that while there was some slippage in the net worth of many White families, there were some who accumulated sufficiently more to pull up the mean even while the median was falling slightly. Whereas, among minority families, the opposite pattern occurred. However, yet again, the failure to sample among the very wealthiest families, virtually all of whom are White, clearly led to some understatement in the upward shift of the mean, and might even have accounted for some modest portion of the decrease in the median.

THE CHANGE IN WEALTH HOLDINGS WITHIN FAMILIES - 1983-1986

The recent work by Avery and Kennickell (1987) also allows us to begin to gain some insight into the changing wealth position within particular households, that is to employ a longitudinal perspective, as opposed to the cross-sectional and comparative cross sectional perspective employed throughout the rest of this chapter. Their longitudinal work is rather preliminary and suggestive, what they refer to as "...the first attempt to use data from the 1983-86 SCF to characterize the dynamics of wealth observed at the household level" (ibid.: 20). However, it is potentially quite useful.[6]

They develop what they refer to as transitional tables showing the population of households by deciles of wealth in both 1983 and 1986, capturing the percentage of households who moved between deciles over the three-year period. While, not surprisingly, the amount of mobility is much less when one focuses on wealth rather than on income, there is still considerable movement. They report that, "Over half (56.3 percent) of the population moved between deciles [in the holding of wealth] between 1983 and 1986; 19.4 percent of the sample moved more than one decile" (ibid.: 19). This compares to 67.3 percent who moved between deciles of income during the same period, including 33.4 percent who moved more than one decile. These changes in wealth position clearly reflect not just changes in the net value of the wealth of the households, but also a whole complex of changes in the structure of households over the life-cycle of its members, including marriage, divorce, retirement, etc.

Avery and Kennickell indicate that the research division of the Board of Governors of the Federal Reserve is continuing to support studies in this area and that related work is in progress.

This will allow for much more detailed analysis of savings and dissavings behavior of households and of the other mechanisms by which wealth is created and destroyed.

THE DISTRIBUTION OF FAMILY NET WORTH AMONG DIFFERENT ASSETS

Tables 7-5 and 7-6 give us a picture of the distribution of the net worth of American families over a variety of different assets. Table 7-5 reports data from the Census Bureau's 1984 SIPP study and Table 7-6 from the Federal Reserve Board's 1986 SCF study. Both are presented because of the different types of information provided. The Census data allow us to compare the portfolios across racial/ethnic groups, while the Fed's data allow us to compare the portfolios of families at very different levels of total net worth. Then, in Tables 7-7 and 7-8, we use the Fed's data to examine the concentration of wealth holdings among the different assets by those who are the wealthiest in America.

Table 7-5 provides some insight into how the net worth was distributed among different types of assets for families as a whole and for families in the different racial/ethnic origin groups in 1984. While these are overall averages, and are not broken down by income or net worth brackets, the table does provide an overview of how families invested their wealth. As expected, on average, one finds that a family's own home was its single most valuable asset and that between the home and the family's motor vehicles about half of its net worth was accounted for. As discussed earlier, this was even more true of Black and Hispanic families than of White families, which is not at all surprising given the far smaller net worth of the former.

It is interesting to note that Hispanic families had a significantly larger proportion of their net worth tied up in their business or profession than was true, on average, for Black families (about 2.5 times as much) and even more than for White families (about 1.6 times as much). On the other hand, it is quite clear that White families tended to have far more invested in interest earning assets, in stocks and in retirement accounts. It is also important to note that the Other Asset/Liability entry was positive for White families, indicating that, net of other liabilities, they had 1.8 percent held in such investments as trust accounts. However, this entry was negative for Black and Hispanic families, indicating that they had net liabilities that had to be subtracted from the assets listed earlier to account for their overall net worth position. These differences between the racial/ethnic groups again demonstrate the importance of disaggregating alone these lines if one wishes to present data that are an accurate representation of the net wealth holdings of American families.

When we turn to Table 7-6, we see how important it is to also disaggregate by the overall amount of wealth. It is really quite true that the very wealthy are not like the rest of us in many quite significant ways, not the least of which is the nature and composition of their portfolio of wealth holdings. In addition, in Table 7-6, we find a somewhat different categorization of the various types of assets. Moreover, it must be kept in mind that the Federal Reserve's Survey of Consumer Finances (SCF), upon which Table 7-6 is based, encompasses a supplementary sample from among the wealthiest portion of our society (though as was pointed out in Chapter 6, they missed the very wealthiest). This goes a long way toward explaining such differences in the overall All Households column as the smaller proportion of net worth tied up in ones Principal Residence, 27.9 percent, in the 1986 SCF study, as compared to 41.3 percent tied up in Own Home in the 1983 SIPP study--since the net value of a household's principal residence accounts for only 5.1 percent of the net worth of those in the wealthiest one-half percent of the population, as compared to 50 percent for those in the first 90 percent.

But before proceeding it is necessary to point out that the reason for lumping a full 90 percent of all households into one group, but then examining in more detail the wealth holdings of the top 10 percent and in particular the wealthiest 1 percent and even one-half percent, is because, as we shall see in detail shortly, the top 10 percent own and control about two-thirds of all the privately held wealth in the nation. By the way, the decision to group the data in this manner was made by the Federal Reserve's researchers.

Looking further at Table 7-6, we can begin to see how very different is the composition of the wealth of those who are truly rich from that of the vast majority of our population. Some 54.3 percent of the net worth of the least wealthy 90 percent of our population in 1986 was in their primary homes and cars, with another 10.1 percent in Other Real Estate that for this group was, one suspects, primarily invested in small summer vacation homes. On the other hand, among the wealthiest one-half percent of the households only 5.1 percent was in their principal residence, 0.1 percent in their automobiles, but 14.5 percent in other real estate, which included second homes and also rental properties held by households whose primary business is not renting property.

Publicly held stocks represented only 2.7 percent of the holdings of the lowest 90 percent, but more that 19 percent of the portfolios of the top 1 percent. Even more striking is the fact that Business Assets represented 5.7 percent of the wealth of the lower 90 percent, but 33.1 percent of that of the top one-half percent and only slightly less, 27.2 percent, of that of the second richest one-half percent. Not surprisingly, the proportion of money kept in checking and savings accounts decreased as wealth increases, from 7.2 percent to 1.2 percent, whereas the use of CDs and money market accounts was rather constant. The Miscellaneous category includes trusts and managed investment accounts, as well as the value of more mundane items as the cash value of life insurance. Hence, it is not surprising that this category assumed more importance the more one's wealth. What is a bit surprising is the unexpectedly lower importance of both this last category and of CDs and money market accounts by the second richest one-half percent, as compared to those both richer and poorer than themselves. I have no ready explanation for this.

The Census Bureau's SIPP data allow us to examine what percent of households owned the each of different types of assets and what the mean values of those holdings were across households with different levels of income and of wealth--which is a slightly different perspective from the issue of the relative proportions of their portfolios in the different assets. However, the highest bracket of wealth holders in the 1984 SIPP study begins at $518,000 (1985 dollars), which, as we shall see shortly, is below the mean wealth of those families in the 90th to 99th percentile in the 1986 SCF data, which indicates the lack of a detailed examination of the wealthiest households. For that reason, these data are not presented in detail here.

However, insofar as they go, these SIPP data do confirm that the percentage of families owning interest earning assets, stocks, rental property, other (than own homes and rental) property, IRA accounts, mortgage notes (owed to the household, not by it), and "other assets" monotonically increase as either income or wealth increase; whereas, except as compared to the poorest households, there is little increase in the percent owning cars or checking accounts. The proportion owning their own home does increase with income and wealth, but only up to a wealth level about equal to the mean of those in the poorest 90 percent in the Fed's SCF data. After that point, the proportion stays constant at about 93 to 94 percent. The mean value of the holdings in each of these categories show a similar pattern.

THE HIGH DEGREE OF CONCENTRATION IN THE OWNERSHIP OF WEALTH

With Table 7-7, we begin the last topic of our analysis of the distribution of wealth. We have examined the distribution of wealth over time since 1962, the different patterns of wealth holdings among families of different racial/ethnic origins and at different levels of wealth. Implicit and explicit throughout these discussions has been the fact that relatively few families own and control a vast proportion of the wealth of our nation. In this section, we will explore this concentration in the possession of wealth in some detail. We will begin by looking at the concentration of wealth in 1986. Then, we will take a look back at the changes that occurred in the pattern of concentration from 1963 to 1983 and then, to see the latest trends, from 1983 to 1986. Since only the Fed's SCF data include even the semblance of adequate data about the wealthiest among us, it is to this material that we turn--keeping in mind, as we have pointed out a number of times already, that even these data apparently failed to sample from among the truly wealthiest of the wealthy, a point to which we shall return later when evaluating some of the figures presented.

The Concentration of Wealth in 1986

Table 7-7 presents data on the concentration of wealth in both 1983 and 1986. However, at this point, we will focus only upon the 1986 figures, returning later to compare these to those in 1983. Table 7-7 provides the information concerning the pattern of concentration, not only in total net worth, but also in the ownership of each of the types of assets about which we have already spoken, and in total income. This allows us to make some important comparisons. Then, in Table 7-8, some actual dollar figures are presented, again in 1985 dollars, to allow for convenient comparisons to the dollar figures presented throughout the book.

For the reasons discussed in Chapter 6, the figures for 1986 are for households with heads aged 25 and older. The figures for 1983 in Table 7-7 are for the same type of households, to allow for comparability. However, for the same reasons, those in Table 7-11 for 1963 and 1983 are for households with heads aged 18 and older.

In both Table 7-7 and 7-11, six columns of percentages are presented. Reading across each row, for each year, the figures in the first four columns add to 100 percent (except for rounding errors) showing the distribution of the ownership of that asset, or group of assets, among households arranged into four groups by the amount of total wealth held by that group. The first column is for all those households who fall into the least wealthiest 90 percent of all households, when the households are ranked by their total net worth. The second column represents the next 9 percent of households in such a ranking, those from the 90th to the 99th percentile. Then, we have those one-hald percent of the households in the 99th to 99.5th percentile, followed by the wealthiest one-half percent. Since it is quite common, in the media and elsewhere, to talk about the wealthiest 1 percent and 10 percent of households, the last two columns present the data for these groups. These two columns merely represent simple addition of the figures in the earlier columns.

Looking at the data for 1986 in Table 7-7, not surprisingly, we find that the severest concentration in the holding of wealth is when it is in the form of stocks, bonds, business assets, and the miscellaneous category which includes trust and managed investment accounts. Thus, we see that 47.2 percent of the publicly owned stock (as distinguished from that stock which is closely held and not publicly traded--hence included in business assets), 38.8 percent of the publicly held bonds (as distinguished from those owned by business, such as banks and insurance companies, and hence, included in the net value of those businesses), 44.5 percent of business assets, and 44.4 percent of miscellaneous assets--all taken at their net value--were owned in 1986 by the wealthiest one-half percent of America's households. Overall, (see the second row from the bottom in the table) 44.7 percent of these assets, which represent the ownership of our nation's means of production, were owned by only this very small proportion of our people.

When we extend our analysis to include the next richest one-half percent, we must include the 13.7 percent of the stock, 10.4 percent of the bonds, 11 percent of the business assets, and 4.5 percent of the miscellaneous assets owned by this group, bringing the total owned by the richest 1 percent to 55.4 percent of these crucial four categories of the net wealth. In a similar manner, if one extends the discussion to the richest 10 percent, one encompasses the ownership of some 87.1 percent of all of this wealth. These figures reflect an astounding degree of concentration of wealth and of power.

If one takes a broader perspective, looking at all the forms of wealth, there is still a very high degree of concentration, though not to the same extent. Clearly, since principal residences, automobiles, and checking and savings accounts are not nearly so overwhelmingly possessed by the rich, when one includes them the degree of concentration drops, though it does remain quite considerable. When we look at the total, we find that the poorest, in terms of net wealth, 90 percent of the households owned a bit more than a third (35.1 percent) of the wealth in 1986, while the richest 10 percent owned the other two-thirds (64.9 percent), with almost one-quarter (24.4 percent) of all of the net wealth having belonged to the richest one-half percent. Another rather striking comparison is to realize that the poorest 50 percent of all American households owned, together, less than 4 percent of the total wealth in 1986, while the richest 5 percent held 55 percent of total wealth and 65 percent of non-housing wealth (Avery and Kennickell 1988: 12).

Table 7-7 allows us to see in a clear fashion how the degree of concentration increases as one moves from consideration of all wealth, to the total minus the three most widely held assets (homes, cars, and checking/savings accounts), to consideration of those four categories which represent the real control of productive wealth, stocks, bonds, business assets, and miscellaneous (primarily trusts and managed investment accounts). For many purposes, it is the latter concentration figures that are the most relevant, figures that reflect a third more to almost twice the degree of concentration in the hands of the rich than do the broader figures.

Moreover, as we often alluded to in earlier portions of this book and as is made quite clear in Table 7-7, the concentration and centralization in the possession of wealth is far higher than for income. Thus, the poorest (again in terms of wealth) 90 percent received 72.7 percent of the 1986 income received by all households with heads aged 25 or older, but held only 35.1 percent of the net wealth; whereas, the richest one-half percent received *only* 6.2 percent of the income, but held 24.4 percent of the wealth. Thus, as unequal, and I would assert inequitable, as is the distribution of income, that problem seems pale and almost minor when compared to the inequalities and inequities reflected in the ownership of our nation's wealth.

This pattern is also reflected in the absolute size of the income and wealth figures, as is shown in Table 7-8. The mean income (all figures being again expressed in 1985 dollars to insure maximum comparability throughout the book) of the poorest 90 percent, that is, of the vast and overwhelming majority of America's households (with heads aged 25 and older), is $25,123 per household, barely above the Minimum Adequacy level discussed in the first part of this book, while their mean net worth is $55,545, only about twice as much--with more than half of that tied up in their homes and cars (recall Table 7-6). On the other hand, the mean income of the richest one-half percent is $388,126, while their mean net worth is $6,946,713, or almost 18 times as much as their income. Even more dramatic is the fact that the mean income of the wealthiest one-half percent is about 15 times that of the poorest 90 percent, while their mean wealth is 125 times as much. There can be little doubt that wealth is highly centralized in the hands of a few and that the amount of these holdings represent a remarkable degree of concentration.

On top of this, one must recall that the 1983 SCF, upon which the 1986 reinterviews were based, included in their supplementary sample of the wealthiest households none which exceeded $93,514,000 in net wealth (in 1985 dollars), and only five which had more than $54 million, at the same time that *Forbes* magazine's survey of the 400 wealthiest individuals indicated that the poorest of this elite group had a net worth of at least $135 million (again in 1985 dollars). That is, the least wealthy among the *Forbes* group had a net worth more than 44 percent above that of the very wealthiest in the SCF sample.

As we discussed in Chapter 6, the combination of the omission of individuals such as these from the SCF sample, with the undersampling of those with between $65 million and $135 million (in 1985 dollars), led to an estimate that the wealth holdings of the richest one-half percent were probably understated by some $1,249 billion in 1983 (in that year's dollars), an omission amounting to 12.4 percent of the reported total net worth in 1983. This, in turn, implies that the proportion of total wealth held by the richest one-half percent of households that year was understated by 8.4 percentage points.

Since the 1986 SCF consisted of merely reinterviewing a subset of those in the 1983 sample, it is not unreasonable to consider that a correction of about the same order of magnitude is again in order. Moreover, the SCF figures indicate that while total net worth held by households (with heads aged 25 and older) increased by some 10.3 percent in real, after inflation dollars, from 1983 to 1986, the gross value of stocks and bonds held by all households increased by 23.3 percent (again in real terms) and accounts with financial institutions, including CDs, showed a similar increase of 25 percent. On the other hand, there was an increase of only 6.1 percent in the value of principal residences net of the increases in home mortgages. Given the disproportionate growth in stock and bonds and in financial accounts and the fact that the wealthiest one-half percent of the households own a disproportionate share of these assets, especially stocks and bonds, an adjustment figure considerably larger than 8.4 percentage points should in all likelihood be employed in 1986. This conclusion is further strengthened by the fact, discussed in Chapter 6, that due to some problems in the survey design, its authors suspect that "aggregate 1986 businesses [that is, their net asset value] still [after some adjustments in the 1986 data] appear to still be significantly underestimated" (Avery and Kennickell 1988: pg 11).

Nevertheless, being conservative and using the adjustment figure of 8.4 percentage points implies that the actual proportion of total wealth held by the richest one-half percent in 1986 was probably closer to 32.8 percent than to the 24.4 percent shown in Tables 7-7--which is to say that in all likelihood this group owned closer to one-third, rather than one-fourth, of total wealth. Moreover, given the especially disproportionate share of stocks and bonds and business assets owned by the richest one-half percent, it is even more likely that the 8.4 percent adjustment figure is very conservative even in 1983, let alone in 1986, when considering the more narrow asset group of stock, bond, business and miscellaneous assets. Thus, I think it can safely be stated that in all likelihood, by 1986, the tiny proportion of our nation's households constituting the richest one-half percent actually controlled in excess of 55 percent of these vital assets, not the 44.7 percent shown and that the richest 1 percent actually owned closer to two-thirds of these assets in 1986, as compared to the 55.4 percent shown in Table 7-7. Similarly, the wealthiest 10 percent probably owned in excess of 95 percent of such assets, compared to the 87.1 percent shown.

Much is often made of the role of the many small businesses in the United States, but as these figures make it clear, at least 89 percent of the net value of private business assets owned directly by households (as opposed to being held through public stock) are held by the richest 10 percent. There is also much talk about the democratizing effect of public stock ownership. But when one realizes that more (probably far more) than 90 percent of all such stock held in private households is held by the richest 10 percent of those households, who also own at least 85.9 percent of the bonds and 74.9 percent of the miscellaneous assets--mostly trusts and managed investment accounts--it would appear that the economic democratization has not gone very far.[7]

When one combines this information with the fact (see Table 7-9) that only 19 percent of all American families directly owned any publicly held stock at all (in 1983) and more than half of those (10 percent of the total) owned stock in but one company, while only 5 percent owned any mutual fund shares (Avery and Elliehausen 1986), the conclusion is inescapable. To wit, while some have held that the combination of direct ownership of small and other business with the "democratization of ownership via the stock market" have meant the elimination of a capitalist class in the United States, that is, a separate class of people/families that own a very disproportionate share of the nation's productive assets, the reality is quite different. About 90 percent of the value of U.S. businesses are held in the hands of the richest 10 percent of the nation's families, with most of the rest holding little or no ownership; while indeed a far smaller group, amounting to one-half percent of the families, own about half or more of our nation's productive assets. It would seem that the talk of the demise of the capitalist class is a bit premature.

In this light, it is interesting to note that Lester Thurow, after reviewing and analyzing the *Forbes* (1984) survey data concerning the richest people in the United States in 1983 (see Table 7-10), concluded that:

This ($2.4 trillion in 1985 dollars) represents 40 percent of all fixed, non-residential private capital in the United States [in 1983]. . . . Great wealth is accumulated to acquire economic power. Wealth makes you an economic mover and shaker; projects will happen, or not happen, depending upon your decisions. It allows you to influence the political process and remold society . . . Economic power is a source of social concern because power entails the ability to order others about. With great inequalities in the distribution of economic power, it is hard to maintain the equality of influence that is the backbone of democracy (Thurow 1984b).

It should be noted that even if one assumes that the 400 individuals are each in a separate family from each other and from the 82 families cited--the number 482 represents only 0.15 percent of the number of families constituting the top one-half percent of households in 1983 and only 0.0008 percent of all American families that year. This is truly the economic elite of America. For these very few people to control some 40 percent of all the fixed, nonresidential private capital in America, with all the power that implies and which Thurow discusses, is to effectively deny that there can be much of an economic basis for democracy in our nation.

Changes in the Concentration of Wealth Since 1963

Let us now look for a moment at what has been happening to the pattern of concentration over the last quarter of a century. In this regard, we will first turn to Table 7-11 to look at the concentration patterns in 1963 and 1983 and then return to Table 7-7 to make comparisons between 1983 and 1986, in order to look for recent trends. In this discussion, we will again use the Federal Reserve's SCF generated data, but the reader should keep in mind the aforementioned discussion concerning some of the limitations in that data as it pertains to the very wealthiest households.

Moreover, the data used in the 1963-83 and 1983-86 tables are not strictly comparable. The subcategories in which the asset and debt data are presented varies; the earlier studies covered all households with heads aged 18 and over, while the latter focused on those with heads aged 25 and over, etc. However, as discussed in Chapter 6, the differences are relatively minor and do give us the best available benchmarks, especially given the fact that the Federal Reserve's researchers found it possible to make adjustments in the 1983 data to first make it as compatible as possible with that from 1963 and then with that from 1986.

Having said all that, the first impression that comes from these data is that when one looks at the broadest category, total net worth, the degree of concentration across the four specified groups is remarkably stable over this 23-year period. Looking first at the 1963-83 period (Table 7-11), one finds no statistically significant change in the concentration of wealth held by either the top one-half percent or the top 1 percent. On the other hand, there is a drop in the amount of wealth held by the lowest 90 percent and an increase in that held by those in the 90th to 99th percentiles of net worth, the latter often being defined of as the upper middle class or the lower upper class.[8] This occurred despite the increase in the proportion of consumer debt held by those in the 90th to 99th percentile.

If one looks at the detailed data by asset type, one finds that the lowest 90 percent saw their share of the net value of principal residences drop from 70.6 percent to 61 percent, their share of other real estate drop from 26.4 percent to 20.9 percent, and of business assets decrease from 19.2 percent to 9.3 percent. The relative holdings of this poorest group in checking accounts, stocks, life insurance, and miscellaneous did show some increase; however, the increase in checking account balances has little significance and the increase in miscellaneous assets primarily reflects that various employee thrift and stock option plans were included in this category in 1983, but not in 1963.

On the other hand, the biggest increase in relative holdings by the 90th to 99th percentile group occurred in the area of Bonds and Trusts assets, an area in which the holdings of the second to the highest one-half percent also expanded--in both cases at the expense, relatively speaking, of the richest one-half percent. It would appear that, at least within the wealthiest 10 percent of American families, the holdings of these particular types of assets became much more common over the 20 years from 1963 to 1983. One suspects that this largely reflects the widening use of trust and managed investment accounts by these families. The relative holdings of Other Real Estate and of Business Assets by the 90th to 99th percentile group actually decreased, as did their relative holdings of savings type accounts and cash value life insurance.

Turning from either total net worth or individual asset categories to look at the important combined asset group of stock, bond, trust, and business assets, one finds that the relative holdings of the poorest 90 percent dropped by a third from 13.6 percent to 9.0 percent, while that of the upper middle class (90th to 99th percentile) increased by the same 4.6 percentage points. In general, the increase in the relative share of net wealth held by the top 10 percent (from 63.8 percent to 66.6 percent) came because of the increased holdings by those in the 90th to 99th percentile group at the expense of the poorest group, with little significant change in the proportions held by the richest 1 percent. Thus, in relative terms, it was this upper middle-class group that was the winner during this 20 year period, despite their increased relative burden of consumer debt. It is somewhat misleading, though, to use the term "middle", even "upper middle," to describe a group that is wealthier than 90 percent of all households, even if their mean income ($42,427 in 1985 dollars) would rank at the upper level of what we have previously referred to as a middle-class income.

There are two areas in which the richest one-half percent did substantially increase their relative holdings during the twenty years from 1963 to 1983, namely Other Real Estate and Business assets, with the former going from 19.3 percent to 30.5 percent and the latter from 31.2 to 37.2 percent. This, in part, reflects the widespread increase in real estate values and in real estate speculation during this period. On the other hand, their relative holdings of bonds and trusts, as we discussed just above, dropped very considerably from 76.1 percent to 51.1 percent.

The pattern of a greater degree of concentration in the holdings of stock, bond, trust, and business assets than for net worth generally, or of net worth less the value of one's home, checking account, auto and consumer debt, was true at both the beginning and end of this 20 year period. Moreover, the concentration in the ownership of all three of these asset groupings was far greater than that in the distribution of income. The bottom four rows in Table 7-11 make this quite clear. Thus, in 1983, the wealthiest one-half percent held about one-fourth of total net worth (24.3 percent), about one-third (32.8 percent) of the total less the value of one's principal residence, checking account, autos, and consumer debt, and an amount approaching one-half (42.8 percent) of stock, bond, trust, and business assets. Given our earlier discussion of the weakness in the data, especially in these latter categories of holdings by the very rich, the latter figure probably is, indeed, quite close to one-half.

Returning to Table 7-7, we can look at the recent trends that seemed to be emerging as we compare the data for 1983 and 1986. Here it is important to keep in mind the differences in the definitions of the asset categories from those used in the earlier 20 year comparison and not try to make direct comparisons between 1963 and 1986 within particular categories. It is also relevant to keep in mind that the latter data are for households with heads aged 25 and older, while the earlier comparisons were for households with heads aged 18 and over; although, this difference should have little impact given that here we are looking at relative changes, not absolute dollar values and given the small holdings of households with young heads, as was discussed in Chapter 6.

Overall, there were not large shifts in this three-year period, but the direction of the shifts that did occur is interesting. Looking first at Total Net Worth, we find that the wealthiest 1 percent saw a small increase in its relative holdings (30.8 to 31.8 percent), as did the poorest 90 percent (34.4 to 35.1 percent), while the upper middle class, 90th to 99th percentile group saw its relative position weaken from 34.8 to 33.1 percent. This reverses the changes that occurred between 1963 and 1983. Thus, by 1986, the richest 1 percent were at precisely the same level (31.8 percent) they were at in 1963, while the poorest 90 percent held a bit smaller relative portion in 1986 (35.1 percent) than they had in 1963 (36.1 percent). The upper middle class, 90th to 99th percentile group, despite a bit of slippage in the 1983-86 period, still held a slightly larger proportion in 1986 (33.1 percent) than in 1963 (32.0 percent). But all of these overall shifts are quite small and the most notable result of this comparison is the relative stability in the pattern of concentration in the holdings of total net worth over a period of almost a quarter of a century.

However, there is a more significant degree of change in the 1983 to 1986 period when one focuses on stock, bond, business and miscellaneous (which here includes trust and managed investment accounts) assets. Both the poorest 90 percent and the upper-middle class, 90th to 99th percentile group saw their relative position in the holding of these vital assets decrease, while the second to the richest one-half percent, and especially the very richest one -half percent saw their relative holdings increase. For the poorest 90 percent, as best we can tell given the asset category definitions, this continued the trend found in the 1963-83 comparison. However, for the 90th to 99th percentile group those three years from 1983 to 1986 reversed the pattern of the preceding twenty years. In fact, given the limitations imposed by the different asset category definitions, it seems to have rather fully wiped out the relative gains of those earlier two decades leaving this group with 31.7 percent of these pivotal assets in 1986 compared to 37.3 percent in 1983, and to 32.5 percent of a roughly similar group of assets in 1963. Meanwhile, the richest 1 percent saw their holdings of these assets increase from 49.1 percent in 1983 to 55.4 percent in 1986- -and, as we have often discussed, the figures for this richest group are in all likelihood quite conservative.

CONCLUSION

We have seen that the distribution of wealth is indeed far more concentrated and far more unequal, dare I say inequitable, than that of income. To the extent to which the stock of wealth that a family owns yields of itself a stream of income and also a stream of direct services (such as a place to live and a mode of transportation), it is clear that this extremely skewed distribution of wealth in itself is a cause, as well as a result, of the skewed distribution of income. That is, those with great wealth, as we saw, typically enjoy large incomes, in part, derived from that wealth, especially when it is in the form of financial or business assets. And we have seen that the vast majority of households in the United States, some 90 percent of them, own a very small proportion of the business assets and of many of the most critical financial assets.

Moreover, we know that the possession of wealth gives one the opportunity to acquire even more wealth, without the need for further savings from current earned (wage and salary) income. Homes appreciate in value, interest and dividends can be reinvested, business assets appreciate and produce increased wealth and income. Certainly there are no magic guarantees for a given family at a given moment in time; there are risks and wealth can decrease in value, as with the fall in the stock market in October 1987. However, all in all, those with wealth are better able to acquire more wealth. In addition, they tend to live a far more secure existence and can protect themselves from the vicissitudes of changes in earned income in a manner and to a degree simply not possible for those who do not posses such wealth.

Furthermore, as we have briefly discussed, those with wealth, especially with large amounts of it, tend to exercise a degree of political and economic power that often escapes even those who have considerable current income, but little wealth, and which is certainly not available to individuals and families who possess both little wealth and income. Given this distribution of wealth, the distribution of income described in the first part of this book becomes not very surprising at all. Moreover, the facts concerning the distribution of wealth raise very serious questions as to whether any truly significant progress is likely to be made in redistributing income in a more equitable manner if something is not also done to break up the centers of wealth and power reflected in the data in this chapter.

Thus, the maldistribution of wealth in the United States makes the problems associated with the maldistribution of income even worse and harder to solve. But solve them we must if we are to avoid the destructiveness and social disintegration that is the likely consequence of the vast disparities in income and wealth that exist in America today. What a far better and more decent society we might all live in if we could find ways to reverse many of the destructive patterns in the changing distributions of income and wealth in the U.S. In the next and concluding chapter I will summarize some of the trends and patterns we have observed in the course of this book and I will try to identify some avenues we might go down in the pursuit of that better society.

NOTES

1. In fact, even among those with income of $50,000 to $100,000, 31 percent of their net worth is tied up in their homes, with an additional 21 percent tied up in other (nonbusiness) properties (Avery and Elliehausen 1986: 169).

2. The data that are available as of this writing from the Fed's 1986 SCF do not allow a direct comparison of the distribution of wealth by such categories of net wealth holdings. However, as we shall see in Table 7-3, they do allow us to compare 1983 to 1986 in terms of net wealth holdings by families at different income levels

3. The S.I.P.P. study, upon which this table is based, obtained information from each family via four interviews taken in consecutive months. Each month the family was asked about its income, and then the average income over the four months was included in the published statistics. I merely multiplied this by three to get an annual equivalent estimated income, in order to render the tables reported here for wealth compatible with those reported earlier for income.

4. See the previous endnote for a discussion of these periods.

5. In the Federal Reserve's 1983 SCF, Hispanics were defined as persons of Spanish origin (which presumably includes those of Indian and other ethnic backgrounds from Latin American countries), which is the same as the Bureau of the Census's definition. But, unlike the Bureau, the Federal Reserve survey results exclude Hispanics from the "White's" totals.

6. The _Forbes_ magazine reports on the wealthiest individuals and families in America have begun to adopt some of this longitudinal perspective as well, as they continue to offer some basis for comparison to the government's studies based upon more

traditional sampling techniques. Thus, in its most recent report (October 24, 1988), the editors of <u>Forbes</u> not only describe the current wealthiest 400 individuals and 100 families (the latter being separate from the former), but also talk about what happened to those individuals on earlier published lists who are not included in the current one and also about some of those who just missed this list but are likely to appear on later ones.

7. Looking more closely at bond holdings, earlier data from the 1983 SCF indicated that the richest 10 percent owned "only" 35 percent of the government savings bonds, but 92 percent of the municipal bonds, and 72 percent of the other (mostly corporate) bonds. Of all American families, 21 percent owned savings bonds, but only 2 percent owned municipal bonds and only 3 percent other bonds (Avery and Elliehausen 1986).

8. The mean income in 1983 of those in the zeroth to 90th percentile of net worth was $19,153, while those in the 90th to 99th percentile had a mean income of $42,427, those in the 99th to 99.5th percentile had $80,846, and those in the top one-half percent had mean incomes of $232,794, all in 1985 dollars.

TABLE 7-1
Distribution of Families by Net Worth
in 1962 and 1983,
Using Federal Reserve Board's Survey of
Consumer Finances
(in constant 1985 dollars)

Net Worth (in 1985 dollars)		Percent of Families		
		1962	1983	Change
Negative		11%	13%	2%
None		5	4	-1
$1 to	3,536	12	10	-2
$3,537 to	17,711	17	13	-4
$17,712 to	35,369	15	11	-4
$35,370 to	88,451	23	22	-1
$88,452 to	176,903	10	14	4
$176,904 to	353,699	4	7	3
$353,700 to	707,561	1	4	3
$707,562 to 1,768,931		1	2	1
$1,768,932 or more		*	1	1
Total		100%	100%	

Note: * Indicates too few to report meaningful
      figure.

Source: Avery and Elliehausen 1986: 167.

TABLE 7-2
DISTRIBUTION OF HOUSEHOLD NET WORTH BY RACE/ETHNIC GROUP, INCOME, AND TYPE OF HOUSEHOLD, USING BUREAU OF THE CENSUS S.I.P.P. DATA FOR 1984
(in 1985 dollars)

Net Worth in 1985 dollars	Race/Ethnic Origin of Household				Type of Household			Equivalent Annual Income * in 1985 dollars			
	White	Black	Hispanic	All	Married -Head	Female -Head	Male -Head	Less than $11,184	$11,185 to $24,859	$24,860 to $49,724	$49,725 to and more
Negative or Zero	8.4%	30.5%	23.9%	11.0%	6.0%	19.3%	15.5%	24.5%	9.7%	4.6%	2.2%
$1 - $5,179	14.0	23.9	26.3	15.3	10.5	20.3	25.1	25.3	18.9	8.8	1.8
$5,180 - 10,359	6.3	6.8	7.6	6.4	5.6	6.4	9.7	6.9	8.1	6.2	1.5
$10,360 - 25,899	12.2	14.0	11.4	12.4	12.2	12.2	13.3	11.5	13.5	14.6	5.9
$25,900 - 51,799	15.0	11.7	9.5	14.5	15.6	13.5	11.6	12.5	14.5	17.7	10.3
$51,800 - 103,599	20.7	9.3	13.1	19.3	22.7	15.3	13.0	11.8	19.1	23.9	23.5
$103,600 - 258,999	16.9	3.3	5.1	15.3	19.5	10.3	8.0	6.2	13.6	18.3	31.0
$259,000 - 517,999	4.4	0.5	2.1	4.0	5.3	2.0	2.6	1.0	2.1	4.6	13.4
$518,000 or more	2.1	0.1	1.0	1.9	2.7	0.6	1.4	0.3	0.5	1.3	10.4
Totals	100.0%	100.0%	100.0%	100.0%	100.0%	100.0%	100.0%	100.0%	100.0%	100.0%	100.0%

Note: * Average monthly income over four sample months multiplied by twelve.

Source: U.S. Department of Commerce 1986c.

TABLE 7-3
Median and Mean Net Worth by Income, Race/Ethnic Group, and Type of Household,
Using Bureau of the Census S.I.P.P. Data for 1984
(in 1985 dollars)

| | Median Net Worth | | | | Mean Net Worth | Distribution of: | |
	White	Black	Hispanic	All	All	Net Worth	Number of Households
Annual Income*							
Less than $11,184 "The Poor"	$8,747	$91	$453	$5,263	$30,727	9.7%	25.7%
$11,185 to $24,859 "Low Income"	31,820	4,370	3,809	25,534	54,617	20.5	30.6
$24,860 to $49,724 "Middle Class"	52,348	16,552	25,698	48,427	82,957	31.8	31.3
$49,725 and more "High Income"	132,854	60,873	103,074	127,919	250,769	38.0	12.4

						Median Net Worth without Home Equity
Type of Household:						
Married-couple	$56,135	$13,531	$11,213	$51,920	$105,587	$12,767
Female-Headed	23,310	695	$495	14,385	46,555	3,084
Male-Headed	12,252	3,131	$2,800	10,239	50,654	4,693

	White	Black	Hispanic	All	Net Worth & Income Ratios Black/White	Hispanic/White
All Households:						
Median Income	$21,876	$13,524	$16,716	$20,844	61.8%	76.4%
Median Net Worth	40,544	3,519	5,090	33,843	6.2	12.6
Mean Net Worth	89,440	20,970	37,327	81,568	23.4	41.7
Distribution of:						
Net Worth by Race/Ethnic Group	95.2%	3.0%	2.0%	**		
Households by Race/Ethnic Group	86.8%	11.0%	4.8%	**		

Notes: * Average monthly income over four sample months mulitiplied by twelve.
       ** Can not add three groups since Hispanics can be of any race.

Source: U.S. Department of Commerce 1986c.

193

Table 7-4
Distribution of Net Worth by
Family Income and by Race/Ethnic Group,
Using Federal Reserve S.C.F. for 1983 and 1986
(in 1985 dollars)

	1983 Net Worth Median	1983 Net Worth Mean	% of '83 Population	1986 Net Worth Median	1986 Net Worth Mean	% of '86 Population
Family Income						
Less than $10,800	$5,732	$30,701	22.6%	$10,225	$30,767	24.0%
$10,800 - 21,599	30,872	56,186	26.1	24,078	60,294	25.6
21,600 - 32,399	42,808	83,160	19.3	40,288	80,594	18.6
32,400 - 53,999	82,145	124,661	21.1	82,863	143,445	21.0
54,000 - 107,999	170,883	333,126	8.8	192,220	360,464	8.8
108,000 and more	973,031	2,115,310	2.2	852,897	2,157,384	1.9
All Families	43,208	139,788	100.0	41,865	141,187	100.0
White Families	52,811	161,697	82.7	51,069	164,386	82.2
Non-White &	7,414	35,302	17.3	8,806	34,230	17.8
Hispanic Families						

Source: Avery and Kennickell 1988.

TABLE 7-5
Distribution of Net Worth Among Different Assets
by Race/Ethnic Group,
Using Bureau of the Census S.I.P.P. Data for 1984

Type of Asset	White	Black	Hispanic	All
Own Home	40.5%	64.7%	50.5%	41.3%
Motor Vehicles	5.9%	11.1%	7.9%	6.0%
Other Real Estate	13.0%	14.8%	13.9%	13.4%
Business or Profession	10.5%	6.7%	17.3%	10.3%
Checking Accounts	0.6%	0 .9%	0 .6%	0.6%
Interest Earning Assets at financial institutions or in Government Savings Bonds	15.2%	7.0%	9.6%	14.9%
Other Interest Earning Assets	3.2%	0.7%	0.0%	3.1%
Stocks and Mutual Fund Shares	7.1%	0.8%	2.2%	6.8%
IRA or Keogh Accounts	2.2%	.9%	1.0%	2.2%
Other Assets (Liabilities)	1.8%	-7.6%	-3.0%	1.4%
Total	100.0%	100.0%	100.0%	100.0%

Notes: Own Home is valued as equity in "own home," and does not
include "vacation" homes.
Other Real Estate includes both vacation homes and other
real estate.
Interest Earning Assets at Financial Institutions include
passbook savings accounts, money market accounts, CDs, and
interest earning checking accounts.
Other Interest Earning Assets include money market funds,
government and private bonds, and other interest earning
assets.
Other Assets include unit trusts, amounts owed to the
household from mortgages from the sale of real estate or
notes from the sale of a business, and moneys in other
financial investments not included elsewhere.

Source: U.S. Department of Commerce 1986c.

Table 7-6
Distribution of Net Worth Among Various Assets
for Households with Heads Aged 25 or More
Holding Varying Proportions of Total Net Worth
Using Federal Reserve 1986 SCF Data

Asset	All Households	Percentile of Total Net Worth Held			
		0-90th	90-99th	99-99.5th	Upper 1/2
Principal Residence	27.9%	50.0%	23.8%	11.5%	5.1%
Other Real Estate	14.5	10.1	18.5	17.7	14.5
Publicly Held Stock	10.3	2.7	9.3	19.1	19.9
Bonds	3.7	1.5	4.1	5.2	5.9
Check/Savings Accounts	4.7	7.2	4.7	4.2	1.2
IRA & Keogh Accounts	3.7	3.8	4.3	2.7	2.9
CDs/Money Market Acct.	6.4	7.3	7.9	3.5	7.1
Business Assets	18.2	5.7	18.4	27.2	33.1
Automobiles	2.1	4.3	1.6	0.5	0.1
Profit Sharing/Thrifts	2.8	3.1	2.5	4.9	2.1
Miscellaneous	6.0	4.3	4.7	3.7	11.0
All	100.0	100.0	100.0	100.0	100.0

Notes: Principal Residence is market value, net of first and second
mortgages.
Other Real Estate includes value of secondary homes, rental
property, and land, all net of mortgage debt, includes some
property that conceptionally are business assets.
Publicly Held Stock does not include stocks held as part of
IRA or thrift accounts or those held in a pension or trust
accounts. Includes mutual funds.
Bonds, as with stocks, excludes those held in IRA, thrift,
pension or trusts.
Business Assets includes the net market value of the household's
share of all sole-proprietorships, partnerships, and
non-publicly held corporate assets, not reported elsewhere.
Automobiles is the average retail "Blue Book" value, net of all
installment debts owed by the household. This includes debts
on automobiles, but also those on other durables and
installment payment personal and home improvement loans.
Hence, this category is actually understated with regard to
automobile value, and Total Net Worth is understated by the
exclusion of the retail value of other consumer durables.
Profit Sharing and Thrifts includes the withdrawal value of
employee thrift, profit sharing, stock option, and 401K plan
accounts.
Miscellaneous includes the cash value of life insurance,
trusts, managed investment accounts, and the outstanding
principal on all notes and debts owed the household, minus
the outstanding principal owed on all debts except mortages
and installment loans.

Source: Avery and Kennickell 1988.

Table 7-7
The Concentration of Wealth Holdings in 1983 and 1986
Among Households with Heads Aged 25 or More
by Types of Assets and by Percentage of Total Net Worth Held,
Using Federal Reserve SCF Data

	Percentile by Amount of Net Worth Held											
	0-90th		90-99th		99-99.5th		Top 1/2%		Top 1%		Top 10%	
Assets	1983	1986	1983	1986	1983	1986	1983	1986	1983	1986	1983	1986
Principal Residence	62.6%	63.8%	28.1%	28.6%	4.2%	3.1%	5.1%	4.6%	9.3%	7.7%	37.4%	36.3%
Other Real Estate	22.0	24.4	40.5	42.3	7.4	9.0	30.0	24.4	37.4	33.4	77.9	75.7
Publicly Held Stock	10.7	9.2	32.3	29.9	7.6	13.7	49.4	47.2	57.0	60.9	93.2	90.8
Bonds	10.0	14.0	41.8	36.7	10.5	10.4	37.7	38.3	48.2	49.2	90.0	85.9
Check/Savings Accts	66.1	53.7	26.1	33.4	3.6	6.7	4.2	6.3	7.8	13.0	33.9	46.4
IRA & Keogh Accts	31.7	36.0	41.2	39.4	8.6	5.4	18.6	19.2	27.2	24.6	68.4	64.0
CDs/Money Mkt Accts	48.7	39.8	38.2	40.6	3.9	4.0	9.1	15.6	13.0	19.6	51.2	60.2
Business Assets	10.2	10.9	41.2	33.5	12.4	11.0	36.2	44.5	48.6	55.5	89.8	89.0
Automobiles	70.3	72.4	25.3	24.7	1.8	1.7	2.6	1.2	4.4	2.9	29.7	27.6
Profit Share/Thrift	37.4	38.8	48.6	29.8	4.5	12.8	9.5	18.5	14.0	31.3	62.6	61.1
Miscellaneous	34.3	25.0	27.4	26.0	3.4	4.5	35.0	44.4	38.4	49.9	65.8	74.9
Total Net Worth	34.4%	35.1%	34.8%	33.1%	7.1%	7.4%	23.7%	24.4%	30.8%	31.8%	65.4%	64.9%
All but Prin Res, Ck/Sav Acct & Auto	19.8	20.5	38.4	35.2	8.6	9.4	33.2	34.8	41.8	44.2	80.2	79.4
Public Stock, Bonds Business & Miscel.	13.6	13.0	37.3	31.7	9.9	10.7	39.2	44.7	49.1		55.4	86.4	87.1
Distribution of Income	72.2	72.7	19.3	18.6	2.9	2.4	5.6	6.2	8.5		8.6	25.5	27.1

Note: See Notes at the bottom of Table 7-6 for the definition of assets.

Source: Avery and Kennickell 1988.

Table 7-8
Concentration in the Dollar Holdings of Net Worth and in the Receipt of Income,
and Mean Net Worth and Income, All by Percentile Holdings of Net Worth
Among Households with Heads Aged 25 or More, Using Federal Reserve
1986 SCF Data (Assests in 1985 dollars)

Asset	All Households	Percentile by Amount of Net Worth Held			
		0-90th	0-99th	99-99.5th	Upper 1/2%
Total Net Worth	$11,858.6	$4,158.2	$3,926.4	$ 877.5	$2,896.5
Total Income (Gross)	$2,591.0	$1,884.5	$482.1	$62.6	$161.8
(above in billions)					
Mean Net Worth	$142,493	$55,545	$524,141	$2,096,369	$6,946,713
Mean Income	31,109	25,123	64,377	149,558	388,126
Minimum Net Worth	$-95,477	$-95,477	$263,484	$1,618,751	$2,736,634
Maximum Net Worth	110,311,960	262,763	1,605,928	2,726,013	110,311,960
Number of Households	83,207,536	74,880,352	7,491,641	418,587	416,956

Notes: Number of Households refers to the number in the population in 1986.
   Minimum and Maximum Net Worth reflect that actually reported by
   households in the sample interviewed and are in 1985 dollars.
   The Mean Net Worth and Income figures are in 1985 dollars.
   The Total Net Worth and Total Income figures are in billions of 1985
   dollars.
   See notes at the bottom of Table 7-6 for details about asset definitions.

Source - Avery and Kennickell 1988.

Table 7-9
Distribution Among American Families of Ownership of
Publicly Traded Stocks from the Federal Reserve's
1983 Survey of Consumer Finances

Number of Stocks Owned	Percentage of Families
0	81%
1	10%
2-4	4%
5-9	2%
10-19	1%
20 or more	1%

Source: Avery and Elliehausen 1986.

TABLE 7-10
The Net Worth of the Wealthiest Americans in 1983
(in 1985 dollars)

Wealthiest	Minimum Net Worth per Individual or Family
400 Individuals	$135 million
82 Families	$215 million

Combined Holdings of 482 Wealthiest Individuals & Families	
Direct Ownership of Business Investment Assets	$179 billion
Business Investment Assets Controlled Directly and Indirectly	$2,369 billion

Note: The 82 Families are separate from the 400 Individuals.
No single member of the families held in his/her own name
sufficient net worth to qualify among the 400 wealthiest,
but each family did "show enough cohesion--in financial
matters, at any rate--to be considered as entities"
(Forbes 1983: 146)

Source: Thurow 1984b.

Table 7-11
The Concentration of Wealth Holdings in 1963 and 1983 Among Households with Heads Aged 18 or More by Types of Assets and by Percentage of Total Net Worth Held, Using Federal Reserve SCF Data

	Percentile by Amount of Net Worth Held											
	0-90th		90-99th		99-99.5th		Top 1/2%		Top 1%		Top 10%	
Assets	1963	1983	1963	1983	1963	1983	1963	1983	1963	1983	1963	1983
Principal Resid.	70.6%	61.0%	23.2%	29.4%	2.4%	4.1%	3.8%	5.5%	6.2%	9.6%	29.4%	39.0%
Other Real Est.	26.4	20.9	47.1	41.5	7.2	7.1	19.3	30.5	26.5	37.6	73.6	79.1
Public Stock	8.6	10.0	29.2	32.1	15.6	8.4	46.6	49.4	62.2	57.8	91.4	89.9
Bonds & Trusts	7.2	6.7	13.1	35.4	3.5	6.8	76.1	51.1	79.6	57.9	92.4	93.3
Checking Accts.	47.2	54.7	29.4	31.5	5.0	5.6	18.5	8.3	23.5	13.9	52.9	45.4
Savings, CDs, & Money Mkt.	53.4	49.4	37.3	36.6	2.6	4.4	6.7	9.6	9.3	14.0	46.6	40.6
Life Ins. C.V.	55.3	61.8	30.4	21.5	5.3	4.6	9.0	12.0	14.3	16.6	44.7	38.1
Business Assets	19.2	9.3	40.8	39.9	8.8	13.6	31.2	37.2	40.0	50.8	80.8	90.7
Automobiles	79.9	79.2	17.2	17.5	1.7	1.5	1.4	1.8	3.1	3.3	20.3	20.8
Miscellaneous	28.9	39.1	38.0	43.2	15.4	5.3	17.7	12.3	33.1	17.6	71.1	60.8
Less Cons. Debt	70.2	69.3	13.3	17.5	4.1	6.9	12.4	8.5	16.5	15.4	29.8	32.9
Total Net Worth	36.1%	33.4%	32.0%	35.1%	7.2%	7.2%	24.6%	24.3%	31.8%	31.5%	63.8%	66.6%
All but Prin. Res, Ck Acct., Auto, Cons.Debt	23.8	20.8	34.9	37.5	9.0	8.8	32.3	32.8	41.3	41.6	76.2	79.1
Pub. Stk., Bds., Trusts & Business Assets	13.6	9.0	32.5	37.1	10.5	11.1	43.5	42.8	54.0	53.9	86.5	91.0
Distribution of Income	76.2	72.4	16.8	19.1	1.8	2.7	5.2	5.8	7.0	8.5	23.8	27.6

Notes: Principal Residence is net of first and second mortgages.
   Other Real Estate includes second homes and rental property, all net of
      mortgages, and some business property such as farms.
   Public Stock includes mututal funds & investment clubs, but not trusts, IRAs,
      or those held in pension or thrift accounts.
   Bonds and Trusts includes all assets held in trusts and all gov't and corporate
      and other bonds, except gov't savings bonds.
   Savings, CDs & Money Market Accounts also includes Money Market mutual funds and
      IRA and Keogh accounts, plus gov't savings bonds.
   Business Assets is net of all debts of the business, unless owed to the household
      and includes non-publicly traded stock. Some business holdings, particulary
      farms, are included with Other Real Estate. Includes the household's share of
      all sole-proprietorships, partnerships, and non-publicly held corporate assets
      not reported elsewhere.
   Automobiles are listed at gross market value, using the "Blue Book" in 1983.
      Debt due on automobiles is included in Consumer Debt.
   Miscellaneous includes notes and mortgages due to the household, plus gas leases
      and patents. In 1983, includes withdrawal value of employee thrift, profit
      sharing and stock option plans. Only profit sharing was included in 1963.
   Consumer Debt includes debts on cars, home improvements (unless in form of second
      mortgage), and other loans with and without regular payment schedules.

Source: Avery, Elliehausen, and Kennickell 1988.

PART III

AN OVERVIEW OF WHAT IS AND WHAT COULD BE

8

Summary and Recommendations

SUMMARY: A DOZEN IMPORTANT CONCLUSIONS

There are a number of interesting and provocative conclusions
that can be drawn from the evidence cited in this study. While I
would not pretend that a basically descriptive overview of the data
concerning the distributions of income and wealth in the United
States is sufficient in and of itself to conclusively prove all of
these points, I do propose them as viable hypotheses, for which
there is considerable supporting evidence, hypotheses that warrant
careful consideration and further study.

**1. The U.S. is in the midst of a serious polarization in the
distribution of income.**

The standard of living of the already poorer sections of our
population deteriorated far faster during the decade from 1972 to
1982 than did that of families in the upper portions of the income
distribution. Since then, the median incomes of those with
relatively higher income has increased faster than those who were
already among the poorest. Thus, the gap between the rich and the
poor continued to grow wider, both in relative terms and in terms
of the actual number of dollars involved. The poor are receiving
an ever smaller portion of the nation's income to share among
themselves, while the rich are getting an increasing share.
Meanwhile, the image of a vast, expanding, relatively affluent
American middle class is seen to be a myth. Those in the middle
are becoming an endangered species as the American society becomes
more polarized.

2.   Poverty in America is at unacceptably high levels, both in absolute and historical terms.

While much has been made of the modest improvement in the official poverty rate in the years since 1983, as we have discussed at length, this improvement only looks good when one forgets to mention the serious increase in the extent of even official poverty during the decade from 1973 to 1983.   Moreover, there are some recent signs that for some sectors of our population the incidence of poverty began to increase again by 1987.   Overall, in terms of both the rate of poverty and the number of people and families affected, poverty in America in the late 1980s is as big a problem as it was in the late 1960s.   In this regard, our nation has made virtually no progress in 20 years.

3. The official definition of poverty vastly understates the extent of the problem.

The official definition of poverty has little usefulness beyond that of a statistical reference point.   The basis for the original level chosen was so inadequately supported by responsible research and so arbitrary that to base our social programs or our vision of the nature and extent of the problem of poverty upon it is simply unacceptable.   We need to do the necessary work to determine how much it really costs people in our society to live at a level that is not an insult to human dignity and an embarrassment to a nation that prides itself as being the richest in the world (a dubious claim in many ways, but that is a separate discussion).

The point here is that when one tries to use alternative standards against which to judge the extent to which families in the United States are forced to live at income levels that do not allow for adequate housing, food, medical care, etc., one gets estimates that are in excess of fully one-third of our families, not the 15 percent or so commonly talked about when one uses the official poverty standard.

Moreover, when one extends the analysis to talk about families which, while not suffering in a physical sense from inadequate income, nevertheless live with an amount of income that does not enable them to enjoy the basic amenities of life that our society defines as minimally reasonable in a modern society, we begin to get numbers that exceed half the population.

How is this possible? It must be kept in mind that the median income, the 50 percent point so to speak, is but one interesting statistical measure of central tendency, it is not a number with any particular meaning in terms of describing a particular absolute standard of living.   Thus, as the median family income fell in real terms for much of the late 1970s and early 1980s and as real weekly wages continue to fall, on average and in many industries, such an measure as median family income just charts a picture of a falling standard of living.   In light of this and keeping in mind that the median real (constant dollar) family income in 1987 barely surpassed that in 1973, a period during which the real costs of such necessities as housing and medical care rose far faster than the costs of many other items (to become a much larger proportionate burden on the incomes of many families), is it really any wonder that more than half of America's family do not live with reasonable access to many of the basic needs and amenities of life in a modern society?

4. A significant and growing proportion of Americans live at a very high standard of living, by any absolute or historical standard, and live in a style that is almost as different from that of America's poor as the classical image of life in the United States is as compared to that in many Third World countries.

This upper portion of U.S. society enjoys an ever increasing proportion of the nation's resources and has watched with amazing unconcern as the gap between the affluent and the poor widens dramatically in both absolute and relative terms. This part of America has managed to design for itself such things as marvelously advanced and sophisticated forms of medical care, and even such medically defined necessities as weight control and exercise classes, while upwards of 37 million Americans, including more than one-fifth of all of our nation's children have no medical insurance and little access to medical care of any sort, including even the most rudimentary preventative health facilities. Similar contrasts exist when one talks about housing, diet, education, vulnerability to crime, and many other basic elements of life. The affluent, on the one hand, and the poor and low income earners on the other hand have truly come to live in two very different societies, and the gaps between these societies is growing as is their membership.

5. This polarization is taking on increasingly racial and ethnic overtones.

Thus, while the majority of the poor are now and have always been White, the incidence of poverty among the Black and Hispanic portions of our population remains at levels many times that experienced by the White community. In addition, the most recently available data (for 1987) indicates that while the poverty rate among Whites has recently improved modestly, it has worsened considerably among Blacks and Hispanics. Moreover, the evidence suggests that the racially based discrimination in earnings is also getting worse in recent years, not better, and that this discrimination spans across the whole spectrum of industries and occupations. On top of this, the distribution of wealth between White families, on the one hand, and Black and Hispanic families, on the other, is vastly more inequitable than the distribution of income and greatly increases the vulnerability of these latter families to economic disaster whenever there is any pressure on the family's current income position.

While one can not address the problems of poverty, low income, and a lack of significant wealth as if these were the problems of the Black, Hispanic, and other minorities exclusively, we must nevertheless still acknowledge the particularly high incidence of poverty and low income and the lack of assets in these communities and come to terms with the reality that across every educational level, across the full range of industrial and occupational categories, discrimination based on race, color and ethnic origin is still a very integral part of the United States, even for those lucky enough to be working full-time all year. It will simply not be enough to address the problem of our inequitable distributions of income and wealth without special attention and focus on overcoming the causes and results of this discrimination.

6. The distribution of income also severely discriminates against women.

Thus, while there has been some narrowing of the gap between White women and White men, especially when they both work full-time, that gap remains far wider even than that between Blacks and Whites, as both Black and Hispanic males consistently earn more than White women. Moreover, the increasing presence of female-headed households and the remarkably high incidence of poverty and very low net worth among them, suggest an increasing degree of polarization between these households and the rest of society. The economic discrimination visited upon women in the United States can not be separated from our attitudes toward children and families. We must face the obvious fact that until and unless we formulate a program to address the needs of mothers, we will be unable to fully address the needs of women.

7. The highest incidence of poverty in America has been forced upon our children who are the least able to overcome it, and this problem is getting worse, not better.

By consigning one-fourth to one-half of our youngest children and one-fifth to one-third of all of our nation's children to poverty, we are laying the seeds for a degree of social degeneration and deterioration perhaps never before experienced in a modern industrialized nation. By condoning a situation where millions of our children live in intolerable conditions of poverty and low income, with all that implies about poor diet, poor health care, inadequate housing, exposure to being criminally victimized, and an education that leaves them illiterate and uneducated, we have come to virtually institutionalize a form of what can only be viewed as societal child abuse.

Beyond that, are we really so naive as a nation not to realize that the results of such shortsighted mean-spiritedness is a crucial part of the cause of the drug and crime problems about which we seem to care so much? We talk of the unfair competition with other nations. But how can this or any other society possibly hope to compete in the modern world if its children are deprived of the possibility of preparing to successfully function in that world?

If we are to have a future as a nation that we are to take any pride in we must start today to deal with the effects of our distributions of income and wealth upon our children. Better still, we must effectively change that distribution.

8. Education, especially through the high school level, has become part of the problem, not the solution, to overcoming the effects of our distributions of income and of wealth.

We once held out the hope that education would overcome the racial, ethnic, and sexual discrimination that is so evident in our distribution of income, but this has not happened. We have found that despite the attainment of more and more education, the discrimination between the racial/ethnic groups and the sexes continues with little closing of the income gaps--although there is real movement up the income scale.

While it is beyond the scope of this book, there are many related problems with our educational system as it leaves many of its graduates illiterate, with little or no knowledge of history or geography, and not even the rudiments of mathematics and science. In study after study, U.S. children fall farther and farther behind those in other countries in terms of their knowledge of the tools of science, mathematics, and language that will be necessary for them, and for us as a nation, to succeed in a modern and rapidly changing world. Perhaps as we try to address the other problems discussed in this book, we need to ask whether we should not also be thinking about fundamentally changing how our educational system is funded, how the teachers are trained, evaluated and paid, how performance is measured for both teachers and students, how curriculums are designed and textbooks chosen, how teachers and administrators are used and misused, and who should make the basic decisions about how to answer and respond to these and other questions.

9. The view that poverty is primarily a function of unemployment and part-time employment is simply false--the basic structure of our wage system is a major part, perhaps the most significant part, of the problem.

When the minimum wage leaves even a full-time, full-year worker with an income well below the poverty level necessary to support a family, when the average real wage in industry after industry is so low as to leave even full-time workers below   a   modestly defined low income level, and while no industry pays an average wage sufficient to enable a full-time worker to reach a moderate income level, then unemployment and part-time employment can not alone be blamed for the poverty problem or for our poor distribution of income. Hence, attempts to solve the poverty problem simply through job training and employment services will simply not suffice.

This is not to say that these efforts are not needed. Efforts to expand employment, just as efforts to bring immediate relief to those in poverty via public assistance of one form or another, of course, are needed and crucially so. But, the primary cause of poverty and low income in the United States is the structure of wages. The point that comes across time and time again is that even when one takes the most conservatively optimistic point of view by looking at only those people who are able to work full-time, full-year, one still finds real poverty and unacceptably low income.

Hence, it is clear that significant progress in closing the gap between the rich and the poor in the United States requires a restructuring of the entire wage system. To put it in terms that may sound rather polemic, but are nevertheless accurate, only if we significantly reduce the exploitation of the vast majority of the American work force can we begin to substantially move the distribution of income toward some more equitable structure. When the majority of the U.S. labor force finds itself living at unacceptably low levels of income, despite working full-time, and when this majority has to watch the so-called Yuppies (and the others who make up the one-third or so who live at increasing levels of affluence) consume the output of the majority, something is sorely wrong.

This is not a new observation, but it is one that many of us had begun to lose sight of as we were told that the War on Poverty had largely been won and the time of affluence for the majority was upon us. Well, that war was not won, affluence by any real criteria remains a distant goal for the vast majority of Americans, and the problems go far beyond unemployment and job training. The entire structure of the economy and the manner in which wages are determined need to be examined and overhauled.

Ironically, this occurs at the same time as it has become quite clear to even the most uninformed that the historical period of American economic dominance over the rest of the world is long past--having ended during the early 1970s. The United States is now forced to compete more with the modern industrial nations of Europe and Asia than at any point in the last 100 years, as well as with such "newly industrializing nations" as Korea and Singapore. At the same time, to meet this competition, American corporations seek, throughout much of the Third World, new, low-wage areas in which to locate production facilities.

In the midst of all this, the myth has been propagated that the reason for the lack of international competitiveness of the United States is its "high paid" or "over-paid" workforce. But there is growing evidence that, compared to a number of other industrialized nations, such as Germany and Sweden, we are becoming a low wage area.[1] Moreover, as has been shown, the vast majority of American workers are not even adequately paid, let alone overpaid. While the U.S. has succeeded in creating literally millions of new jobs in recent years, these have primarily been low paid, nonunionized, and often part-time jobs which offer little security.[2] Many writers have analyzed this nation's economic problems and have concluded that the competitive problem is not one of workers who are too highly paid, but of low productivity due to inadequate modernization of facilities, non-productive use of investment funds, primitive and even barbaric conditions of labor relations and work organization, and an almost total lack of long-term, integrated, strategic economic planning that involves labor, business, and government.[3] Perhaps if the United States began to face these problems it would be able to pay reasonably livable wages to more of its workers, reduce the inequalities in income, take care of all of its children, and begin again to address the tragic discrimination against Black, Hispanic, and female workers.

10. The distribution of wealth in the United States is far more unequal than that of income and vastly worsens the negative impact upon families of periods of either low income or of an interruption in the stream of income--with the growing problem of homelessness being but one reflection of this situation.

As we saw in Chapter 7, the average net worth of the wealthiest 0.5 percent of American families in 1986 was 125 times that of the least wealthy 90 percent, while the ratio of the mean incomes of the two groups was "only" 15:1--making wealth more than eight times more concentrated. If one focuses only upon wealth held in the form of publicly traded stocks, bonds, business assets, and miscellaneous assets (trust and managed investment accounts), the ratio of the mean values of the holdings of the two groups leaped to an astounding 566:1, with the average holdings of just these assets by the wealthiest 0.5 percent having been in excess of $5 million, while that of the least wealthy 90 percent was some $8,851 (1986 current dollars). Thus, the concentration in the holding of these assets is four and a half times higher than for wealth generally, and 38 times higher than for income.

There is little doubt, therefore, as to the fact that possession of wealth in the United States is far more concentrated than is the receipt of income. Nor is there any doubt that this concentration is even far higher when one focuses on those assets that are indicative of the ability to exercise power in the economic arena. In addition, we also saw that the differentials in wealth between White families on the one hand, and Black and Hispanic families on the other hand, were far wider than those found when looking at the distribution of income. Finally, we saw that for the least wealthy 90 percent of American families the majority of the wealth they do possess is tied up in their homes and cars. Only a small part of it is very liquid and available.

This lack of available wealth, especially for those in the lower 20 percent or even 40 percent (let alone the lower 90 percent), implies that these American families always lead a perilous economic life. For many, if not most, of these families, the jobs of their principal breadwinner--the only breadwinner in many of the poorest families--carries little security. Layoffs and unemployment, not to mention plant closings, are all too regular an occurrence. The so-called safety net of unemployment insurance and welfare is, as we have discussed at some length, full of very large holes through which a majority of the poorest families fall through. Yet, without any wealth of their own,[4] these families are dependent on these often inadequate social programs to avoid such disasters as homelessness when their stream of income is interrupted for reasons that are typically totally beyond the control of the family itself. In this circumstance, is it any wonder that we have seen the remarkable rise of homelessness in America in the last decade--and this is but one symptom of this economic vulnerability.[5] (For some details on the size, nature and causes of the problem of homelessness in the United States, see this endnote.)

11. The concentration of wealth in the hands of a very small portion of the population undermines the very foundation of America's aspirations to be a truly democratic society and lies at the root of why this nation has been unable to address some of its most severe economic problems.

As was suggested when the figures on the distribution of wealth and on the intense concentration of assets were discussed, the existence of a small group of Americans who control a vast portion of our nation's wealth implies a grip on both economic and political power by this group of Americans and their cohorts that belies much of this nation's claim to be democratic.[6] These individuals and families who have "won" the economic game in the United States, obviously feel very little need to change the rules of that game.

For them, it is very convenient to laud the virtues of *laissez-faire*, of a supposedly free enterprise capitalistic system, of the doctrine that that government governs best which governs least. But, in fact, much of the basis for the profession of such ideological positions is self-interest. The last thing they want is a political economic system that would interfere with their control of wealth and power or that would seriously attempt to redistribute either income or wealth.

I am reminded of the words of John Kenneth Galbraith as he critiqued the classical concept of consumer sovereignty, the concept which he labeled as the "accepted sequence," which states that the people control the economy, and business simply functions to meet the needs expressed by the people. Galbraith (1967, 1973) argued persuasively that, in fact, the reverse is true, that the corporate structure is sovereign, that it controls the economy in its own (and I would argue its owners') interests, and that the consumers, the people, are the ones being controlled. Galbraith argued that:

> The accepted sequence also raises barriers against a wide range of social action which, though in fact inconvenient to [corporate] organization . . . is held by the [accepted] theory to be inimical to this maximization of satisfaction by the individual. . . . The doctrine thus outlaws a wide range of government interference and does so in the name of the individual. . . . A doctrine that celebrates individuality provides the cloak for organization. . . . Once it is agreed that the individual is subject to management in any case--once the revised sequence is allowed--the case for leaving him free from

government interference evaporates. It is not the individual's right . . . that is being protected. Rather, it is the . . . right to manage the individual (1967: pp. 226-227).

Galbraith went on to comment on the importance of those in control maintaining the traditional ideology that cloaks their power, when he pointed out that,

It is possible that people need to believe that they are unmanaged if they are to be managed effectively. . . . were it recognized that . . . [we are] subject to management, we might be at pains to assert our independence. Thus we would become less manageable (1967: 228).

If we are to begin to design a program that would redress the vast inequities that are inherent in the current distributions of income and of wealth in the United States, we must free ourselves from the false ideologies that are used to keep us from even considering practical ways to redistribute income and wealth. If this requires a major restructuring of our economy, then so be it.

12. The total effect of these conclusions is to paint a picture of a nation in deep trouble, a nation that must consider major restructuring of the ways in which it distributes its income and wealth.

While it may seem trite and old fashioned, the only possible way I see to solve these problems is if the people most affected-- the minorities and women and poor, the people who work so hard and yet earn so relatively little, in combination with those who have been given the tools to explain and clarify what is happening and why--come together and begin to build a serious political movement. This movement must aim not just at finding immediate relief in the form of welfare reforms and the like (though those efforts are also needed), but rather this movement must begin to come to grips with the need for a fundamental restructuring of the United States' economy. While, sadly, I see little evidence that this is happening, I see even less hope if it does not.

In the final section of this book, I will try to outline some of the parameters that I feel are essential to that restructuring.

RECOMMENDATIONS

I have presented a detailed examination of the distributions of income and wealth in the United States and have made quite clear my opinion that those distributions are in many different ways very unacceptable both on the grounds of ethics and humaneness. Also unacceptable are the inefficiencies with which they burden the society which loses so much of the potential contributions that could be made by those who suffer at the low ends of these distributions. It is only reasonable, therefore, that I be asked: So, what do you think should and can be done? Fortunately or unfortunately, the limitations of this book preclude a full and detailed exposition of what should be done to overcome these inequities. However, I will attempt to very briefly outline the directions in which I think we should move in the United States.

Discussion of the nature of an overall solution to these multifaceted problems must be approached in a systematic manner. First, we must somehow move as rapidly as possible to come to the aid of those millions of American families and their children whose suffering can not wait for long-term solutions as to the causes of the maldistributions of income and wealth. Simple humaneness requires that we prevent the homelessness, the malnutrition, the lack of decent medical care, the inadequate education of the children, and the criminal violence that plagues the lives of these people every day. Second, we must correct and eliminate the barriers that prevent many of the poor who wish to work from doing so. Third, we must change the way wages are determined so that those who do put in a full day's work earn enough to support their families at a standard of living that allows these people to participate fully and with dignity in the life of their communities and their nation. Fourth, we must correct the distribution of wealth so that all families who have helped to build and create the vast wealth that this nation possesses have some share in the streams of income that wealth generates, and not just in the form of wages and salaries, so that all families have some measure of control over how that wealth is employed. It should be clear to even the casual reader that many books can and have been written on each of these topics, and not just in recent years. This final chapter is not the place for me to review all of that literature (though I will make reference to some of it and many of the relevant works are listed in the Bibliography), nor is it the place for me to go into great detail into how to address each of these four levels of the needed solution. But, without begging or avoiding the question, I will lay out some basic principles and some specific suggestions.

Addressing the Basic Needs of Poor and Low Income Families

Medical Care

It is long overdue for the United States to finally enter the twentieth century[7] and accept the necessity of providing the full range of top quality medical care to all of our people regardless of their ability to pay. This must include the full range of preventative health care, including pre and postnatal care, and the treatment of acute illnesses. The outlines for such a minimal program are well-known: every employer must provide *as a paid benefit* access to either a group health insurance program and/or to a health maintenance organization that covers both the worker and the worker's family. In the case of two or more workers in a family, coordination of payment between the programs will prevent duplication of costs and should help further reduce the direct out-of-pocket expenses of the family. Every business must simply come to accept that the normal cost of doing business is to include such health plans as part of the overall compensation of its workforce.

This health coverage must be available and provided to part-time and temporary workers, as well as to those working full-time. This will provide the necessary incentive to businesses to keep their costs as low as possible by maximizing their use of full-time workers, rather than the current practice of trying to avoid these costs by using part-time and temporary workers, many of whom would prefer regular full-time employment. For those who are not working, *regardless* of the reason, coverage must be provided via a government insurance program, similar to Medicaid and Medicare.

The health coverage provided must be complete, that is, it must include vision care, dental care, maternity benefits, prescription drugs, etc. The extraordinary costs of very long-term medical care, nursing care, and so-called catastrophic treatment programs are probably best handled by a national supplementary health insurance paid for out of *general* tax revenues, not special taxes on a particular age group as in the recent addition of catastrophic coverage under Social Security.

Once it is clear that all employers will have to participate fully in such a program and that all taxpayers will have to support the supplementary plan, there should finally be a constituency that is large enough and powerful enough to take on the medical and hospital professions and force upon them a comprehensive program of cost constraints. This might begin with the requirement that substantial portions of the medical profession be placed on salaries that are capped at some reasonable level, with a vision of the application of comprehensive (dare one say holistic) medical programs that are based on the full range of medically related professions, without the overemphasis on surgery that is now the case, and that place far more emphasis on the prevention of illness rather than simply on treatment.

In addition, we must begin to develop a national system of public neighborhood health clinics in all low income areas and in all areas, urban or rural, where there are inadequate private facilities. These clinics would provide basic preventative and curative health care, pre and postnatal care, and first level emergency care. We can simply not tolerate a medical delivery system wherein large urban neighborhoods and many small towns and rural areas have virtually no access to local, convenient, quickly available medical care. If our private medical system is incapable or unwilling to fill this obvious need, a need recognized by every civilized society, then our public system must do it. Providing health insurance to our people is useless if there is no place for many of them to go to receive medical attention.

Housing

No family or individual in the United States should be without a decent home in which to live, no matter what the circumstances. For decades, this nation has abandoned to the free market the provision of housing, when that market, by its very nature, is incapable of and unwilling to respond to the needs of the poor. I am well aware of the housing programs that have existed in the past, but all of them were never, even at their peak, able to adequately deal with the size and nature of the problem. The massive, one might very well say cruel and mean spirited cuts in even these inadequate programs by the Reagan administration simply made a bad problems far, far worse.

What is needed is a national commitment to the following concept. Every family should be expected to pay no more than a reasonable amount of its annual income for housing, say 30 percent, by which I mean to include a reasonable package of utilities. If that amount of money is inadequate to provide rental housing services in the area in which the family is living and working, then the family should be provided with vouchers in an amount sufficient to enable them to pay for housing. Families who wish to pay more than the suggested percentage are, of course, free to do so.

In many high cost areas, the government will likely find it less expensive to provide publicly built and administered housing, rather that rely totally upon the private market. But such housing must be very low density and well spread throughout the community to avoid the many problems that we have seen in the large, centralized housing projects located in the midst of poverty areas. Residents in these public housing units must be given some control over their administration and a stake in seeing that they are maintained and passed on in good condition. A system of financial incentives to encourage this can rather easily be designed.

Nutrition

Similarly, each family should be expected to pay no more than a reasonable percentage of its income on food, say 33 percent to use the figure the government seemed so fond of when it defined the poverty level. If that amount is insufficient to provide an appropriate amount of nutritional food for that family given the costs of food in that area, an expanded food stamp program should fill the gap.

But this nation also has a severe problem of illnesses due to improper diets. For example, every foreign visitor to this country is simply amazed to find the extent of obesity that is rampant, especially among the poorest segments of the population. Perhaps it is time for us to limit the use of food stamps to such items as milk, dairy products, eggs, meat, fish, poultry, fresh produce, fruit juices (and I mean juices, not these various "fruit drinks") and generic brands of bread and cereals that contain a minimum of sugar and preservatives. No family that has an adequate supply of such items will suffer from malnutrition. If the family wants other food products, fine; but there is no reason for the society as a whole to help provide foods that merely help create problems that our medical system will have to face later. If some elements within our commercial food industry do not like the imposition of these limits, too bad. Let them make their profits selling in the private sector, not to those using public monies; or let them provide products that meet these terms and do so at competitive prices. In addition, we clearly need to do far more to educate our people, especially the poor, about nutrition.

Education

As someone who is a credentialed high school mathematics teacher and worked in that profession before moving on to university teaching, as someone who has raised two children within the American public school system, and who has also observed firsthand a number of European educational systems, and finally as someone who has professionally followed the development of education in this nation, I would like to make a number of suggestions for how to improve our educational system.

The fundamental problem with American education is its basic structure. To state the matter clearly: locally controlled, locally funded education is a disaster and a failure and it is about time we woke up to and admitted that fact. It is simply unacceptable to have the amount of money spent on a child's education dependent on the accident of what community and what state that child happens to go to school. The truth is that there is simply no excuse for any community to have the power to keep its children from having a top notch education; and there is no excuse for those communities who happen to benefit from our unequal and inequitable distributions of income and of wealth to be able to provide such an education to their children, but keep it from the rest of the nation's children by refusing to share their income and wealth with the rest of the nation's families via a progressive national tax on both that income and wealth. We must end forever the system whereby a community has the power to simply refuse to pay a tax for its educational program, or a system in which some communities can not afford to pay for an adequate education program because of the low tax base, in income, wealth, or property, within that community.

Moreover, the way we train, credential, evaluate, use, and pay our teachers is also a disaster and a failure. To have the quality and extent of the professional training of a child's teachers, the basis for the evaluation, promotion, and retention of those teachers, the quality and content of textbooks, and the design of the curriculum vary dramatically from place to place is an absurd, cruel and unacceptable burden to place upon our children.

Sure, we can be sensitive to the need a local community might feel to supplement the basic education with a range of elective courses, extracurricular activities, and out-of-school supplementary educational opportunities, perhaps even funded from some special allocation of funds made available to each and every community. But, we can simply no longer allow local prejudices and ignorance, and the varying tax bases of different communities and states to determine the overall quality of the education our *nation's* children receive.

State and federal funds provided from general tax revenues must be used to guarantee that all of our children have a truly equal educational opportunity. Teacher salaries, and those of educational administrators as well, should be set at a level such as to attract the best and brightest of our young people and the same pay should be paid everywhere in the United States. If we are not willing to pay well, very well, to educate our own children, then what are we really about as a nation? This will mean that teachers will be relatively highly paid in some regions where salaries, and perhaps the cost of living, are generally low. So be it. Perhaps that will attract some of the best teachers out of the high cost areas into these areas where they are sorely needed. In some extremely high cost areas, teachers may have to be given supplementary housing and food vouchers as part of their regular compensation package. But hopefully, that would be a rare situation.

If we are going to pay a lot more for education, then we have a right to demand a lot more of it. As is already the case in many other nations, the educational standards necessary to enter the teaching profession in the United States need to be increased dramatically, both in the area of *proven knowledge of the subject area* which is to be taught and in the area of *proven capability as a teacher*. Extensive preparation and a high grade point average in the subject area, subject matter competency tests, a required period of supervised, closely evaluated probationary teaching, and regular required refresher courses, with examinations that must be passed, is a minimum that can and must be expected of teachers who must be paid well enough to attract those who are capable of and willing to endure such a rigorous professional program. Other countries do it, other professions do it, we can do it with our teachers.

But then we must let them teach. We must relieve teachers of the myriad of nonteaching tasks with which they are burdened. We must reduce the size of our classes so that teachers can work meaningfully with students--25 or 30 should be the upper limit. We must lengthen the time of some classes so that a teacher can develop an idea fully in a period. (What is so magical about 50 minutes?) We must begin to allow for a more flexible schedule, with some classes that meet five days a week, but others only once, or twice or three times a week, to enable more subjects to be covered. Our students do not need a three-month vacation every summer, and, if reasonably employed and paid, neither do our teachers. One month per summer would be sufficient, perhaps on a varying basis between the states, as is done is some European countries to relieve the concentration and spread the vacationing over a three or four month period.

We must begin to standardize our basic curriculum across the entire nation. Are we not capable of bringing the very best minds in America together to design a basic curriculum of mathematics, the sciences, grammar, literature, foreign languages, history, geography, economics, political science, and sociology, with all of the humanities and social sciences courses infused with an international, cross-cultural content? Are we not tired of our children constantly placing among the worse in the industrialized world in virtually every subject field? Are we not concerned that our children must be able to function in a very international, multi-cultural context? If we indeed do share these concerns and if we have the capability to build such a curriculum, then let us get on with doing so as a first priority for our nation.

Child Care and Early Childhood Education[8]

If we are to break what has been called the cycle of poverty, if we are to enable mothers who want to work the opportunity to do so, if we are to begin to help our children, all of our children, to catch up educationally with the rest of the modern world and be able to compete in a modern economy, then this nation must extend its public educational system down to the level of infant care. This means that just as we have public elementary schools, almost all of which include kindergartens, we must build real public educational gardens for all of our youngest *kinder*.[9]

Just as we must train and retrain a whole cadre of teachers for our older children, the same must be done for child care workers, who must begin to be seen as teachers of our youngest children. Various studies have indicated that some of the very basic patterns of learning behavior, how one learns to learn, are in fact taught and learned in the period between the ages of 10 and 18 months of age. The issue is not whether the child will learn *some* learning behavior, the issue is what sort of learning behavior is taught and whether the behavior that is learned is useful and effective. This is not done in the sense of formal education, but is done in the manner in which adults choose to respond to infants as they begin to explore their environments. Many social skills, as well as concepts crucial to learning to read and do mathematics, are also developed before the age of two. Some basic patterns affecting one's appreciation of music and art are developed then as well. All of our children deserve to have a full opportunity to develop these skills and concepts and to have the opportunity for playing with other children in a safe and supportive environment.

I am not proposing that we require all children to attend child care/early childhood development centers. Many families can and do provide similar opportunities for their children at home or through various family and private connections. But for those families who wish to have their children enrolled in such programs, or who need to do so, on a full- or part-time basis, so that parents can work or themselves go to school, we have the responsibility as a nation to provide, free of tuition costs, adequate spaces in specially designed buildings, with teachers fully trained to work with those age groups, teachers who are also paid enough to attract committed professionals.

A Guaranteed Minimum Level of Income

Even if we address the specific, basic problems of food, housing, medical care, and education, as we must, there still remains a host of other needs for which a family must have income. We all know the list: clothing, transportation, household goods, newspapers and books, cultural and recreational activities. It is not so difficult to develop estimates of what a minimally adequate volume of these would cost in a given area. Every family in the United States should be able to live at least at that minimum level. If not, the necessary funds have to be provided. It is as simple and direct as that. The question is how to do it in a manner that is as cost efficient as possible, that reaches everyone who really needs the help, and that encourages those receiving help to fully participate in the society in a manner so as to earn the income that will allow them to provide for themselves.

The basic idea for how to do this has been around for over 20 years. Economists refer to it as the Negative Income Tax. This is a system wherein families file a tax return and then, if their income is below a set minimum, receive a "refund" from the government. This can be paid in monthly installments, in response to perhaps quarterly updated reports. The system can, indeed must have built into it a graduated, sliding scale of slowly increasing taxes and slowly reduced "refunds" as earned income increases so as to provide a reasonable incentive to work one's way up to the point where the "refunds" stop.

A number of studies, and even experiments, have been done with such a system.[10] I am convinced it can work and that, in combination with the food and housing vouchers and the medical insurance program already discussed, can finally allow all American families to live and function with at least a minimum level of dignity and well-being. Moreover, this system would be designed to largely replace the whole range of other public assistance programs and their expensive administrative structures.

A single office could provide families with help in filling out the initial tax return statement and quarterly updates, and could provide various forms of counselling and referral services. The housing and food vouchers would then be sent to the family along with their "refund" checks each month. For families without a worker who receives health insurance, this office would also be responsible for having the government health insurance card issued to the family.[11] The local office would only need to provide the first month's housing and food voucher and issue an initial temporary health insurance card until the permanent one came in the mail. Once a family member found work, they would exchange their government health insurance card for the private one. As part of the government's response to the initial payment of withholding and Social Security taxes, the old government card would be cancelled and the flow of "refunds," food and housing vouchers adjusted as appropriate.

One might ask, if there is to be this negative income tax system to provide a stream of income to those who need it, then why do we need the housing and food vouchers and the public health insurance program? The answer is unfortunately quite obvious and straightforward. We can not necessarily trust that all those who receive the funds will necessarily spend them wisely. We must be particularly concerned to protect and provide for the children involved. Therefore, it is appropriate and necessary that the food, housing, and health care be provided in a form that does not allow for those funds to be used for any other purpose. In special cases, it may even be necessary to provide some clothing vouchers for children's clothing in lieu of an adjusted "refund." In some case, we may have to insist that the children be placed in childcare facilities during all or part of the day, where they can be fed and cared for while parents attend educational or job training classes or drug rehabilitation programs.

In short, we must do what has to be done to insure that poverty in America is a one-generation phenomenon. The whole concept of an intergenerational cycle of poverty is an admission of a fundamental failure of our social system. Whether this phenomenon occurs in White, Black, Hispanic, or other ethnic/racial environments is immaterial. Our society can be sensitive to the special cultural and language needs of each community. We can help those communities to find ways to celebrate and preserve their rich traditions via, for example, assistance for community cultural programs and supplementary educational activities. But no segment of our society should be allowed to flounder in such poverty and misery that its children, who are also *our* children, are deprived of the opportunity to fully participate in the larger society, nor can our nation afford to lose the genius, the creativity, the untold potential that these children have the capacity to contribute to us all.

Opening Up the Labor Market to All Who Want to Work

Unemployment and involuntary part-time employment clearly are contributing causes to poverty and low income among America's families. In addition, there are many others who are not counted among the unemployed because they have been forced to drop out of the labor force due to the lack of affordable, high quality child care, or because of illness or drug related problems, who would also like to work if they could overcome these problems.

The easiest problem to solve is that of child care and that is something we discussed in the preceding section. As for illness, what we need to do is either prevent it or cure it. In this regard, providing equal access to quality medical care to all of our people, regardless of their ability to pay, is the crucial first step to reducing illness as a cause of not working. This, too, we discussed earlier. Once we have provided health care, then for those who are still ill or disabled, and who wish to work, employment opportunities need to be opened up. The truth is that this nation has done much in this area, though we clearly need to do more. However, this is a topic about which I offer no specific suggestions and only identify the issue. Similarly, though I have a number of thoughts about the drug problem, this is an area sufficiently removed from my area of expertise that I will hold those comments for another forum.

Having said all this, what does need to be done to open up the job market so that all of those who want work can find it? There are three things that need to be done: (1) Create more jobs, (2) Educate and retrain workers and potential workers so that they can qualify for jobs that now exist and that will be created in the future, (3) Reduce and redefine the workweek and the workday so that the existing jobs are spread among more people. Beyond finding a job is being sure that the job carries a wage sufficient for the worker to support a family. However, for purposes of expositional clarity, I will separate the topic of the number and availability of jobs from that of the wage level, which I will discuss in the following section.

To begin with, the truth is that creating jobs is something at which our nation would appear to have been quite successful. We have created many millions of new jobs, even in the face of many millions of other jobs which have ceased to exist, such that the net number of jobs has increased in every year, but three, since 1960. The exceptions were the recession years of 1961, 1975, and 1982. However, during this same period not only has our civilian noninstitutional population[1] gone from 117.2 million in 1960 to 182.8 million in 1987, but a larger percentage of that population is either working or wants to work. Thus, the labor force participation rate, the civilian labor force (which includes both employed and unemployed workers) as a percentage of the civilian noninstitutional population, has also increased, with some ups and downs, from 59.4 percent in 1960, to 60.4 percent in 1970, to 63.8 percent in 1980 to 65.6 percent in 1987.

The combination of a larger population and a higher labor force participation rate have put this nation under great pressure to create more jobs. And though we have created many, it has not been fast enough, so that, as we discussed in an earlier chapter, the unemployment rate was at historically very high rates consistently from 1975 through 1987. It was not until late 1988 that the official unemployment rate finally reached the levels of 5.4 to 5.5 percent that we last saw in the early 1970s and before that in the early 1960s. However, during those earlier periods, an unemployment rate of 5.5 percent was considered quite high, the goal being a rate of 3.5 to 4.5 percent, such as was the rule during most of the 1950s and the second half of the 1960s. Thus, while we have indeed created many jobs, it has simply not been enough. Moreover, as we discussed in detail in earlier chapters, far, far too many of these jobs have been part-time and temporary, and even among the full-time jobs, far too many have carried wages so low that no worker could support a family at any reasonable level of living on the resulting earnings.

Creating Jobs: Reversing the Movement to Part-Time and Temporary Jobs Instead of Regular Full-Time Jobs

So, how do we go about creating more full-time jobs paying better wages? Leaving aside the wage question for a moment, we initially must ask ourselves what the incentives are that have led so many employers to prefer to create part-time or temporary jobs. The obvious answer is the cost of such jobs to the employer is lower. Why? First of all, such workers are rarely unionized. The employer is freed from the pressure of collective bargaining and often pays lower hourly wages and lower salaries to such workers. Second, even in most union contracts there are escape clauses that allow the employer to avoid the paying of virtually all benefits to such workers: no health insurance, no retirement contributions, no sick leave, no vacation leave. The cost savings to many employers, even if they otherwise paid the same hourly rate, is often as much as 20 percent, a considerable savings to be sure. One way to discourage the use of part-time and temporary help in lieu of full-time employees, therefore, is to remove this differential by requiring that *all* workers, regardless of the number of hours worked or the number of days or weeks worked, be entitled to a full package of benefits. They should get full medical coverage as I suggested earlier, plus the employer should be required to contribute the same percentage into retirement programs as is done for full-time workers, and allow for the accumulation of sick and vacation leaves according to a reasonable, I might even suggest a slightly generous, prorated schedule.

As for wages, except for the provision of a short probationary period, during which both sides are testing the waters, so to speak, and during which some initial on-the-job training normally occurs, the wages of all part-time and temporary workers should be set at an hourly (or weekly or monthly as the case may be) level equal to that of full-time workers doing the same work.

Such steps would go a long way toward reducing the creation of those part-time and temporary jobs whose existence, in lieu of full-time jobs, are almost totally a function of the ability of employers to exploit these workers. Those part-time and temporary jobs whose existence are dictated by concerns for efficiency, worker productivity in a given context, or the short-term nature of the work itself, would still continue to exist. Obviously, the adoption of the policy suggested would mean more full-time jobs, but almost surely less jobs in total.

Creating Jobs: Redirecting the Flow of Private Investment Funds
There are two sources of private investment funds, or perhaps it would be better to say, two indications of the availability of such funds that could be used to create significantly more jobs in America. During the last decade, we have seen an accelerating wave of corporate takeovers and buyouts, often referred to as LBOs, or leveraged buyouts, to indicate that the corporation doing the buyingout is making use of prodigious amounts of borrowed investment funds, often in the form of what has come to be know as junk bonds. We have also seen United States' corporations that have continued to invest huge amounts of money abroad building new production facilities and creating millions of jobs, often at very low wages, in other nations. The issue is: what have been the market incentives that have encouraged this behavior and is it possible to change the incentive structure or the legal environment so that these funds would be more likely to stay at home and be used to create new jobs here.

I know of very few economists who feel that the leveraged buyouts have increased efficiency or productivity or have resulted in new jobs or new products. They have primarily been motivated simply by the desire of the owners and managers of a given corporation or investment banking firm to increase their own profits by acquiring control over the assets and future profit streams of other firms. This new wave of take-overs occurred in large part because the Reagan Administration made it clear by its lack of any credible enforcement of the antitrust laws that it would not challenge or interfere with any such activities. Bush, during his first few months in office, would appear to be following the same pattern.

What is needed is vigorous enforcement of those laws that already exist and the institution of new laws that place the burden of proof upon the corporation wishing to do the taking over that there are clear economic benefits of increased efficiency, productivity, or competitiveness that would result from such an action. In such an environment, I am convinced that most of these buyouts would not occur. The point is that this activity reveals the existence of vast pools of ready investment funds in the hands of industrial corporations, banks, insurance companies, and the 1 percent or so of families who own so much of our nation's wealth, funds that they seem ready and able to invest in buyouts, but which are not being used in productive ways. The challenge is to use the tactics suggested to block the misuse of these funds and to instead rechannel them into more productive, job-creating uses.

Another indication of the availability of private investment funds is the flow of overseas investment. (And, yes, I am aware that this is occurring at the same time that foreign corporations and individuals are investing in the United States.) I am sensitive to the efficiency arguments which support the need for financial capital to be able to flow across national borders. I am also sensitive to the needs of many of the receiving nations for such investment funds. However, much of this outflow of money occurs because of elements in our tax laws which artificially render such investments abroad more profitable than those at home. Moreover, much of that investment is motivated by the desire to gain access to foreign labor forces that will work at extremely low wages and under unsafe and inhumane conditions and which are prevented from unionizing. The presence of these U.S. corporations in these countries often results in small enclaves which drain labor power, investment capital, and social infrastructural investment away from the rest of the economy with the result that a very small privileged class becomes rich, while the lives of the majority of the people are either not improved or even worsened. This often increases the social and class tensions in the nation and leads to social chaos, revolts, and repression. Ultimately, the majority of workers in both the United States and the Third World nation are hurt, not helped, by much of this flow of investment funds.

If the United States placed high export taxes on such outgoing funds, taxes aimed at eliminating the cost differentials between employing cheap, unorganized foreign labor compared to employing American workers, much of those funds could be kept at home. I am proposing that we institute exactly such a tax policy.

I am well aware of the valid location theory arguments that transportation costs in general, differentials in transportation costs between finished products versus input materials, the need to place production facilities of regionally specialized items near their places of use, the need to place certain production facilities near customers so as to make available service and repair facilities, etc., often provide real gains in efficiency and productivity that warrant the export of capital and its investment abroad. Where these factors are significant, the corporations involved can afford to pay the labor cost differential tax I am proposing and still export their investment funds. Where that is not the case, let them stay at home and invest here.

To the extent to which other nations adopted similar policies aimed at us, so be it. If the primary reason for a foreign firm to invest in the U.S. is to take advantage of our relatively cheap labor, or to avoid strong unions and worker safety laws in its home nation, then let it stay put. That sort of investment we do not need. Where their investment is motivated by other market incentives, it will come anyhow.

Then, we need to adopt a cooperative, national planning environment, similar to that in many other nations, in which labor, business and government work together (1) to identify research and development projects, at both the basic scientific level and at the applied product development level, (2) to identify products and services for which a real social need exists, (3) to identify regions of the nation and specific locations where there are existing pools of labor that need jobs, (4) where existing pools of labor need to be retrained to be able to perform jobs that industry needs and would be willing to provide. Once this is done, then joint projects can be created in which labor, business, and the government cooperate, using mostly private investment funds, but perhaps supplemented in certain cases by government start-up, training, relocation, or research funds. In this way, private investment funds can be channeled from current unproductive and often destructive uses, to the creation of needed jobs and products.

Creating Jobs: Social Investment Projects

The U.S. government creates millions of jobs via such activities as defense expenditures, the space program, and the 30 year-long project to build the interstate highway system. What is now long overdue is an effort by the federal government to identify particular social needs that can or will not be met by the private sector and then embark on the planning effort necessary to satisfy those needs. In choosing projects there should. be a concern for maintaining a broad overview that looks for projects that simultaneously satisfy a variety of social goals and that do not cause social problems that will be costly to correct.

Two such projects were implicit in the earlier discussion. We need to build the facilities and train and hire the personnel necessary to extend our public educational system to include the level of infant and child care and early childhood development. Second, we need to build the facilities and hire and train the personnel necessary to establish a set of medical clinics in those neighborhoods and communities which the private medical delivery system can not or will not service. In addition, much has been written in recent years about the unsafe and deteriorating conditions of our nation's bridges and the need to refurbish and rebuild many of them.

A New Transportation Infrastructure. In addition, I want to propose another project, one that like our highway program would span 30 years or more and that would result in (1) the creation of hundreds of thousands of entry level skilled and semi-skilled jobs that could provide employment for many of those with a minimum of education and training, (2) the resuscitation of our steel and automobile industries providing jobs to tens of thousands of laid-off workers from those industries and employment for other new entrants to the labor force, again at skilled and semi-skilled level jobs, as well as at professional jobs, (3) create a new capacity within the automobile industry that could allow the U.S. to compete in a world market from which we are now excluded, (4) provide a market for high-technology computers and related equipment that would in turn provide employment to many highly skilled professionals, give a major boost to an important industry, and create new capacities within that industry that would enable it, too, to compete in new foreign markets, (5) vastly improve the energy efficiency of the nation and reduce our dependence on foreign oil, and (6) considerably upgrade the infrastructure of the United States, enabling industries across the economy to enjoy increases in efficiency and productivity. This all sounds too good to be true, but it is not.

What I am proposing is that the U.S. undertake to rebuild and vastly redesign and upgrade its entire railroad transportation system and that it integrate that new system with existing and improved airport and trucking facilities so as to provide for the country the capacity to move materials and people far more rapidly, far more efficiently, with far less use of petroleum products and far less pollution. What I have in mind is relaying every foot of track in the United States with welded tracks that are well banked in order to accommodate very high speed trains, trains that can attain speeds of 250 to 300 miles per hour. The laying of this track would take years and provide many of those unskilled and semi-skilled jobs to which I referred.

Designing and building the rolling stock would be the job of a reinvigorated automobile industry, which is already the primary provider of what railroad rolling stock we do still build. These new engines and cars would have to be lighter, more aerodynamic, and stronger than anything we now build. Providing them would reemploy tens of thousands of auto workers. Providing the steel for the rails and the rolling stock would provide a vast new market for our steel industry and thousands of jobs there. Designing, building, programming and installing the computerized control systems that would be needed on every train, at every station, and along the full length of tracks would provide a vast, new market for our computer industry and thousands of new jobs, most of which would be high skilled, professional positions.

In addition, we would need to build new terminal facilities near each major metropolitan area. These hubs should also include facilities to transship materials to trucks for distribution within and around the metropolitan area. Ideally, and where possible, these hubs should be near the major airports that already service each area, so that people and material can quickly move from train to plane, and even more important, so that goods can be trans-shipped between trucks and planes.

What I envision is a system modeled on the containerization that has occurred in the ocean shipping business. Containers of standardized size and design would be loaded at a production facility, placed on a truck for transport to the hub. There, it would be placed aboard a high speed train, or in the case of very light or very perishable items, or items needed very urgently, aboard specially designed cargo aircraft. Upon arrival at another hub, the reverse process would occur. Long-haul trucking would be largely eliminated as far too slow, too expensive, and too wasteful of fuel. A high tax on truck fuel would speed this process and produce some revenue in the interim. Each hub would also connect with local public mass transportation facilities, subways and monorails, that would move people between the train/plane hub and the central cities and suburban areas.

The reader should understand that high speed train systems travelling in excess of 200 miles per hour already exist in France and Japan and are being built in Germany. Much of the technology for the system I envision already exists and is well proven. Some of this same technology is used in new subway systems in cities around the world. We would be playing catch-up in many regards. The sad thing is that when, for example, the San Francisco Bay Area Rapid Transport system was being built, not a single U.S. firm was even able to bid to provide many of the essential components. Were we, as a nation, to develop the capacity to design, provide the materials for, build, and train the operators of such a state-of-the-art national system, we would have attained the capacity to enter what over the next century will be a world market for such systems.

The Recycling Industry. Yet another possible social investment project involves the development of an integrated set of industries to sort and recycle our solid waste, for example, converting currently unusable, nonbiodegradable plastic waste into multipurpose lumber,[13] converting glass and paper products into new usable products, clean burning (that is, with no toxic emissions) other waste to provide electricity,[14] etc. Here again, labor, business, and government could cooperate to design, locate, build, and operate such a system on an integrated national basis, and in the process create thousands of new jobs, develop new exportable products and whole industries, clean up our environment, and make us more energy efficient.

These are the sort of long-term, multi-impact, job-creating, environmentally sound social investment projects that we need. We do not need make-work projects employing our people at dead-end, low efficiency jobs producing products or services for which there is little need. Instead we need to undertake the planning and then the long-term commitment to implement social projects such as these I have proposed that could provide many of the jobs we need, provide new markets for industries that are stagnating, and help us develop new products and industries that would enable us to better compete on the world market.

Finding the Money for Social Investments
The obvious question arises: This is all well and good, but, especially in these days of federal budget deficits that are already

far too high, where is the money going to come from to do these things? The answer is: (1) increased taxes on corporate profits, which have decreased as a share of federal government receipts from 28.6 percent in 1950, to 27.6 percent in 1960, to 16.9 percent in 1970, to 12.5 percent in 1980 and to only 9.8 percent in 1987; (2) increased taxes on those with the highest incomes, reversing the steady downward trend in the highest marginal rates; (3) instituting a progressive wealth tax on the financial and business assets of those individuals and families who own such a vastly disproportionate share of the nations wealth; (4) reductions in the defense budget, in part made possible first, by a slowing, and even a reversal, in the arms race with the Soviet Union, something that seems quite likely as this is being written, and, second, by the reduction of U.S. overseas forces as wealthy allies, with whom we are running substantial trade deficits, are asked to assume more of the cost of their own defense; (5) private investment funds rechanneled from overseas investments and leveraged buyouts (as discussed earlier) that could be used, perhaps as matching funds alongside government monies for some special projects; (6) special user taxes on such things as truck fuel and gasoline generally.

The point is that this nation clearly has the economic capacity to mount the sort of efforts I have outlined and provide the needed jobs. The issue, as we have seen over and over again, is: do we have the political will? Can the majority of the people who are living at either very modest or indecently low incomes and who have little or no wealth forge a political force capable of overcoming the economic and political power of those who would have to pay the taxes and change their business practices under the proposals I have suggested? That is the crucial question, and I do not have a very optimistic answer. All I know is that we must try.

Training and Retraining the Labor Force

Clearly this nation has a major problem when millions of its people are functionally illiterate and millions more are ill-trained for many of the high technology jobs that are emerging. On one hand, many of the new jobs that have been and are being created in the service sector and many of the jobs that could be created with the social investment projects outlined above can be done by people with even a low level of education. They are trainable for these jobs. In this regard, the task is to get these people employed on these jobs and pay them a wage with which they can support their families, while at the same time educating their children so that this is a one-generational problem.

However, having said that, we clearly have a major problem in adult education. These millions of people who are beyond high school age, need to be taught to read and write and do basic mathematics and they need to be taught a marketable skill. This has been said many times by many people. The point is that we have not been willing as a nation to develop and implement an educational program to accomplish this task. However, models for such programs exist in the experience of other, usually Third World nations. Moreover, our institutions of higher education have already shown a remarkable ability to develop curriculums and schedules that have allowed them to attract a very significant number of adult, or so-called continuing education students.

However, reaching the poorest and least educated admittably is a far more difficult task than designing courses that meet in the evening or weekends and that address the needs of already reasonably well-educated people who wish to improve or change careers. We do not have a national cadre of professionals trained to teach basic reading, writing and math skills to adults. But we certainly can educate and train such a corps. The physical facilities already exist, in the form of high schools, community colleges and even church buildings. Attracting the students may require a combination of the carrot and the stick. We can not expect folks to come, if there is no child care for their children while they are in class, if they can not find affordable, safe transportation, if they have to miss work at perhaps very poorly paid and undesirable, but nevertheless very needed, jobs. But once these problems are identified the solutions are obvious: free child care on the premises; using school buses with regular routes and schedules to provide free transportation; and where necessary, supplementary payments to replace lost wages, combined with government-mandated educational leaves.

As for the stick, one can make the payments under the negative income tax system described earlier partially conditioned upon attendance, and even upon performance, in these educational settings. Those involved must view this effort as a job as well as an opportunity. They will be expected to attend, to work hard, and to be successful. Failure to attend or work hard can result in reductions in "refunds," while successful completion might result in a system of bonuses.

There then must be follow-up with movement into more focused work-related skill training and with transfer into regular community college educational programs. If all of this is done, we are capable of overcoming the problem of an ill-educated and under-educated adult population. But, as with other aspects of the program I am outlining, this will take planing, money, competent supervision, and, perhaps most importantly, a long-term commitment. This is an effort that will take years, not months.

Reducing the Length of the Workweek and/or the Workday

Americans are not taught labor history and, when asked, most seem to think that the idea of the 40 hour workweek and the eight-hour workday are somehow permanent, unchangeable concepts. But, the idea of eight hours as a legal norm for a working day is but the most current step in a progression that has gone from as much as fourteen hours, to twelve, to ten, and now to eight. The idea of 40 hours as the legal norm for the work week is even more recent. As late as the 1950s many Americans routinely worked a 48 hour six-day week.

As labor productivity has increased over the decades, our society, and industrialized societies generally, required fewer hours of work from each member of the labor force in order to provide a stream of goods that allowed for not only what was at any given moment seen as a reasonably good standard of living, but for a standard that increased over those decades. Now the time has come to again reevaluate those norms once again.

As we move firmly along with the "Third Wave" of the industrial revolution, as Alvin Tofler described it, we must ask ourselves whether there is any basis to think that we need everyone to adhere to the norm of an eight-hour per day, five-day per week work schedule. I would answer with a resounding no! And as robotics and computerization take on more and more of the work in our factories that will become even more true.[15]

Moreover, there has been a major social change in the composition and nature of our labor force that also argues for a shorter work period norm. The labor force participation rate of women has increased rather steadily from 33.9 percent in 1950, to 37.7 percent in 1960, 43.3 percent in 1970, 51.5 percent in 1980, and 56 percent in 1987, the latter being the highest annual rate on record. Surprisingly, this has occurred in the face of a male labor force participation rate that has decreased over the same period from 86.4 percent in 1950 to 76.2 percent in 1987, its lowest rate on record. In fact, the male rate has not reached 80 percent since 1968. Nevertheless, overall, the labor force participation rate has increased rather steadily over this period. With a larger proportion of our population in the labor force, compounding the effects of increased productivity, one could logically argue that each worker should have to work fewer hours.

Moreover, as women have entered the labor force, as we saw in earlier chapters, more and more families are characterized by having two earners, not the traditional one. In any rational system, if two members of a family are now working, whereas in the past only one supported the family, it would seem that both could work fewer hours than the single breadwinner used to work, while still working more in total, and bringing the family to a higher living standard. For example, both could work 30 hours a week for a total family contribution of 60 hours, 50 percent more than the forty hour norm for one person. This logic also supports the claim that it is time to shorten either the workday or the workweek or both. Beyond this, with both parents working, it could logically be argued that there is a social need for a shorter work period to enable both of them to better take care of their children and their home.

There is one serious counter argument to all of the above. As we discussed earlier in great detail, hourly wages in real terms have been falling and the earnings of women have been held far below those of men. Thus, having two people work has become a necessity for many families to sustain their standard of living and only those with at least two earners are likely to be able to provide even an adequate level of income for a family. As mentioned in an earlier endnote, there would seem to be a sad and tragic validity in Karl Marx's notion that the wage level in a market system tends to be that necessary to just sustain a family, and, hence, logically, if two in a family work, the system will tend to pay each about half that necessary for a family. But our society does not have to accept this tendency. We do not have to accept the idea that two people, or one and half, need to work to earn what one alone used to earn, merely because women have entered the labor force in large numbers.

The time has come to define the normal workweek to consist of 30 hours. Adopting the slogan that began to be heard in Europe three years ago (1986),[16] the movement should be towards "30 for 40", that is, toward a workweek of 30 hours at pay levels at least equal to those now paid for 40 hours of work. This can not be done at once, but it can be phased in gradually and should be set as a national goal to be reached by the turn of the century. The 30 hour week could consist of five days of six hours each. This would have the advantage that in firms using separate shifts to stay in operation all 24 hours a day, four shifts instead of the current three would be needed. Another alternative would be to have workers work four days of seven and a half hours per day, a practice commonly adopted by many professionals already.

The impact of this would mean that more jobs would have to be created, that the existing work would be spread among more people. At least this would have to occur in those industries which wanted to maintain the same hours of service or which wanted to see the same hours of productive activity. It would also mean that the legal point at which overtime would have to be paid would slowly be lowered, which in itself would help to increase the pay of those who did work the longer hours.

Improving the Wage Structure

A central point of this book has been that the problem of poverty, in particular, and, more generally, of low and inadequate incomes for all too many families was not merely a function of unemployment or involuntary part-time and temporary employment. Rather, I have argued that a major cause of low family incomes was a level of real wages that were simply, on average, too low across the entire industrial and occupational spectrum, except perhaps for those paid to White males in the 2 or 3 very top paid white collar professions. Moreover, I have argued that this problem of low wages was especially true for those paid to women and minorities. The issue is: How do we go about restructuring the way in wages are determined and begin to develop a pattern of wages such that, at least on average, those who work full-time, full-year earn enough to at least support a family at an adequate level, rather than at a low income or poverty level or even less?

The first step in this direction is to immediately begin to raise the minimum hourly wage, not up to some percentage of the average wage such as 50 percent, which has been the most progressive proposal heard in Congress in recent years,[17] but rather to a level that would guarantee an income at least above the poverty level for a family of four.[18] No family in which even one person works full-time, full-year should receive from the employer a sum that would require them to live below that miserly and inadequate subsistence level.

Then, we need to begin to think in terms of a national wage policy, perhaps modeled on some of those in place and/or under discussion in places such as Sweden. Some of the steps inherent in such a policy would be the following. We need to do the research necessary, on an on-going and regular basis, to define minimally adequate and socially adequate standards of living derived from pricing appropriately designated "market baskets" of goods and services. These would be akin to the Minimum Adequacy or Low BLS Budget and the Modest but Adequate or Intermediate BLS Budget employed throughout this book. The government would also have to collect wage and salary information on a firm by firm, industry by industry level. Then, the government would be responsible for sitting down with both labor and management, within the context of collective bargaining situations, where they exist, to monitor those discussions and report to both sides how their wage structures compare to the national norms which have been established. Reasonable goals would need to be established such as:

1. no one should be paid below the minimum (poverty) wage
2. the average wage within all occupational and industrial categories should be maintained above the Minimum Adequacy level
3. among workers with longer periods of seniority and or higher skill and/or educational levels, the average should be maintained above the Modest but Adequate level
4. consistent with the earlier discussion, part-time and temporary workers should receive wages that on an hourly basis were equivalent to those of regular full-time workers doing equivalent work
5. female and minority workers doing equivalent work should be paid the same wages as their White male counterparts[19]

Workers and management would of course be free to negotiate higher wages, and given that the goals specified in (2) and (3) are averages, some workers would still earn below them.

The government would have to recognize that some firms in some industries could meet and easily exceed these minimum standards while continuing to make substantial profits. But, there may be some firms and even some industries that could not afford even such minimum wages and still stay in business. In such cases, the burden of proof would be upon the firm to present evidence of this to the government and its workers. If that claim was held to be valid, then the government would need to provide wage subsidies sufficient to guarantee that at least the minimum wage standards enumerated above were met in the short run.

Then, longer term planning, involving management, labor, the federal and also affected local governments, would have to be undertaken to see whether (1) this firm or industry could be restructured so as to make it economically viable if it continued to pay these wages without government subsidy, or (2) the firm or industry needed to be slowly phased out of existence, or (3) in very special situations, the firm or industry needed to be maintained with government subsidies because of the unique product or service it provides. But make no mistake about it, in general, if the only way a business can continue to exist is by paying American workers inhumanly low wages, then in the long-run the nation is better off without it.

Of course, many firms will claim that they must have government wage subsidies, just as so many claimed that they could not afford to meet the environmental standards for clean air and water. However, in the vast majority of the environmnetal cases, the claim was at best a false fear, at worse an outright lie. In fact, many of those firms, for example, in the petroleum refining and chemical industries, soon made additional profits due to the greater efficiencies in production and the sale of reclaimed pollutants. I think that the results would be similar in this situation. Especially if combined with better labor-management relations, more open and honest collective bargaining processes, and new structures that give labor more decision-making power and more flexibility, the increases in productivity and the reductions in labor turnover and in absenteeism, should enable the vast majority of firms and industries to comply with these minimum wage standards and be quite competitive.

A final note to this subsection needs to be added. Some readers who still think that neoclassical marginal revenue product calculations are the appropriate manner in which wages are, or should be set may be distressed by such a wage policy, as will those who, on principle, think that government should have little or no role in the determination of wages. But I am quite convinced that the concept of marginal revenue product wage determination is a myth told to students of economics by faculty who have ample grounds to understand that, in fact, no corporation sets wages in that manner. It is at best a conceptional reference point that is of little relevance in a modern economy, if indeed it ever had any real weight. Any economist who thinks that he or she can make such a standard empirically useful, would be welcome to present their data to either labor and management to be used in negotiations such as these, but I would not hold my breath until that happens.

As for the argument about the government's right to a role in the wage determination process, that is the whole point of this exercise. What the data in this book make very clear are that when left to the private market alone, the resulting structure of wages and the distribution of income are quite unacceptable. While the government can attempt to redress some of the worse outcomes of these wage levels and of the distribution of income via the implementation of such policies as a negative income tax or more conventional welfare and tax programs, it is about time that we faced up to the fact that labor and capital are not coequal partners in the negotiation of wages and that the representatives of capital have secured a structure of wages and salaries that has contributed in a major way to the creation of the problems we have been discussing.

In this context, the working people of a democratic nation have every right to employ their government as an active partner in the wage determination process so as to gain a more equitable structure of wages and distribution of income. Moreover, as this is accomplished, the need for the government to spend large sums of money in such programs as a negative income tax will be greatly reduced, saving everyone a lot of tax monies and administrative expenses that can then be better employed in social investment projects from which the entire nation, business and consumers alike, will benefit.

Coming to Terms with the Distribution of Wealth

In the course of Chapter 7, and in the Summary which constitutes the first part of the current chapter, I made a number of arguments pertaining to the adverse effects and general undesirability of the distribution of wealth in the U.S., a distribution which leaves a remarkably small proportion of our nation's families controlling the vast majority of the nation's wealth. The issue here is what can and should be done about this problem.

Taxes on Current Wealth Holdings
One recommendation was already made a bit earlier--impose a progressive tax on the holdings of business and financial assets aimed primarily at the wealthiest few percentiles in the distribution. This would yield a not inconsiderable revenue to the government which could be used to fund some of the programs discussed earlier. As an example, given the Federal Reserves' estimate that the net worth, not counting the net value of principal residences, of the wealthiest 1 percent of America's families in 1986 was $3,591.4 billion, or almost $3.6 trillion, even a tax of only 1 percent would yield $35.9 billion dollars, an amount equal to 4.1 percent of all federal government receipts that year. If one considers the net wealth, again not counting principal residences, of the wealthiest 10 percent, the sum almost doubles to $6,641 billion, which at a 1 percent tax rate would obviously yield some $66.4 billion in revenue. Imposing a small tax on such wealth, so as to provide funds to protect those with little income and almost no wealth seems quite reasonable and appropriate, though I recognize that others might not share that view.

Taxes on Inherited Wealth
Beyond the imposition of taxes on the current holders of large sums of wealth, an even more important potential source of revenue would involve closing the loopholes and raising the tax rates on the estates of the wealthy when they die. This would include, for example, imposing taxes on funds that have been lodged in trusts in the names of others, specifically in order to escape estate taxes, and imposing taxes on the capital appreciation of assets that occurred during the life of the deceased.

Wealth Taxes in Kind
One could even build an argument that the government should impose some wealth taxes in kind, rather than in dollar equivalents. That is, that a portion of the taxes should be collected in the form

of a percentage of the stocks and bonds and in the form of a percentage interest in the business assets held by the wealthy. The government might then hold these assets in trust in the name of the people generally, using the stream of income that would be generated over the years to fund various transfer and social programs. Meanwhile, the growing portfolio might give the government some direct leverage in discussions as to the wage patterns that should emerge and as to the firm's investment decisions.

Federal Chartering of Corporations and the Redefinition of Boards of Directors

One of the crucial concerns that stems from the highly concentrated ownership of wealth is the economic power that flows from such ownership, the access to and the control of economic information, the ability to influence economic decisions that affect the lives and well-being of millions of persons. As one important step in decentralizing and democratizing that power, I would propose that the chartering of corporations that are engaged in interstate commerce be assumed by the federal government. As we saw in the various landmark civil rights cases, virtually all corporations can be so defined, given the sources of their supplies, if not the locations of their customers and clients.

Then, that federal chartering should specify that all corporations with more than some threshold number of employees, such as 50 to exempt truly small business and closely held small family operations, and all corporations that publicly trade their stock, be required to establish boards of directors consisting of three classes of persons, (1) elected representatives of the stock holders/owners, as is already the case; (2) elected representatives of the employees of the corporation, excluding the CEO and other top officers; and (3) nonvoting representatives of the government.

The presence of the labor representatives on the board would be designed to guarantee that those who work for a firm are privy to all financial information about the firm, have a voting voice in the major decisions made by that firm, and are regularly consulted and informed by the management team. It would also give those working for a firm some voice in the selection of those who will manage it. West Germany has such a system, which they refer to as codetermination. Many Italian firms have a system related to this, whereby elected worker councils must be consulted by management on all major decisions and may inspect the books of the corporation upon request. The American system desperately needs to have injected into it an element of economic democracy to bring some balance to the concentration of power that currently exists. Once this is done, and assuming that management and stockholders operate in good faith, such things as unexpected plant closing would become a thing of the past, since the board of directors would need to be consulted about any such major move, and the board would contain representatives of both labor and government.

The presence of representatives of government would be to guarantee that the civil authorities had direct and first hand knowledge of the firm's plans and performance and could thereby monitor the firm's compliance with regulations concerning the setting of wages, environmental pollution, occupational health and safety, product safety and investment planning. These representatives would be nonvoting and would be there to advise and consult with the rest of the board, to mediate disputes between board members, especially as between the representatives of labor and owners, and to guarantee that the broader public interest was at least informed of what the firm was doing, had some opportunity to influence through persuasion the actions of the firm, and had the timely knowledge necessary to support judicial intervention if that became necessary.

I should acknowledge that I fully understand that such a change in corporate chartering and in the structure and function of the board would be fiercely resisted by the current owners and managers of corporate America and would be criticized by them and others as socialistic. I also understand that should such a program be implemented there would, for some time, be efforts to circumvent and nullify it. But my concern here is not with taking over corporations, but with infusing them with a modicum of democracy. Moreover, this proposal must be seen as part of a larger scheme by which business, labor, and government begin to act in a coordinated and cooperative way to improve the standard of living of all of our people and enable the United States to better compete in a world marked by many successful nations where such cooperation, in one form or another, already exists. If those who now own and control vast quantities of our nation's wealth are unwilling to engage, democratically, in such an effort with the other major segments of our society, then they invite more hostile reactions that might be less in their own interests and less in the interests of the nation.

CONCLUSION

The problems presented by the distributions of income and wealth in the United States are formidable:

--the millions living in poverty
--the more millions living with inadequate income, always
  on the edge of disaster
--the vast numbers of our nation's children who are forced
  to suffer in families that can not adequately provide for
  them
--the women and minorities who must work for wages that
  are substantially below those of their White male cohorts
--the unacceptably low wages that are so typical and that
  leave so many families with inadequate incomes even when
  members are working full-time all year
--the millions of families headed by women with little
  chance of earning enough to adequately provide for the family
  and a lack of childcare that often makes any effort to work
  difficult and painful at best
--the lack of wealth that leaves the vast majority of our
  families so very vulnerable to any slight interruption in
  their income

   --the concentration of wealth that subverts and makes a
   mockery of many of our claims to be a democratic nation.

But the point of this last chapter is to say that as bad and as
difficult as these problems are, solutions do exist.
   The fundamental problems are ultimately not really economic
since economic solutions can be readily identified for many of these
issues. The fundamental problem is political, and it is cultural
and ideological. It is: Do we as a nation, as a people, have the
political will and the social courage to seek out and pursue the
solutions that exist? Can we begin to build the political movement
that is necessary as a vehicle to attempt to implement solutions?
While I am not optimistic about the building of such a political
consensus, I feel that those of us who are concerned with these
matters have no alternative but to try. My hope is that some
readers of this book may be motivated to join in that effort.

NOTES

   1. For example, a study by the Council on Competitiveness
revealed that, ". . . in 1980 dollars, . . . in 1986, the average
German worker earned $19,594 to $16,522 for the American worker,"
while the same study showed that a measure of the standard of living
defined as Gross Domestic Product divided by the number of
employees, "to take into consideration the growth of two-income
families," provided a German level of $34,400 to an American level
of $28,400. In commenting upon this study, which also examined
relative differences in productivity growth in various countries,
John Young, CEO of Hewlett-Packard, said these figures demonstrate
that the U.S. is "losing its competitive edge." (Quotes are from
AFL-CIO News 1988.)
   2. A report by the staff of the Senate Budget committee
released September 26, 1988, stated that ". . . half the new jobs
created in the past eight years were at wages below the poverty
level for a family of four . . ." and concluded that ". . . both
high-paying and low-paying jobs have grown at the expense of a
shrinking middle class" (Columbus Dispatch 1988). Recall also the
extensive discussion of these trends in Chapters 4 and 5.
   3. See for example, Bluestone and Harrison (1982), Steinberg
(1985), Alperovitz and Faux (1984), Carnoy and Shearer (1980),
Magaziner and Reich (1982), Reich (1983), Leckachman (1982),
Ackerman (1984), Center for Popular Economics (1986), Lodge (1986).
   4. Recall from Chapter 7, that as of 1983 the poorest (in
wealth terms) 13 percent of families actually had a negative net
worth position, with an additional 4 percent who had zero net worth.
Even the next 10 percent had less than $3,536 in total net worth.
(See Table 7-1.)
   5. Some facts about the problem of homelessness in the United
States:

   It is true that drug addicts, alcoholics and the severely
   mentally ill make up the hardest core of the homeless .

. . [but] they add up to less that half of the total
homeless population . . . one-third of all homeless were
families with young children. About 22 percent had full-
or part-time jobs . . . 40 percent of the men in city
shelters were veterans. The fastest growing group was
made up of kids under six years of age (Mathews 1988).

Twenty percent more people sought emergency shelter [in
1987 than in 1986]. Nearly two-thirds of the [26] cities
[surveyed] had to turn away some people because their
shelters were full. In two-thirds of the cities, waiting
lists for publicly assisted housing are so long that
officials won't take any more applications. People
already on the list must wait an average of 22 months for
housing . . . [and] the problem is just getting a lot
worse every year [Hey 1987, reporting on a study by the
U.S. Conference of Mayors].

The issue of just how many people are homeless is a matter of
some debate. The lowest estimates include a 1984 report by the U.S.
Department of Housing and Urban Renewal of 250,000 to 350,000 and
another by Richard Freeman of Harvard "who puts the number at
approximately 350,000" in a study for the National Bureau of
Economic Research. High estimates run to as much as 3 million in
reports from various advocacy groups (Baker 1986). Looking at the
problems associated with housing our nations people a bit more
broadly, the National Association of Housing and Redevelopment
Officials:

estimate that more than 25 percent of American households
cannot find decent, safe housing at affordable prices.
These Americans live in sub-standard, over-crowded homes,
or they are spending an unreasonable portion of their
income on housing. Typically, the poorer a household, the
higher the percentage of its income is spent on housing.
. . . Housing problems have reached crisis proportions in
urban centers, suburbs, and rural areas (Irwin 1987).

Waiting lists for public housing in New York are 18 years
long. Welfare budgets allow only $270 a month for rent
in a metropolitan area, where even minimal space in
outlying boroughs costs $350 or $400 (Gardner 1988, in a
review of the book by Kozol 1988).

At the same time, according to Jonathan Kozol, at one "welfare
hotel" in New York:

Despite leaky plumbing, peeling lead paint, trash-filled
hallways, broken windows, and a large population of
rodents and roaches, its tiny rooms rent for as much as
$1,900 a month. The owners grossed more than $8 million
in 1986, all of it from welfare funds paid by the City
of New York (Gardner 1988).

Kozol goes on to condemn a policy which allows private owners of such slum buildings to "profit from the suffering of those whose anguish they cannot alleviate" (ibid).

Looking at the federal government's response to this problem, one finds that:

> Since 1981, . . . the federal budget for housing has dropped more than 70 percent, from $30 billion per year to $7.3 billion in 1987. . . . from $32 billion in 1980 to $9 billion in 1986 . . . When Jimmy Carter was President, 300,000 units of subsidized housing were constructed; under Gerald Ford, 200,000 units. By contrast, in 1986, the Department of Housing and Urban Development, subsidized construction of only 25,000 units (Mathews 1988).

Moreover, the problem is almost sure to get worse before it gets better. The General Accounting Office (GAO) predicts that:

> 240,000 to 890,000 low-income units could be lost by 1995, and an additional 800,000 could disappear by 2005. . . . [because] restrictions on subsidized federal housing from the 1960s and Nixon years are expiring. Owners will soon be able to sell or rent them at prevailing market prices--astronomically beyond reach of the homeless (ibid.: 58)

The GAO concludes that "Losses on this scale could be catastrophic" (ibid.). The government programs that have been passed simply fail utterly to keep up with the magnitude of the problem. For example, in 1987, the McKinney Homeless Assistance Act was passed, and though it called for the spending of $1 billion (hardly a adequate sum to begin with), it was funded for less than $700 million, and that over a 2 year period. Then, to make matters worse, "Since then [1987], attorneys for the homeless have had to sue the Department of Education, HUD, the Department of Defense, and the Veterans Administration to get them to stop foot-dragging on provisions of the McKinney Act and a number of other [related] programs" (ibid.).
Another law designed to encourage, through a system of tax credits, middle-class families to invest in projects to build housing for the poor has not been at all effective, in fact on December 31, 1987 about $240 million was ". . . tossed onto the federal budget scrap pile. The money, targeted to build housing for the poor, . . . [is] in the form of tax credits [and] is not being used" (Hill 1987).
In light of the cutbacks in public funds and the cruel and ineffective implementation of policy under the Reagan administration, and in the context of the overall situation described in the main text concerning low wages and incomes and the lack of wealth, is it any wonder that we have a growing problem of homelessness in the United States? It might be more surprising if we did not.

6. There exists a vast literature on this point, only a small part of which can be cited here. However, many of these works contain extensive bibliographies, some of them annotated, that can guide the interested reader further. The key point here is that, while there is some debate about the exact nature and role of America's elite, there is little doubt that it exists and exercises an inordinate amount of both economic and political power and it does so with little or no regard to the formal institutions of democracy. In this regard, see Mills 1956, Kolko 1962, Domhoff 1967, 1970, and 1980, Lundberg 1968, Winter-Berger 1972, Green, Fallows and Zwick 1972, Dye 1976, Dye and Zeigler 1978, Katznelson and Kesselman 1979.

7. One could argue that we should enter the 19th Century, for it was in the late 1890s when Bismark in Germany first began to introduce the concept of socially provided medical care.

8. There are many other aspects of what is internationally known as a national family policy that I can not here address in even the brief detail possible in the main text. But these include such matters as fully paid material leaves immediately before and after birth, paid parental leaves especially during the first few years of a child's life, special children's allowances, and guarantees of medical care and child care. The United States and South Africa are the only two industrialized nations without national parental leave policies (and without national health insurance) and we spend far less than do most other industrialized nations, as a percent of our GNP or on a per child basis, to provide care for our children or the opportunity for parents to care for them when they are very young or ill. A brief but good article that speaks to some of these issues and makes some more detailed international comparisons is Fried 1988.

9. For an excellent review of the current system of federal support for child care, which can be broadly construed to include elements of some 22 different programs, including Head Start, the Child Care Food Program, provisions for Child Welfare Training (under Title IV-B of the Social Security Act, as amended in 1967) and the Dependent Care Assistance Program of tax credits, see Robins 1988. Robins not only identifies all of the currently available programs, but also examines the gaps and overlaps between them and the pattern of funding levels over the years. This shows that, "Excluding the tax credit, federal spending for child care declined by almost 25 percent in constant dollars from 1977 to 1986." Moreover, he found that it was the nontax credit programs that primarily benefitted the poor; whereas the tax credits, as expected, primarily went to middle and upper income families. Overall, he finds that there has been a decided shifting of total federal spending (including tax spending) for child care away from the poor. He goes on to propose a two-tiered system consisting of an expanded tax credit program (so-called demand subsidies) and the direct provision of free or low cost child care for the poor (supply subsidies). Once this were implemented, he would then phase out a number of other programs which would have become redundant.

10. To name just a few, see U.S. Department of Health, Education and Welfare 1973 and 1976 and Green 1967. For a recent overview of current poverty programs and a set of proposals which include a negative income tax, see Haveman 1988. His proposed plan would set a rather low floor under family income, one-half to two-thirds of the poverty level, and like all such programs would be sensitive to the size and composition of the family and the amount and sources of other income. He also makes an interesting proposal to establish "A universal personal capital account for youth" as a way to overcome some of the disadvantages of the unequal distribution of wealth by providing young people, upon turning 18, with a basis upon which to either go on to college or begin careers.

11. By the way, it would be important that the government health insurance card be indistinguishable from that provided by the government to all federal employees. In fact, there should be only one program for everyone, that is, both for government employees and for those who do not have, for what ever reason, insurance through a private employee. This would be an important way to eliminate much of the discrimination that now is visited upon Medicaid and Medicare patients by all too many private providers of medical services. Moreover, there is no need, objectively, for more than one program. The whole idea is for everyone to have the same basic medical insurance.

12. Here, I am avoiding the issue of the changing size of the military or of the institutionalized population, most of which is in jail.

13. Pilot projects to do just this exist already in the U.S. and Europe wherein old plastic and other materials, even some metal, is melted down and reformed into a full range of lumber that is strong, nailable, fire resistant, and noncorrosive.

14. Such a plant now exists in Columbus, Ohio.

15. This argument obviously touches on the issue of the changes, the increases, in the productivity rate of our labor force, and also involves us quickly in the difficult questions surrounding the debate as to how to measure productivity. For more information on that topic see Mandel 1988, which also contains a short but useful list of references on this topic. See also the articles by Fischer, Griliches, and others in the report of the Symposium on The Slowdown in Productivity Growth in *The Journal of Economic Perspectives*, vol 2, no. 4, Fall 1988. Indeed, much has been written about the declining rate of productivity increases in the United States. Focusing on the official estimates of the annual increases in output per hour of labor in the nonfarm business sector, the most relevant figure for our purposes, the facts are these. From 1948 through 1964, the U.S. average annual increase in productivity was 2.7 percent; from 1965 through 1972, it was 1.9 percent; and from 1973 through 1987, it was only 0.9 percent. A variety of reasons have been offered for this slowdown, especially given that our's is one of the poorest records among the industrialized nations, although many of them also saw a slowdown in productivity, but not as severe. These reasons include: inadequate investment and modernization within the private business sector, the bleeding off of too much scientific and technical

personnel and resources into purely military and space-related activities, a poorly educated labor force, primitive labor-management relations, poor work conditions, a downturn in the production of relevant knowledge (but there the question is why), the effects of the oil price shock in the early 1970s, government interference in the economy, the growing federal budget deficit as a drain on available savings, and the list goes on.

Nevertheless, in all but five years since 1948, output per hour of labor in the nonagricultural business sector had increased such that it was 58.4 percent higher in 1964 than in 1948, 16.3 percent higher in 1972 than in 1964, and 13.7 percent higher in 1987 than in 1972. Looking at the period which is the primary focus of this book, 1960 to 1987, output per hour increased 52.7 percent. (Figures are computed from tables B-46 and B-47 in the Economic Report of the President 1988.)

16. The West Germany trade union representing steel and auto workers went out on strike over this issue in 1986 and won a gradual reduction of the work week to 35 hours to be phased in over a five to seven year period.

17. This 50 percent figure would imply a considerably higher minimum wage than the proposal that, as of this writing, seems likely to pass Congress in 1989--and even that seems destined for a Presidential veto at the hands of a President who pledged to work toward a kinder and more gentler nation. Words, indeed, are cheap.

18. In 1989, this would require an hourly minimum wage a bit in excess of $6, whereas Congress is talking about trying to pass a bill that would achieve a minimum wage of $4.55 in stages over a three year period. A person working 40 hours per week, 52 weeks per year at $4.55 an hour in 1989 (not three years from then) would earn about $3,200 *less* than the amount needed in 1989 for a family of four to surpass the poverty level, given the apparent inflation rate of about 4.5 percent per year as this is being written. Such a minimum wage is clearly inadequate.

19. I fully understand that far more is involved here than simply trying to get equal pay for equal work. The definition of equivalent work is difficult, but I think not insurmountable. Overcoming the racism and the sexism that are often the real basis upon which the unequal and inequitable wage and salary structures have been built and maintained is a problem the solution to which goes far beyond the bounds of this book. But, if we can gain some measure of economic parity, of "comparable pay for comparable work," then I think we will have a better basis upon which to attack the ideological and cultural elements inherent in sexism and racism as social phenomenon.

In addition, for "the most comprehensive assessment to date of the relative status on minority groups in the United States " (to quote from one review), a study which examines not just the poverty of Blacks and Hispanics generally, but which also looks at the different specific groups within the Hispanic community and at American Indians, see Sandefur and Tienda 1988.

Bibliography

Ackerman, Frank. *Hazardous to Our Health: Economic Policies in the 1980's.* Boston: South End Press, 1984.

AFL-CIO News. "Industrial Erosion Topples U.S. Living Standard," pp. 3, June 11, 1988.

Albelda, Randy. "Let Them Pay Taxes: The Growing Tax Burden on the Poor" *Dollars and Sense*, 135, pp. 9-11, April 1988a.

---. "Women's Income Not Up to PAR--Wage Gap Narrows, Income Gap Grows," *Dollars and Sense*, 138, pp. 6-8, July/August 1988.

Albelda, Randy, Lapeidus, June, and McCrate, Elaine. "What Price Economic Independence? Women's Economic Status in the Postwar Period." (Unpublished manuscript, Deparment of Economics, Univ. of Mass., Amherst), 1988.

Alperovitz, Gar, and Faux, Jeff. *Rebuilding America: A Blueprint for the New Economy.* New York: Pantheon Books, 1984.

Amott, Teresa. "Re-Slicing The Pie: Government Policy and Income Inequality," *Dollars and Sense*, 146, pp.10-11, May 1989.

Avery, Robert B., and Elliehausen, Gregory E. "Financial Characteristics of High Income Families," *Federal Reserve Bulletin*, 172, pp. 163-175, March 1986.

Avery, Robert B., and Kennickell, Arthur B. "Savings and Wealth: Evidence From the 1986 Survey of Consumer Finances." Paper presented at the National Bureau of Economic Research's Conference on Research in Income and Wealth, Washington, D.C., May 1988.

Avery, Robert B., Canner, Glenn B, and Gustafson, Thomas A. "Survey of Consumer Finances, 1983", *Federal Reserve Bulletin*, 172, pp. 679-92, September 1984.

Avery, Robert B., Elliehausen, Gregory E. and Kennickell, Arthur B. "Measuring Wealth with Survey Data: An Evaluation of the 1983 Survey of Consumer Finances," *Review of Income and Wealth*. Forthcoming.

Baker, Amy Brooke. "US Homeless Organize, Get Attention," *The Christian Science Monitor*, p. 3, August 27 1986.

Bane, Mary Jo. "Household Composition and Poverty: Which Comes First?" in *Williamsburg Conference Papers*. Madison, WI: Institute for Research on Poverty, 1984.

Belsie, Laurent. "Hard Times for Many Part-Timers--Underemployment Not Falling as Fast as Joblessness," *The Christian Science Monitor*, p. 3, Feb. 11, 1988.

Block, Fred; Cloward, Richard A.; Ehrenreich, Barbara, and Piven, Frances Fox. *The Mean Season: The Attack on The Welfare State*. New York: Pantheon Books, 1987.

Bluestone, Barry, and Harrison, Bennett. *The Deindustrialization of America*. New York: Basic Books, 1982.

---. Untitled paper presented at the annual Summer Conference of the Union for Radical Political Economics, Sandwich, MA., August 1984.

---. "The Growth of Low-Wage Employment: 1963-86," *The American Economic Review--Papers and Proceedings*, 78-2, pp. 124-28, May 1988a.

---. *The Great U-Turn: Corporate Restructuring and the Polarizing of America*. New York: Basic Books, 1988b.

Bradbury, Katharine L. "The Shrinking Middle Class," *New England Economic Review*, pp. 41-55, Sept./Oct. 1986.

Broida, Arthur L. "Consumer Surveys as a Source of Information for Social Accounting: The Problems," *The Flow of Funds Approach to Social Accounting*, Conference on Research on the Distribution of Income and Wealth, 26. Princeton: Princeton University Press, 1962.

Bronfenbrenner, Martin. *Income Distribution Theory*. Chicago: Aldine-Atherton, 1971.

Buhmann, Brigitte, et al. "Equivalence Scales, Well-Being, Inequality and Poverty: Sensitivity Estimates Across Ten Countries Using the LIS Database," *Review of Income and Wealth*, pp. 115-42, June 1988.

Carnoy, Martin, and Shearer, Kerek. *Economic Democracy: The Challenge of the 1980's*. White Plains: M.E. Sharpe, 1980.

Center for Popular Economics. *Economic Report of the People: An Alternative to the Economic Report of the President*. Boston: South End Press, 1986.

The Christian Science Monitor. "The Economy . . . ," p. 21, Nov 10, 1986.

---. "Minorities and Education", p. 17, Nov. 9, 1987.

Coder, John, Rainwater, Lee, and Smeeding, Timothy M.   "LIS Information Guide," *LIS-CEPS Working Paper No. 7.* Walferdange, Luxembourg, Nov. 1988.

---. "Inequality Among Children and Elderly in Ten Modern Nations: The United States in an International Context," *American Economic Review: Papers and Proceedings*, pp. 320-24, May 1989.

Cohen, Stephen S., and Zysman, John. *Manufacturing Matters: The Myth of the Post-Industrial Economy.* New York: Basic Books, 1987.

Congressional Budget Office. *The Changing Distribution of Federal Taxes: 1975-1990.* Washington, D.C.: U.S. Government Printing Office, 1987.

---. *Trends in Family Income: 1970-1986.* Washington, D.C.: U.S. Government Printing Office, 1988.

The Columbus Dispatch. "Safety Net Programs: Are Thety Reaching the Poor," p. 10, Oct. 3, 1986.

---. "Minimum Wage Bill Pulled," p. 4A, Sept. 27, 1988.

---. "More U.S. Kids Live in Poverty," p. 12A, October 27, 1988.

Curtin, Richard T., Juster, F. Thomas, and Morgan, James N. "Survey Estimates of Wealth: An Assessment of Quality," NBER Conference in Income and Wealth, Baltimore, March 1987.

Daniels, Lee A. "Experts Foresee a Social Gap Between Sexes Among Blacks," *The New York Times*, pp. 1, 30, Feb. 5, 1989.

Danziger, Sheldon and Weinberg, Daniel, eds. *Fighting Poverty, What Works and What Doesn't.* Cambridge, MA: Harvard University Press, 1986.

Danziger, Sheldon, Haverman, Robert, and Plotnick, R. "Anti-poverty Policy: Effects on the Poor and Nonpoor," *Conference Papers.* Madison, WI: Institute for Research of Poverty, University of Wisconsin, March 1985.

Danziger, Sheldon, Gottschalk, Peter, and Smolensky, Eugene. "How the Rich Have Fared, 1973-87," *American Economic Review: Papers and Proceedings*, May 1989.

Dayton Daily News. "Studies Paint Dismal Picture of Life for U.S. Blacks," pp. 1A, 4A, March 17, 1989a.

---. "Blacks Have Less Incentive to Wed, Study Says," pp. 4A, March 17, 1989b.

Dollars and Sense. "Defining Away the Poor," p. 9, Jan./Feb. 1987.

Domhoff, G. William. *Who Rules America?* Englewood Cliffs, NJ: Prentice-Hall, 1967.

———. *The Higher Circles.* New York: Random House/Vintage Books, 1970.

———, Ed. "Power Structure Research II," a special issue of *The Insurgent Sociologist,* 9 (2-3), Fall 1979/Winter 1980.

Dye, Thomas R. *Who's Running America? Institutional Leadership in the United States.* New York: Prentice-Hall, 1976.

Dye, Thomas R., and Zeigler, L. Harmon. *The Irony of Democracy: An Uncommon Introduction to American Politics,* 4th ed. North Scituate, MA: Duxbury Press, 1978.

Eberts, Randall W., and Swinton, John R. "Has Manufacturing's Presence in the Economy Diminished?" *Economic Commentary.* Cleveland, OH: Federal Reserve Bank of Cleveland, January 1, 1988.

Economic Policy Institue. *The State of Working America.* Washington, D.C.: Economic Policy Institute, 1988.

Economic Report of the President. Washington, D.C.: U.S. Government Printing Office, February 1988.

Ferber, Robert. "The Reliability of Consumer Surveys of Financial Holdings: Time Deposits," *Journal of the American Statistical Association,* 60, pp. 148-63, March, 1965.

———. "The Reliability of Consumer Surveys of Financial Holdings: Demand Deposits," *Journal of the American Statistical Association,* 61, pp. 91-103, March 1966a.

———. *The Reliability of Consumer Surveys of Financial Assets and Debts.* Urbana, IL: Bureau of Business and Economic Research, 1966b.

Ferber, Robert, Forsythe, John, Guthrie, Harold, and Maynes, E. Scott. "Validation of a National Survey of Consumer Financial Characteristics," *Review of Economics and Statistics,* 51, pp. 436-44, November 1969.

Fischer, Stanley. "Symposium on the Slowdown in Productivity Growth", *The Journal of Economic Perspecitves,* 2 (4), pp.3-9, Fall 1988.

Flaim, Paul O., and Sehgal, Ellen. "Displaced Workers of 1979-83: How Well Have They Fared?" *Monthly Labor Review,* pp. 3-16, June 1985.

Forbes. Special Issue on "The *Forbes* Four Hundred," Fall, 1983.

---. Special Issue on "The *Forbes* 400: 1988," October 24, 1988.

Francis, David R. "US Taxes Hit Poorest Hardest," *The Christian Science Monitor*, p. 9, April 18, 1989.

Fried, Mindy. "Who's Minding Our Children?", *Dollars and Sense*, 138, pp. 13-15, July/August 1988.

Galbraith, John Kenneth. *The Affluent Society.* Boston: Houghton Mifflin, 1958.

---. *The New Industrial State.* New York: Signet Books Division of The New American Library, Inc., 1967.

---. *Economics and The Public Purpose.* Boston: Houghton Mifflin, 1973.

Gardner, Marilyn. "Children of the '80's: Our Choices, Their Future," *The Christian Science Monitor*, Sept. 16, 1986.

---. "In Need of Sheltering: Families with No Place to Call Home," a review of *Rachel and Her Children: Homeless Families in America* by Jonathan Kozol, *The Christian Science Monitor*, p.B4, April 1, 1988.

Garfinkel, Irwin. "The Evolution of Child Support Policy," *Focus*, pp. 11-16. Madison, WI: University of Wisconsin, Institute for Research on Poverty, Spring 1988.

Gilbert, Dennis, and Kahl, Joseph. *The American Class Structure: A New Synthesis.* 3rd ed. Chicago: The Dorsey Press, 1987.

Gilder, George. *Wealth and Poverty.* New York: Bantam Books, 1982.

Green, Christopher. *Negative Taxes and the Poverty Problem.* Washington, D.C.: Brookings Institute, 1967.

Green, Mark J., Fallows, James M., and Zwick, David R. *Who Runs Congress?: The President, Big Business, or You?* New York: Bantam/Grossman Books, 1972.

Griliches, Zvi. "Productivity Puzzels and R & D: Another Nonexplanation", *The Journal of Economic Perspecitves*, 2 (4), pp. 9-22, Fall, 1988.

Halverson, Guy. "Behind the Impressive Data on Jobs, Some Hidden Problems," *The Christian Science Monitor*, p. 12, March 22, 1988.

Hamermesh, Daniel S., and Rees, Albert. *The Economics of Work and Pay*, 3rd ed. New York: Harper & Row, 1984.

Harkness, Laurence P. "On The Critical List: Remedy Needed for Children's Health Care Shortcomings", *The Dayton Daily News*, pp. 11A, November 11, 1988.

Harrington, Michael. *The Other America: Poverty in the United States*. New York: Penguin Books, [1962] 1981. (Reprint with a new introduction and afterword.)

---. *The New American Poverty*. New York: Holt, Rinehart and Winston, 1984.

Harrington, Michael, and Levinson, M. "The Perils of a Dual Economy," *Dissent*, pp. 417-426, Fall 1985.

Haveman, Robert H. "The Changed Face of Poverty: A Call for New Policies," *Focus*, 11(2), pp. 11-14. Madison, WI: University of Wisconsin, Institute for Reseach on Poverty, Summer, 1988a.

---. *Starting Even: An Equal Opportunity Program to Combat the Nation's Poverty*. Old Tappan, NJ: Simon and Schuster, 1988b.

Helmore, Kristin and Laing, Karen. "Exiles Among Us: Poor and Black in America, Part I," *The Christian Science Monitor*, Nov. 13, 1986a.

---. "Exiles Among Us: Poor and Black in America, Part II," *The Christian Science Monitor*, Nov. 18, 1986b.

---. "Exiles Among Us: Poor and Black in America, Part III," *The Christian Science Monitor*, Nov. 19, 1986c.

---. "Exiles Among Us: Poor and Black in America, Part IV," *The Christian Science Monitor*, Nov. 20, 1986d.

Hey, Robert P. "Families hit by US Economy," *The Christian Science Monitor*, p. 4, Oct. 14, 1987.

---. "Washington Takes a Lood at Rural Poverty," *The Christian Science Monitor*, p. 8, April 14, 1989.

Hicks, Jonathan P. "Steel Industry Employment Is Up After Years of Decline," *The New York Times*, pp. D1, D5, Feb. 27, 1989.

Hill, Mary Jo. "Poor Losing Out as Housing Plan Flops," *The Christian Science Monitor*, p. 6, December 17, 1987.

Horrigan, Michael W. and Haugen, Steven E. "The Declining Middle-Class Yhesis: A Sensitivity Analysis," *Monthly Labor Review*, pp. 3-13, May 1988.

Horvath, Francis W. "The Pulse of Economic Change: Displaced Workers of 1981-85," *Monthly Labor Review*, pp. 3-12, June 1987.

House Select Committee on Children, Youth, and Families. *Safety Net Programs: Are They Reaching Poor Children?* Washington, D.C.: U.S. Government Printing Office, October 1986.

Irwin, Victoris. "Senate Pursues $15 billion Housing Bill Despite Veto Threat," *The Christian Science Monitor*, p. 7, Nov. 17, 1987.

Jain, Shail. *Size Distribution of Income: A Compilation of Data.* Washington, D.C.: The World Bank, 1975.

Kahan, David. *The Next Frontier: Relieving State Tax Burdens on the Poor.* Washington, D.C.: Center on Budget and Policy Priorities, 1987.

Kantrowitz, Barbara. "Who Cares About Day Care?" *Newsweek*, p. 73, March 28, 1988.

Kassalow, Everett M. "Four Nations' Policies Toward Displaced Steel Workers," *Monthly Labor Review*, pp. 32-34, July 1985.

Katznelson, Ira, and Kesselman, Mark. *The Politics of Power: A Critical Introduction to American Government*, 2nd ed. New York: Harcourt Brace Jovanovich, 1979.

Katz, Michael B. *In The Shadow of The Poorhouse: A Social History of Welfare in America.* New York: Basic Books, 1986.

Kolko, Gabriel. *Wealth and Power in America.* New York: Praeger Publishers, 1962.

Kozol, Jonathan. *Rachel and Her Children: Homeless Families in America.* New York: Crown Publishers, 1988.

Kutscher, Ronald E. "Projections 2000 - Overview and Implications of the Projections to 2000," *Monthly Labor Review*, pp. 3-9, September 1987.

Kuttner, R. "The Declining Middle," *Atlantic Monthly*, pp. 60-72, July 1983.

Lampman, Robert J. *The Share of Top Wealth Holders in National Wealth: 1922-1956.* Princeton, NJ: Princeton University Press, 1962.

Levitan, Sar A. *Programs in Aid of The Poor*, 5th ed. Baltimore: Johns Hopkins University Press, 1985.

Lawrence, Robert Z. "Sectoral Shifts and the Size of the Middle Class." *Brookings Review*, pp. 3-10. Washington, D.C.: The Brookings Institute, Fall 1985.

Leckachman, Robert. *Greed is Not Enough: Reaganomics.* New York: Pantheon Books, 1982.

Lodge, George C. *The American Disease: Why the American Economic Systems is Faltering and How the Trend Can Be Changed with a Minimum of Crisis*. New York: New York University Press, 1986.

Lundberg, Ferdinand. *The Rich and the Super Rich*. New York: Lyle Stuart, 1968.

Magaziner, Ira, and Reich, Robert. *Minding America's Business: The Decline and Rise of the American Economy*. New York: Vintage Books, 1982.

Mandel, Michael. "Is Productivity a Problem? - Good and Bad Ways to Fix the Productivity Drop," *Dollars and Sense*, 141, pp. 16-19, November 1988.

Mandell, Lewis and Lundsten, Lorman L. "Some Insight into the Underreporting of Financial Data by Sample Survey Respondents," *Journal of Marketing Research*, 15, pp. 294-99, May 1978.

Marshall, Marilyn. "The Alarming Decline in the Number of Black College Students", *Ebony*, pp. 44-48, September 1987.

Marx, Karl. *Wage Labor and Capital*. New York: International Publishers, 1969a.

---. *Value, Price and Profit*. New York: International Publishers, 1969b.

Mathews, Tom. "What Can Be Done? - Homeless in America," *Newsweek*, pp. 57-58, March 21, 1988.

McBride, Nicholas. "Not Only Do Rich Get Richer, They Vote More, Too," *The Christian Science Monitor*, pp. 1, 32, May 5, 1988.

McIntyre, Robert S. "The Populist Tax Act of 1989 - Stop Coddling the Rich," *The Nation*, pp.461-463, April 2, 1988.

McLanahan, Sara, Cain, Glen, Olneck, Michael, Piliavin, Irving, Dansiger, Sheldon, and Gottschalk, Peter. *Losing Ground: A Critique*, Special Report #38. Madison, WI: University of Wisconsin, Institute for Research on Poverty, 1985.

McNeil, John M, and Lamas, Enrique J. "Year-Apart Estimates of Household Net Worth from the Survey of Income and Program Participation," NBER Conference of Research in Income and Wealth, Baltimore, March, 1987.

McMahon, Patrick J., and Tschetter, John H. "The Declining Middle Class: A Further Analysis," *Monthly Labor Review*, pp. 22-27, Sept. 1986.

Mellor, Earl F. "Weekly Earnings in 1985; A Look at More Than 200 Occupations," *Monthly Labor Review*, pp. 28-32, Sept. 1986.

---. "Workers at the Minimum Wage or Less: Who They Are and the Jobs They Hold," *Monthly Labor Review*, pp. 34-38, July 1987.

Meyer, Peter. "Notes of the Distribution of Income," *Working Papers*. State College, PA: Dept. of Community Development, Pennsylvania State University, 1977.

Mills, C. Wright. *The Power Elite*. New York: Oxford University Press, 1956.

Monmaney, Terence. "Preventing Early Births," *Newsweek*, p. 70, May 16, 1988.

Moynihan, Daniel Patrick. "Our Poorest Citizens--Children", *Focus*, pp. 5-6. Madison, WI: University of Wisconsin, Institute for Research on Poverty, Spring, 1988.

Murray, Charles. *Lossing Ground: American Social Policy 1950-1980*. New York: Basic Books, 1984.

Nardone, Thomas J. "Part-time Workers: Who Are They?", *Monthly Labor Review*, pp 13-19, February 1986.

---. "Have the Poor Been 'Losing Ground'?" *Political Science Quarterly*, 100(3), pp. 427-45, Fall 1985.

Osberg, Lars. *Economic Inequality in the United States*. Armonk, NY: M.E. Sharpe, 1984.

Palmer, John, Smeeding, Timothy M., and Torry, Barbara B. *The Vulnerable*. Washington, D.C.: Urban Institute, Sept. 1988.

Peckman, Joseph. *Who Paid the Taxes, 1966-85?* Washington, D.C.: Brookings Institution, 1987.

Projector, Dorothy S., and Weiss, Gertrude S. *Survey of Financial Characteristics of Consumers*. Washington, D.C.: Board of Governors of the Federal Reserve System, 1966.

Reich, Robert B. *The Next American Frontier: A Provocative Program for Economic Renewal*. New York: Penguin Books, 1983.

Reschovsky, Andrew, and Chernick, Howard. *Unfair Burdens: Taxation of the Poor in Massachusetts*. Boston: Tax Equity Alliance for Massachusetts, 1988.

Robins, Philip K. "Federal Support for Child Care: Current Policies and A Proposed New System", *Focus*, 11(2), pp. 1-9. Madison, WI: University of Wisconsin, Institute for Reseach on Poverty, Summer 1988.

Rodgers, Harrel R., Jr. *Poor Women, Poor Families: The Economic Plight of America's Female-Headed Households.* New York: M.E. Sharpe, 1986.

---. *Beyond Welfare: New Approaches to the Problem of Poverty in America.* New York: M.E. Sharpe, 1988.

Rosenthal, Neal H. "The Shrinking Middle Class: Myth or Reality?" *Monthly Labor Review,* pp 9-22, March 1986.

Saikowski, Charlotte. "Mayors to Editors: Growing 'Underclass' Is Survival Issue for U.S.," *The Christian Science Monitor,* p. 6, April 15, 1988.

Samuelson, Robert J. "Progress and Poverty," *Newsweek,* p. 41, Aug. 24, 1987.

Sandefur, Gar D., and Tienda, Marta. *Divided Opportunities: Minorities, Poverty, and Social Policy.* New York: Plenum Press, 1988.

Schwartz, Marvin. "Trends in Personal Wealth, 1976-81," U.S. Department of Treasury's *Statistics of Income Bulletin,* 3, pp. 1-26, Summer 1983.

---. "Preliminary Estimates of Personal Wealth, 1982," U.S. Department of Treasury's *Statistics of Income Bulletin,* 5, pp. 1-19, Winter 1985.

Smeeding, Timothy M. "Generations and the Distributions of Well-Being and Poverty: Cross National Evidence for Europe, Scandinavia and the Colonies" presented to Symposium on Population Change and European Society, Florence, Italy: December 9, 1988.

Smeeding, Timothy M., and Torrey, Barbara B. "Poor Children in Rich Countries," *Science,* pp. 242, 873-78, November 11, 1988.

Smith, James D., and Franklin. Stephen. "The Concentration of Personal Wealth, 1922-1969," *American Economic Review, Papers and Proceedings,* 64(2), pp. 162-167, May 1974.

Smith, Ralph E., and Vavrichek, Bruce. "The Minimum Wage: Its Relation to Incomes and Poverty," *Monthly Labor Review,* pp. 24-30, June 1987.

Steinberg, B. *Deindustrialization and the Two Tier Society.* Washington, D.C.: AFL-CIO Industrial Union Department, 1985.

Thurow, Lester C. *Generating Inequality: Mechanisms of Distribution in the U.S. Economy.* New York: Basic Books, 1975.

---. *The Zero-Sum Society: Distribution and The Possibilities for Economic Change.* New York: Penguin Books, 1980.

---. "The Disappearance of the Middle Class," *The New York Times*, p. F3, Feb. 5, 1984.

---. "The Wealthiest Americans", *International Herald Tribune*, p. 5, October 25, 1984.

Tucker, Robert C. *The Marx-Engels Reader*. New York: W. W. Norton, 1972.

U. S. Department of Commerce, Bureau of the Census. Current Population Reports, Series P-60, No. 137. *Money Income of Households, Families, and Persons in the United States: 1981*. Washington, D.C.: U.S. Government Printing Office, 1983.

---. Current Population Reports, Series P-60, No. 143. *Money Income of Households, Families, and Persons in the United States: 1983*. Washington, D.C.: U.S. Government Printing Office, 1985.

---. Current Population Reports, Series P-60, No. 154. *Money Income and Poverty Status of Families and Persons in the United States: 1985 (Advance Data From the March 1986 Current Population Survey*. Washington, D.C.: U.S. Government Printing Office, 1986a.

---. Technical Paper 55. *Estimates of Poverty Including the Value of Noncash Benefits: 1984*. Washington, D.C.: U.S. Government Printing Office, 1986b.

---. Current Population Reports, Series P-70, No. 7. *Household Wealth and Asset Ownership: 1984*. Washington, D.C.: U.S. Government Printing Office, 1986c.

---. Current Population Reports, Series P-60, No. 156. *Money Income of Households, Families, and Persons in the United States: 1985*. Washington, D.C.: U.S. Government Printing Office, 1987a.

---. Current Population Reports, Series P-60, No. 158. *Poverty in The United States 1985*. Washington, D.C.: U.S. Government Printing Office, 1987b.

---. Current Population Reports, Series P-60, N. 155. *Receipt of Selected Noncash Benefits: 1985*. Washington, D.C.: U.S. Government Printing Office, 1987c.

---. Current Population Reports, Series P-60, No. 157. *Money Income and Poverty Status of Families in the United States: 1986 (Advance Data from the March 1987 Current Population Survey)*. Washington, D.C.: U.S. Government Printing Office, 1987d.

---. Current Population Reports, Series P-60, No. 159. *Money Income of Households, Families, and Persons in the United States: 1986*. Washington, D.C.: U.S. Government Printing Office, 1988a.

---. Current Population Reports, Series P-60, No. 160. *Poverty in The United States 1986*. Washington, D.C.: U.S. Government Printing Office, 1988b.

---. Current Population Reports, Series P-60, No. 161. *Money Income and Poverty Status of Families in the United States: 1987 (Advance Data from the March 1988 Current Population Survey)*. Washington, D.C.: U.S. Government Printing Office, 1988c.

---. Current Population Reports, Series P-60, No. 164-RD-1. *Measuring the Effect of Benefits and Taxes on Income and Poverty: 1986*. Washington, D.C.: U.S. Government Printing Office, 1988d.

U.S. Department of Health Education and Welfare. *Summary Report: New Jersey Graduate Work Incentive Experiment--A Social Experiment in Neagative Taxation Sponsored by the Office of Economic Opportunity*. Washington, D.C.: U.S. Government Printing Office, December 1973.

---. *The Rural Income Maintenance Experiment - A Summary Report*. Jointly published: Washington, D.C.: U.S. Government Printing Office and Madison, WI: University of Wisconsin, Institute for Research on Poverty, November 1976.

U.S. Department of Labor, Bureau of Labor Statistics. *Employment and Earnings*. Washington, D.C.: U.S. Government Printing Office, December 1986.

---. *Employment and Earnings*. Washington, D.C.: U.S. Government Printing Office, April 1988.

Watts, Harold W. "Special Panel Suggests Changes in BLS Family Budget Program," *Monthly Labor Review*, pp. 3-10, December 1980.

Winnick, Andrew J. *Final Report: The Characteristics, Education, and Earnings of Technicians*. Washington, D.C.: Manpower Administration, U.S. Dept. of Labor, 1970.

---. "Manpower and Occupational Analysis: Concepts and Measurements--A Review," *Journal of Human Resources*, 10(1), Winter 1975.

---. "Reaganomics and Supply-Side Economics: An Evaluation," *The Insurgent Sociologist*, Spring 1985.

---. "The Changing Distribution of Income in the U.S.," *Economic Digest*. Wilberforce, OH: Central State University, November 1988.

---. "Children in Poverty in America: An American Tragedy," *Economic Digest*. Wilberforce, OH: Central State University, January 1989.

---. "The Homeless in America: Who Are They and Why Are They Homeless?" *Economic Digest.* Wilberforce, OH: Central State University, Forthcoming.

Winter-Berger, Robert N. *The Washington Pay-Off: An Insider's View of Corruption in Government.* New York: Dell Publishing Co., 1972.

Wolff, Edward N. "Estimates of Household Wealth Inequality in the U.S. 1962-1983," *Working Papers*, C.V. Starr Center for Applied Economics. New York: New York University, October 1986.

Wolff, Edward N., and Marley, Marcia. "Long-term Trends in U.S. Wealth Inequality: Methodological Issues and Results," NBER Conference on Income and Wealth, Baltimore, March 1987.

Wright, Eric Olin. *Class, Crisis & The State.* London: Verso, 1979.

Zigler, Edward F., and Watson, Rita E. "Investing in Human Capital," *The Christian Science Monitor*, p. 13, March 23, 1988.

Index

Affluent Society, The
  (Galbraith) 1
Alan Guttmacher Institute 96
Albelda, Randy 123
American Council on Education
  74
Amott, Teresa 28
Assets, distribution of wealth
  among different 178
Average hourly earnings, fall
  in 42
Avery, Robert B. 161, 164,
  167-68, 174, 183

Bane, Mary Jo 80
Belous, Richard 46
Belsie, Laurent 45
Black women, full-time income
  ratios of vs. Black men,
  White women 121
Blacks:
  changes in median family
  income 70
  children in poverty 73
  college drop-out rates 74
  compared to "Blacks and
  Other Races" 51
  declining college
  enrollments 74
  distribution of income
  among 32, 34, 72
  distribution of income
  among families 35
  distribution of wealth
  172-175
  distribution of wealth
  among assets 178
  educational experience of
  poor 90
  employment history of poor
  82
  employment history of poor
  family householders 83
  employment history of poor
  female family householders
  84

Blacks (continued):
  female-headed households
  78
  geographical location of
  poor 93
  income by occupation 129
  less incentive for marriage
  95
  "Non-White" wealth in 1983
  vs. 1986 177
  number of earners per
  family 88
  occupational earnings since
  1982 134
  proportion of the poor 71
  rate of poverty 71
  teenage motherhood 77
  tension between men and
  women 95
  and welfare 71
  unemployment rates 72
  vs. Hispanics, full-time
  income ratios 120
  vs. Whites, full-time
  income ratios 119, 122
  vs. Whites, income
  differentials by education
  126
Bluestone, Barry 39-43, 45-
  48, 53
Boards of directors,
  need to restructure
  corporate 233
Bonds, concentration in
  ownership 181
Bradbury, Katharine L. 37,
  43, 70

Canner, Glenn B. 161
Capitalist class, not dead
  184
Chartering of corporations
  233
Child care facilities:
  availability of 98
  need for 98

Children:
  bonding behavior of 98
  in female-headed families
  79
  and Head Start opportunity
  cost 99
  health insurance coverage
  inadequate 99
  highest incidence of
  poverty 206
  and illiteracy 74
  infant mortality rates 99
  parental leave, need for
  98
  in poverty 73
  and welfare programs 75
Children and poverty:
  in female-headed families
  79
  international comparisons
  76
  teenage motherhood 77
  and welfare programs 75
Civil rights movement 121
Clark, John Bates 3, 8
Coder, John 39, 76, 95
Cohen, Stephen S. 52
Comparable pay 240
Competitiveness:
  loss of by U.S. 208
  related to U.S. wage
  structure 208
Concentration in wealth
  holdings:
  adjusted figures 183
  as compared to
  concentration in income
  181
  by type of asset 181
  changes since 1963 185
  increasing concentration in
  stock, bond, etc. holdings
  187
  stability in overall
  figures 1963-86 187
Consumer sovereignty, myth of
  210
Contingent workers, growth in
  46
Corporate boards of directors,
  need to restructure 233
Corporate profit taxes 226

Corporations, need for federal
  chartering 233
Current Population Reports,
  new series P-70 and the
  SIPP 162

Daniels, Lee A. 74
Danziger, Sheldon 34, 68
Deindustrialization of
  America, The (Bluestone and
  Harrison) 39
Distribution of wealth vs.
  income:
  across income brackets
  174;
  by racial/ethnic groups
  174

Early 1970s: (See also
Nineteen seventy-two, Nineteen
seventy-three):
  turning point for
  occupational earnings 135
  turning point in
  Black/White full-time
  income ratios 120
Earnings by industry 136
Earnings vs. income for
  full-time workers 122
Eberts, Randall W. 52
Economic Policy Institute 47
Education:
  and absolute income
  differentials 125
  and adult programs 226
  critical issues 207
  curriculum standardization
  needed 216
  and discrimination 207
  early childhood 217
  and full-time income 124
  funding system unacceptable
  215
  higher standards needed for
  teachers 216
  historical data concerning
  effect on economic
  discrimination 126
  impact on income without
  regard to employment 127
  national pay standard for
  teachers 216

Education (continued):
  need for national standards
    215
  recommendations for reform
    215
  and sexual/racial income
    discrimination 124
Educational experience:
  of the poor 89
  of poor by race/sex 90
  of poor female householders
    91, 92
  of poor householders 91
  of poor householders by
    race 91
Educational system, basic
  questions about 207
Efficiency and the
  distribution of income 5-6
Efficiency 4
  ethical basis of 8
Ellenberger, James 96
Elliehausen, Gregory E. 161,
  164, 167-8
Employment by broad industrial
  groups 40
Employment history:
  of families below 125
  percent of poverty 86
  of families below Minimum
  Adequacy 87
  of poor 82
  of poor family householders
    83
  of poor female family
  householders 84
  of poor since 1960 89
  reasons for not working
  full year 84
  of secondary workers in
  poor households 85
Employment projections by
  race/ethnic group 42
Equitable distributions,
  alternative definitions of
    7
Equity and the distribution of
  income 6
  ethical basis of 8
Export tax on outgoing funds
  222
Families, poverty rate
  understanted 32

Family, definition of 21
  definitional problems 22
Farley, Reynolds 95
Federal chartering of
  corporations 233
Female. See also Women
Female householders, part-time
  employment history 85
Female vs male occupational
  earnings:
  new peak in 1982 135
  data since 1982 134
Female vs. Males, full-time
  income ratios 120
Female-headed familes:
  compared to single
  male-headed 79
  employment history of those
  below 125 percent of
  poverty 86
  not primary cause of
  poverty 79
Female-Headed households 78
  and poverty 78
  and wealth holdings 173
Flaim, Paul O. 95
Forbes magazine's survey of
  the wealthy 183
Foreign investment 222
Francis, Norman 74
Franklin, Stephen 160

Galbraith, John Kenneth 10,
  210
Gardner, Marilyn 236
Garfinkel, Irwin 75
Gilder, George 2
Gottschalk, Peter 34
Guaranteed minimum income 217
Gustafson, Thomas A. 161

Halverson, Guy 47
Harkness, Laurance P. 99
Harrington, Michael 1, 52
Harrison, Bennett 37, 39-45,
  47-48, 53
Haugen, Steven E. 37
Haveman, Robert H. 238
Head Start, opportunity cost
  of 99
Health insurance
  coverage for children 99

Helmore, Kristin 73, 75, 79,
    95, 96
Hey, Robert 236
Hicks, Jonathan P. 40
High school dropouts among
    poor householders 92
Hill, Mary Jo 237
Hispanics:
    changes in median family
    income 70
    children in poverty 73
    distribution of income
    among 32, 34, 72
    distribution of wealth
    among 172-175
    distribution of wealth
    among assets 178
    educational experience of
    poor householders 92
    female-headed households
    78
    geographical location of
    poor 93
    income by occupation 129
    male vs. female full-time
    income ratios 121
    nineteen eighty-three vs.
    1986 wealth 177
    number of earners per
    family 88
    occupational earnings since
    1982 134
    rate of povery 71
    vs. Blacks, full-time
    income ratios 120
    vs. Whites full-time income
    ratios 120
    vs. Whites, full-time
    income ratios 122
Home ownership as a proportion
    of wealth 178
Homelessness 210
    extent, nature, and causes
    235
Horrigan, Michael W. 37
Horvath, Francis W. 95
Hourly earnings, nineteen
    seventy-two as peak year
    137
Household, definition of 21
    definitional problems 22
Housing recommendations 232

In-kind wealth taxes 2232
In-kind transfers 18
    different valuation
    techniques 18
Income:
    after-tax 19
    alternative definitions of
    20
    BLS standard levels of 24,
    25
    defining standard levels of
    22
    definition of 17
    and taxes 18
Income data, problems of
    underreporting 168
Incomes policy, national 229
    criteria 230
Industry specific earnings
    136
Infant mortality rates 99
Investment, redirecting the
    flow of private 221
Investment:
    new priorities 223
    recycling industry 225
    social criteria for project
    selection 223
    sources of funds 225
    transportation
    infrastructure 223

Junk bonds 221

Kantrowitz, Barbara 99
Kassalow, Everett M. 95
Kennickell, Arthur B. 161,
    164, 167, 177, 183
Kozol, Jonathan 236
Kutscher, Ronald E. 41
Kuttner, R 52

Labor cost differential tax
    222
Labor force participation
    rate:
    decreasing for males 228
    increasing for women 228
Laing. Karen 73, 79, 95, 96
Lamas, Enrique 163
Lampman, Robert 160
Lapidus, June 123
Lawrence, Robert Z. 42

Leveraged buyouts (LBOs) 221
Levinson, M. 52
Longhaul trucking reduced 225
Losing Ground (Murray) 2

Male-headed families, no wife
    present 78
Marginal revenue product and
    wage determination 231
Marshall, Marilyn 74
Marx, Karl 3, 100, 228
Mathews, Tom 236
McCrate, Elaine 123
McMahon, Patrick J. 37, 42
Means of production,
    concentration of ownership
    in 181
Medical benefits:
    as a device to discourage
    part-time jobs 213
    and part-time work 221
Medical care:
    as a paid benefit 213
    clinics for urban areas and
    small towns 213
    proposed reforms in 212
Meyer, Peter 34
Middle class:
    definition of 26
    shrinking of 35, 36
    shrinking of and
    demographics 43
    shrinking of and part-time
    employment 43
    shrinking proportion of
    wealth holdings 172
Minimum income guarantee 217
Minimum wage:
    increases in necessary to
    improve wage structure 229
    need to raise it to surpass
    poverty level 229
    and poverty 81
Mishel, Larry 45
Monmaney, Terence 99
Mothers in the labor force:
    by age of children 98
    changing proportions of 98
    growth in 98
Moynihan, Daniel Patrick 76
Murray, Charles 2, 71

Nardone, Thomas J. 44, 53

National planning 223
Negative income tax 218
Nineteen seventy-three:
    peak year for occupational
    earnings 132
    poverty low point 31
    as a turning point 32, 33,
    69
    as a turning point in
    occupational income data
    133
Nineteen seventy-two
    peak year in hourly
    earnings 136
    turning point in industry
    specific earnings 137
Nutrition and recommendations
    for a food program 214

Occupational definitions 129
Occupational earnings 42
Occupational income data:
    consistency problems with
    historical data 131
    racial/ethnic and gender
    ratios 130
Other America, The
    (Harrington) 1

Palmer, John 76
PAR (Per Capita Access to
    Resources) index 123
Parental leave policy 98
Part-time work and medical
    benefits 221
Part-time work, new definition
    of 44
Per capita Access to Resources
    index. See PAR
Planning, national 223
Polarization:
    between female-headed
    families and others 206
    in distribution of income
    203
    racial/ethnic overtones of
    206
Poor, the:
    definition of 3
    deteriorating absolute
    position of 68
    deteriorating relative
    position of 67

Poor, the (continued):
  educational experience of
  89
  employment history of 82
  geographical location of
  92
  racial/ethnic composition
  of 71
Poverty:
  among elderly 72
  among unrelated individuals
  66, 72
  caused by low wages 207
  children in 73, 74
  children per poor family
  66
  defintion of 21–23
  and employment history 82
  extent of, under
  alternative definitions
  204
  by family size 65
  number of persons in 34
  official definition of 23
  proportion in female-headed
  families in 79
  stopping the
  intergenerational cycle of
  219
  a relative view of 33
Private investment,
  redirecting the flow of
  221
Projector, Dorothy S. 160

Racism, institutional and the
  welfare system 75
Railroad transportation
  system, rebuilding the 224
Rainwater, Lee 39, 76, 95
Reagan administration 2, 31–
  34, 134
  budget cuts and the SIPP
  during 162
  cuts in housing
  expenditures programs
  during 214, 237
  and income standards 24
  no enforcement of antitrust
  laws during 221
  peak near-poverty years
  during 72

Reagan Administration
(continued):
  peak poverty years during
  72
  poverty program cut backs
  during 35
  recession in early 32
  and welfare programs for
  children 75
Recycling industry 225
Retraining poorly educated
  workers 226
  developing incentives for
  227
Ricardo, David 3
Rich vs. poor, contrasts
  between 205
Rich, the:
  definition of 3
  different pattern of wealth
  holdings of 178
Roosevelt, Franklin Delano 70
Rosenthal, Neal H. 41

Sandefur, Gar D. 240
SCF (Survey of Consumer
  Finances):
  as follow-up to 1962
  original 130
  assets and liabilities
  included 171
  comparison to SIPP asset
  definition 172
  importance of high income
  sample 164
  missing data on the very
  rich 164
  nineteen eighty-six
  reinterview of 1983 group
  161
  underestimation of wealth
  and holdings of richest
  individuals 164
  vs. estate tax estimates of
  wealth 166
  vs. Flow of Funds (FOF) 165
  vs. SIPP 163
Schwartz, Marvin 160
Second earners:
  importance of 34
  in a family 88
  in poor households 85
Sehgal, Ellen 95

Service sector:
  growth in employment in 40
  projected future growth of
  41
  relative growth in output
  of 41
Single earner families,
  insufficient income
  potential of 89
SIPP (Survey of Income and
  Program Participation):
  asset definition compared
  to SCF 172
  definition of income used
  174
  interview design 162
  interview pattern 174
  purpose and origin 160
  vs. SCF 163
Smeeding, Timothy M.   39, 76,
  95
Smith, James D. 159
Smolensky, Eugene 34
Social investment,
  establishing new priorities
  223
Steel industry employment 40
Steinberg, B. 52
Stocks, concentration in
  ownership of 181
Survey of Consumer Finances.
  See SCF
Survey of Financial
  Characteristics of
  Consumers done in 1962 160
Survey of Income and Program
  Participation. See SIPP
Swinton, John R. 52

Taxes:
  higher upper marginal rates
  226
  in-kind on wealth 232
  need for progressive wealth
  tax 226
  on corporate profits 226
  on current wealth 232
  on inherited wealth 232
Teachers, higher standards
  needed for 216
Teenage motherhood 77
Thurow, Lester C. 5, 7-9, 52
Tienda, Marta 240

Tofler, Alvin 228
Torrey, Barbara B. 76
Trade-off between racial vs.
  gender income gaps 121
Transportation infrastructure,
  need to redesign and
  rebuild 224
Tschetter, John H. 37, 42
Tucker, Robert C. 100
Two-earner families, as a
  basis for shorter work
  norms 228. See also
  Second earners

Unemployment compensation,
  fewer receive benefits 96
Unemployment rate pattern 220
Unrelated individuals:
  definition of 21
  higher incidence of poverty
  among 31

Vouchers, the need for 218

Wage policy:
  criteria for 230
  need for national 229
  need for subsidies 231
Wage system, need for
  restructuring 208
Watson, Rita E. 98
Wealth:
  as hallmark of rich 159
  changes in concentration
  since 1963 185
  changing holdings within
  families 1983-86 177
  degree of concentration
  180
  distribution among
  different assets 175
  distribution among
  different types of families
  173
  distribution among
  racial/ethnic groups 173
  distribution more unequal
  than income 209
  distribution of
  inconsistent with democracy
  210

Wealth (continued):
    distribution of value of
    different assets among
    households 180
    early studies of 160
    estimates from estate tax
    data 160
    increasing concentration in
    stock, bond, etc. holdings
    187
    interrelationship with
    distributions of income
    189
    more unequally distributed
    than income 175
    stability in overall
    concentration 1963-86 187
    vs. income distribution by
    racial/ethnic groups 175
    vs. income distributions of
    1983 and 1986 175
    vs. income distributional
    comparisons for difference
    groups of assets 209
Wealthiest quite different
    than others 178
Wealth and Poverty (Gilder) 2
Wealthy:
    a special subsample of the
    161
    tendency to secretness 159
Weekly earnings, nineteen
    seventy-two as peak year
    137
Weiss, Gertrude S. 160
Welfare programs,
    racial/ethnic participation
    in 71
Wilson, William Julius 95
Winnick, Andrew J. 53
Women:
    full-time income ratios of
    Black and Hispanic 121
    educational experience of
    poor 90
    employment history of poor
    82
    income by occupation among
    129
    vs men, income
    differentials by education
    126

Women (continued):
    White less likely to work
    than Black 127
Women's liberation movement
    121
Workday, need to reduce 227
Workweek, need to reduce 227

Zigler, Edward F. 74, 98
Zysman, John 52

About the Author

ANDREW J. WINNICK is Associate Professor and Chairman of the Department of Economics at Central State University (Ohio). Previously, he taught at the University of California-Santa Barbara, Antioch College (Ohio), San Francisco State University, and the European division of the University of Maryland. He also served on the research staffs of the President's Council of Economic Advisors and of the Federal Reserve Bank of San Francisco. He is a founding member of the Union for Radical Political Economics and serves on the editorial board of its journal, the *Review of Radical Political Economics*. He is the author of numerous articles, both in professional and popular publications, and has lectured widely in the United States and Europe. He has been a consultant to a wide range of organizations, including labor unions, public service and political groups, and governmental advisory bodies.

Dr. Winnick holds a B.A. in Economics and Mathematics from the University of California-Berkeley and an M.A. and Ph.D. in Economics from the University of Wisconsin-Madison.